D0654094

Come Wind or Weather

CLARE FRANCIS

Come Wind or Weather

PELHAM BOOKS
LONDON

First published in Great Britain by
PELHAM BOOKS LTD
52 Bedford Square
London
WC1B 3EF
1978

©Clare Francis 1978

All Rights Reserved. No part of this
publication may be recorded, stored in a
retrieval system, or transmitted, in any form
or by any means, electronic, mechanical,
photocopying, recording or otherwise,
without the prior permission of the
Copyright owner.

ISBN 0 7207 1104 5

Filmset in Monophoto Times 327
by A. Brown & Sons Ltd., Hull,

Printed and bound in Great Britain by
W. S. Cowell Limited, Ipswich

Frontispiece: *ADC
Accutrac* at the start
of her seven-month
voyage (*photo: The
Observer*).

CONTENTS

ACKNOWLEDGMENTS

In a large and complex enterprise like a world voyage one needs all the help one can get from suppliers, manufacturers and those who possess that invaluable commodity, expert knowledge. There were many people who offered us all kinds of assistance and, to those whom I do not have room to mention below, I would say that we were extremely grateful for every particle of help we received.

My principal thanks must go to our sponsors, BSR Limited, who provided the most tremendous support for our venture, both financial and otherwise. Having a successful, forward-looking and enthusiastic company as our sponsor was one of our greatest assets.

Other companies who provided unfailing support were Marconi (Coastal Radio Limited), who loaned us one of their excellent Falcon II radio telephones, almost the only set among the fleet that did not break down; Chloride, who supplied a bank of heavy-duty batteries, as well as torches and dry batteries; and Olympus, who provided the excellent camera equipment which ttook most of the pictures in this book.

Brookes and Gatehouse supplied additional instrumentation to supplement the existing bank of B & G equipment thus providing a superb range of robust yet sensitive instruments (it must stressed that the troublesome radio direction finder was *not* made by B & G). Matthew Gloag and Sons kindly donated some of their delicious Grouse Scotch whisky, which warmed many a cold stomach in the Southern Ocean. Reads lent us one of their Sailmaker sewing machines which was subjected to the most terrible treatment but always survived to mend yet another sail. Francis Searchlights gave us one of their powerful signalling lamps, while Taylor's Para-Fin provided a Kenyon cooker for the galley. Kim Products donated twelve safety harnesses and Man Overboard Limited two experimental lifebuoy release systems.

We were grateful to receive a variety of specialised clothing, particularly the Puffa down-filled quilted vests which proved extremely warm against the cold. We also took James North lightweight oilskins, Aiglesport boots from France, Aquairland's Sealfur polar suits – also invaluable against the cold – and heavy oiled wool sweaters provided by Douglas Gill International.

In the food and galley line, donations included paper plates and plastic glasses from Bender's, Melamine Swallow tableware from Swift's of Exmouth, Five Pint powdered milk (the best we have ever come across) and Long Life milk from Unigate. A Fresh-Ness filter kept the water tasting sweet and fresh.

General Motors provided us with cars at each stop, BUPA with health care and insurance and British Oxygen with nitrous oxide.

The Royal Naval Sailing Association carried out the thankless task of organising the race with efficiency, patience and understanding, while Whitbread, as sponsors of the race, were helpful, enthusiastic and, as one would hope, generous with their beer. Also, the RNSA and Whitbread should be commended for running the race for the benefit of the competitors, and not the organisers. We particularly appreciated being met at the end of each leg by representatives of the RNSA and Whitbread, whatever the time of day or night.

A special thank you must go to Charles Williams, an extraordinarily generous person who gave us our stereo cassette system with 100 music cassettes and sent marvellous surprise parcels to each stop. The enjoyment we received from his thoughtful gifts was immeasurable.

I am very grateful to Mary Reid for her help in typing the manuscript of this book, answering all the letters and generally holding the fort.

Last but not least I must thank my crew, both for their faith in coming along in the first place, and for their enthusiasm and hard work during the race.

PICTURE ACKNOWLEDGMENTS
Unless otherwise credited all photographs are by Clare Francis and Jacques Redon.
Line drawings in Appendix A are by Peter Milne; all others are by David Charles.

CHAPTER 1

The Man on the Train

In the autumn of 1975 there was one sailing event which occupied all my thoughts and plans, the *Observer* Singlehanded Transatlantic Race to be held the following summer. The idea of entering another major event after that was far from my mind. The Transatlantic was a difficult, challenging and demanding race which required long and careful preparation. The last thing I wanted, or could manage, was to plan another. Besides which, I was harbouring a lovely vision of a rose-covered cottage where, after the forthcoming race, Jacques and I would live quietly all the year round, going sailing on weekends and holidays – and then only when the weather was fine. As the race drew nearer, this dream was becoming more and more appealing.

Sometimes, on a quiet evening by the fire, Jacques and I would talk about the future, but it always turned out to be rather a vague future; probably Jacques would continue to teach, possibly we would become involved in the boat trade, or possibly set up a small business of our own. But most of the time we didn't worry about it at all and talked, instead, about more immediate events like the Transatlantic Race or the state of our vegetable patch, wrested by back-breaking toil from the overgrown garden at the back of the old farmhouse.

If the Whitbread Round the World Race was mentioned it was usually by Jacques, reminiscing about the first race in 1973–4 when he had crewed on *Burton Cutter*, a boat which was never to complete the course. The hull had started to break up at the start of the second leg from Cape Town and the boat had returned to South Africa for repairs. By the time the aluminium hull had been rewelded it was too late to rejoin the fleet and they had sailed to Rio to wait for the start of the fourth and last leg back to Portsmouth. It had been a sad disappointment for Jacques and the rest of the crew. They had missed the excitement of racing through the Southern Ocean and round Cape Horn, the high points of the event. Under the circumstances it was natural that Jacques should want to do the race again, just to to be able to complete the course. But the next race was still a long way off, in 1977–8, and if his old skipper, Les Williams, was planning an entry he hadn't announced it yet. Being a person who didn't worry about anything until it happened, Jacques would decide whether to go on the race only when Les entered and asked him to join his crew. But one thing was certain – I would not be invited along. As a matter of principle, Les always had an all-male crew.

Jacques and I didn't consider the possibility of organising our own entry. Big boats and big events needed money, and not just thousands but hundreds of thousands of pounds. That kind of cash was so far beyond our reach as to be unattainable.

It was not surprising, therefore, that my response to the enigmatic letter I received one day that grey autumn was merely one of mild curiosity. The letter read, 'Dear Miss Francis, I am writing to you in the hope that we may arrange a meeting to discuss a possibly mutual sailing interest, namely the 1977 Whitbread Race. A colleague and myself would be delighted if you would dine with us to discuss our project. Please write, giving telephne (*sic*) no', that we make contact soonest.' It was signed Robert Jackson.

It was not hard to guess what the proposed project would involve. The men would, in some way, want my help to obtain sponsorship for the race. Like many other people they would imagine that, due to my success in finding sponsorship three seasons running, I could help them find backing for the Whitbread. Few people realised that I had only ever received small amounts of sponsorship and that I always worked hard to give the sponsor good value in return, by writing plenty of articles, by assiduously attending interviews and photo sessions, and once taking film for a TV programme. I knew that obtaining money and keeping the sponsor happy were always hard work. But at the same time, Jacques and I were curious about this project. 'If we don't meet this chap, we'll never know what kind of crazy idea he's got,' said Jacques. 'He might even have the money!'

Robert Jackson and Robin Buchanan did not have the money nor, it transpired, did they have much sailing experience. Robert – young, extrovert and naturally optimistic – was the one with the enthusiastic ideas. He told us they were both keen to do the race but didn't know of any entry that might

Robert (*left*) and Robin; their unlikely dream was to come true.

take them. They had decided, therefore, to get their own entry off the ground and felt that a boat with a woman skipper would have the best chance of finding sponsorship. Would I be interested? Robin, the opposite of the ebullient Robert, was quiet, reserved and every inch an accountant. He talked about the finances. He admitted they had no firm idea of how much it would cost, but thought £30,000 to charter a boat and £20,000 for expenses might cover it. What did we think?

It was a credit to their enthusiasm and spirit that Robert and Robin still harboured some optimism for the project after Jacques and I had finished listing the problems and obstacles we could foresee. We predicted that three or four times as much money would be needed, that most companies would be very unlikely to provide such a sum for sailing, so far from being a spectator sport, and that no PR person would consider me worth that much money in publicity terms – if they'd ever heard of me at all! Furthermore, I had to admit that I was not very interested in doing the race. Now that we were actually discussing another event, I realised how much I cherished my dream of the rose-covered cottage. Ahead of me lay the toughest race I would ever take part in, not only physically but mentally. In the dark of the night, when I thought of the dangers of sailing the Atlantic alone and the emotional difficulties of separation from Jacques, the vision of a secure, land-bound future was monumentally important. Although entering the Whitbread would not mean separation from Jacques, it would still mean seven long months in the wet, miserable conditions endemic to sailing. It was more than I could bear to contemplate. However, rather than put a complete damper on the idea, I offered a compromise and promised to skipper one leg of the race if that would help the search for sponsorship. I could not promise more.

Their enthusiasm only a little dimmed, the two young men went away to start bombarding industry with proposals. But as the months went by we were not surprised to hear they had met with little success. Few companies showed any interest and those that did had too little money to spare. Like my present sponsors, Robertson's the jam manufacturers, most companies had promotional budgets which were severely limited and very far from bottomless.

It seemed as though Robert and Robin's idea would die and, as Jacques and I became more engrossed in preparations for the Transatlantic Race, we thought it had.

It is difficult, even now, to appreciate how much the Singlehanded Transatlantic Race changed everything. I finished the race thirteenth out of 120 starters and took the women's singlehanded transatlantic record by three days, a result with which I was very happy considering the size of my boat, the 38-foot *Robertson's Golly*, and the difficult weather conditions during the race.

However, it was not so much the result itself that brought about the major change in our lives, as the sequence of events that followed. At first, life seemed the same as before. Immediately after my return from America, I took part in the *L'Aurore* Singlehanded Race in France, an event I had been committed to for some time. But after the hardships and rigours of the Transatlantic Race, during which a good friend, Mike McMullen, had been lost, my heart was no longer in the event and at the finish I announced my retirement from singlehanded racing. Jacques and I returned to the farmhouse and settled back into our quiet, undisturbed life.

By October I had finished writing my story of the Transatlantic Race, *Come Hell or High Water*, to be published the following January. Not counting an earlier effort that had never been published, it was my first book, and I was unprepared for the publicity that preceded its publication. I was also unprepared for the impact of the film I had made for the BBC during the race. When it was shown that autumn, the effect was immediate and overwhelming. Possibly because, in addition to the joys, I had shown some of the miseries of taking part in the race – when tired and lonely, I had actually cried in front of the camera – everyone suddenly wanted to interview me, to take pictures, to hear my views on being alone.

Jacques and I had an ambivalent attitude to this wave of publicity. On the one hand, we wanted to enjoy our quiet life and remain undisturbed in the country. On the other hand, we began to appreciate that the publicity could lead to sponsorship and the opportunity to do a major event or a long cruise which would otherwise be impossible for lack of finance. As this realisation dawned on us, I could see the rose-covered cottage fast receding into the background. Now that I was safely back from the Transatlantic Race, the dream was not as powerful as it had been before – although it was still attractive enough to give me some doubts. However, the idea of doing a long event was becoming even more attractive and, with sponsorship in mind, we decided that, for the moment at least, I should accept all invitations to be interviewed. Inevitably, there were disadvantages to this strategy. The sailing establishment is very traditional and proud of its continuing amateurism; I could almost hear the murmurs of 'commercialism', 'professionalism', and 'she's just in it for the publicity (therefore money)'. True, we were trying to find money – but only in the form of sponsorship. On a personal level, I was making little, and probably a lot less than most of the works teams who go in for so-called amateur events and, when they win, benefit directly from increased boat or equipment sales.

Not surprisingly, the first reaction to this publicity came from my current sponsors, Robertson's. They were delighted with the coverage they were getting and wanted to know if I was going to do another event which they could sponsor. After years of asking for money, of spending weary months writing letters and putting forward proposals, it was quite a change to find money being offered. It seemed that our strategy was paying off. But now we had to decide what event, if any, we wanted to do. 'If there's money going, and they're enthusiastic, why not put up a proposal for the Whitbread Race?' suggested Jacques, innocently puffing away at his pipe.

And indeed, when we came to examine all the possibilities, we discovered there were no other events we wanted to do. Singlehanded events were out – and there were none coming up during the next year anyway – while the majority of other sailing events were so-called 'amateur' races in which the distances were relatively short and sponsorship was forbidden. If you wanted to race a large boat you had to have well over £50,000 to spare.

This left the Whitbread Race, starting on the 27th August, 1977, one year away. With sponsorship a serious possibility, we decided it would be madness not to consider the matter very carefully. I have always believed that you should make the most of opportunities, particularly when they involve doing something you love, like sailing, and something which stretches you to achieve a difficult objective. The Transatlantic had been difficult certainly, but once such a thing is done, it's done and in the past. It was time to look to the future again. I believe it is important to make every project, however small and apparently insignificant or great and 'important', an achievement and source of satisfaction to yourself. The question was, whether this opportunity was one that should be taken. I was not at all sure! On the one hand, I could imagine finding a great deal of satisfaction in leading a quiet life, writing books and tending the garden. On the other, I felt the old urge for adventure, that strange desire to overcome difficulties and reach an objective.

Jacques, too, had a history of adventures and, although he had now reached the great age of thirty-three and was working steadily as a teacher, he was still a world traveller at heart. As soon as he had qualified as a teacher in France, he

Jacques.

had taken a job at a school in Tunisia, a welcome alternative to national service. Later, he had joined an expedition crossing the Sahara in two Renault 4s. When the expedition tried to continue south, their path had been blocked by war, and Jacques had suddenly decided to see Russia and the Far East instead. Stranded in Singapore with malaria, no money and a government unfriendly to 'hippies', he took a job crewing on a yacht bound for Darwin and discovered the advantages of sailing. After two years in Australia, he returned to France, converted an old fishing boat to sailing rig and set off round the world. He got as far as Gibraltar, not a very long way. But it was there that he met Les Williams and dropped everything to help Les in the building of *Burton Cutter* for the Round the World Race. When Jacques and I met, it was not surprising that it should be on a sailing race, this time the Round Britain.

We were both very tempted at the idea of the Whitbread Race. For once we could sail together, an idea that delighted us. Jacques had done more than anyone to make sure my singlehanded events had been a success, working hard on preparing the boats and providing me with tremendous support. I could not imagine sailing without him now, nor indeed being left behind while he went round the world in the crew of another boat. With our own entry we could plan, prepare, sail and race together.

Then there was the lure of the race itself. The more we thought about the difficulties, the more we were fascinated by them. It is 27,000 miles around the world by the three Capes and, sailing west to east, it would take about seven months including three stopovers at Cape Town, Auckland and Rio de Janeiro. The yachts that could be entered were limited to Class One ocean racers, that is, boats between about forty-five and eighty feet in length. They had to be raced with a full crew, which meant that the racing would be hard, fast and very competitive. Apart from the great distance involved, the main attraction of the race was the tremendous variety of weather and conditions that would be met on the course. From the mixed conditions of the Atlantic we would sail into the famous, much-feared Southern Ocean, the sea that stretches around the world south of South America, Africa and Australia. We would have to weather the legendary Cape Horn, the Roaring Forties, and the Screaming Fifties, renowned for their harsh weather, large seas and drifting icebergs. It would be very satisfying to complete the course in one piece.

The race was fascinating, difficult and challenging. Yet it was still hard to take the final decision. Jacques was philosophical. 'If we get the money, we do it. If we don't, we don't,' he would say. I was still very torn. After several years without a proper home – we had lived on our boat for a while, then in the rented, dilapidated farmhouse – I could think of nothing nicer than settling into a home of our own. Like a mother hen in search of a roost, I was starting to make clucking noises. On the other hand, it could probably wait another year, although I tried not to remember how much of that time would be spent in damp, cramped conditions. Seven months on a yacht with ten or so other people was not something to be undertaken lightly. But, as Jacques pointed out, it was not necessary to take a final decision immediately, for we might not find a sponsor anyway. Of course, it was not really possible to put the decision

14

off in this way; if we were offered the means of going on such an adventure, we would be incapable of turning it down. However, we pretended we still had our options open and awaited Robertson's decision with interest. We had asked them to buy or charter a boat for us, and to provide running expenses of £50,000. But, despite their initial enthusiasm, they came back to us with disappointing news. They had decided that the amount of money involved was too great, and that they would be unable to offer us backing.

This was something of a setback, but having now got the idea in our heads, we decided it was worth pursuing elsewhere. Robertson's had enjoyed such success with their sponsorship that we felt there was a reasonable chance that another company would be interested in our project. In the event it took time, many letters and several meetings before we found two companies who were seriously interested – although not in a great hurry to commit themselves. By this time it was nearly January and the race was a mere seven months away, a very short time in which to prepare for such a long and involved project. To hurry things along and to ensure we had covered all the possibilities, we decided to announce our search for sponsorship in the press. This brought an immediate response in the form of a shoal of letters which we tore open with great eagerness. To our chagrin, then our amusement, we discovered that they came from a hundred and one people who wanted to join us as crew. Not one letter offered money, the thing we really needed!

The London Boat Show was the deciding time. If we had not found the money by then we would probably never find it at all. It was a frantically busy time for me. Between signing sessions and promotional activities for *Come Hell or High Water*, which had just been published, and showing people over the *Golly* which was on display at the exhibition, I was trying to finalise arrangements with the two potential sponsors. The new school term had started and Jacques was back teaching, so I was alone. I was to miss Jacques' help for, when the final *dénouement* occurred, it had all the confusion, rushing around and misunderstanding of a stage comedy.

One day, in the middle of signing books, I was called to the phone. Over the din of the show, I could just make out the voice of Eric, my publisher.

'Hope I'm not interrupting anything,' said Eric. I assured him I had only been signing books.

'Oh!' exclaimed Eric hastily. 'I won't keep you, then! It's just that something very exciting has come up, and I *had* to tell you about it. There's this man on the train, you see, a chap I travel with every morning . . . . He might have found you a sponsor!'

'A man on the train?' I repeated. It all sounded rather unlikely to my tired and bemused mind. Men on trains did not suddenly produce hundreds of thousands of pounds . . . or did they? Poor Eric, I decided. Only trying to help but obviously got the wrong end of the stick somewhere. Many friends had kindly offered to put me in touch with people who might know a company, who might sponsor us. These introductions rarely came to much. Usually the sponsorship was unsuited to the company or vice versa. I appreciated Eric's attempt to help – but a man on a train?

Eric rang off, promising more information the next day. Meanwhile I hurried off to see one of my 'possibles', the chairman of the British branch of one of the largest electrical companies in the world. We had arranged to meet on the *Golly* but I had some difficulty finding him, owing to the large number of my family and friends and the *Golly*'s owners, relatives and friends who were crammed in the saloon, to the sound of clinking glasses. Eventually I located Sponsor Number One sitting on some pump spares in the fo'c'sle. Unfortunately he was unable to give me conclusive news, only the assurance that he was still pursuing the matter at board level.

The next day I rushed off to have lunch with Sponsor Number Two, who was more promising; he would make an offer within two days, although he was unlikely to be able to provide all the money we needed.

Then Eric phoned again. 'Keep it under your hat,' he whispered conspiratorially, 'but I think we've got it! I'll bring *him* along tonight.'

'Who?' I asked.

'Why, the man on the train, of course. Except, he's not the actual sponsor, that's someone else. But I'll explain all that later.'

I didn't know what to say. Certainly I found it hard to believe that, through the very unpromising medium of a chance conversation on a train, we had found a sponsor. Even when Eric arrived in company with the mystery man, Gerry Jones, who identified himself as the marketing and advertising adviser to a large company called BSR, I didn't take it in. Only after I had talked to Gerry for some time, had met John Ferguson and Garth Wooldridge, the two top men at BSR, and had discussed the details with them, did I realise that the project was on and we had actually found the money.

BSR Limited was a large British company which made turntables for record players. It was extremely successful and exported to the USA and Japan. Not only were BSR prepared to sponsor us, but they agreed to provide all the money we needed. The boat, which they would buy, would be called *ADC Accutrac; ADC* after a new range of top-quality products they were launching under the name of their US subsidiary, Audio Dynamics Corporation, and *Accutrac* after the first product in this new range, a computerised turntable. The name was not very romantic, but it had a certain air of efficiency about it. BSR would buy whatever boat I chose, on the understanding that it would be reasonably resaleable, so enabling them to recoup most of their money after the event.

It was also understood that I was to be the skipper. Although I had often crewed on large boats, I had never actually skippered one. However, I looked on the job as an exciting challenge. When it comes to the actual sailing, the principles are the same on a large boat as on a small one. The techniques of sail-handling would differ, but with Jacques and a good crew to back me up we should be able to learn how to work the boat together. Every boat is a different animal and every one needs different handling, regardless of size. At the same time I was well aware that big boats are more powerful and therefore more dangerous and intolerant of mistakes. Learning to handle the boat would be a demanding and exciting exercise.

With the money now being offered on such reasonable terms, there was no question of not doing the race. As soon as he heard the news Jacques' burst of enthusiasm and excitement revealed how much he had been looking forward to taking part. I too was very excited now that our entry was confirmed. The idea of leading a quiet life was pushed into a corner of my mind, ready to be reborn on our return.

From the moment that the sponsorship was confirmed the rush was on. There was so much to do of such a varied nature that I often felt like a juggler with ten clubs in the air. First, we had a boat to find. While the Boat Show was still on, I made the rounds of the major yacht brokers to find what they had on their books. It was too late to build a new boat from scratch, although this was what we would have dearly loved to do. Such is the rate of advance in design and building techniques that boats quickly go out-of-date and only the latest type is likely to do well in close competition. However, on a long-distance race we did not feel that a boat built 'to the rules' – that is, built to take every advantage of the complex handicap rules – would necessarily be the best. Just as important was a well-tried boat with great proven strength. Such a boat was the Swan 65, the type of boat which had won the first Round the World race. Of all the large boats on the market, the Swan seemed the toughest and, because of its great reputation, the most easy to resell after the event.

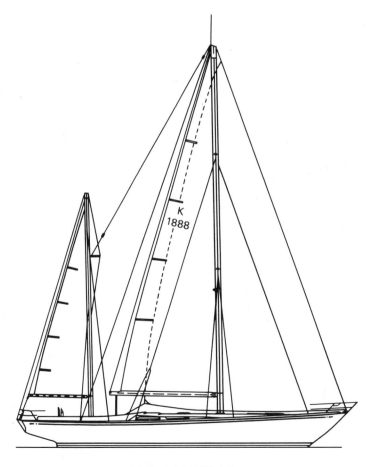

ADC ACCUTRAC

The Boat Show was also an opportunity to find crew members from among our sailing friends and acquaintances. We would have no difficulty in finding 'winch-fodder' as ordinary deck crew are called. Indeed, we were daily being besieged by requests and letters from a wide variety of people. But it was more difficult to find really experienced sailors to be watch leaders or sail trimmers, people who could also take eight months away from work. Some dearly wanted to, but couldn't afford to. Others, although free to take time off, wanted to concentrate on other types of event. Perhaps others had no desire to sail under a woman, although they were too polite to say so!

To our delight, the first person we asked to join the crew accepted immediately. One day I had been signing books at the show when I looked up to see the quietly smiling face of Beat Güttinger. Beat – pronounced Bee-at – was a sailing Swiss, a fairly unlikely combination until one remembers that the Mediterranean is not far from the Swiss border. Beat was a first-class sailor. We had met him on the 1974 Round Britain Race when he and his crew, Albert, had sailed a tiny quarter-tonner called *Petit Suisse* to an impressive second place on handicap. Despite gales and bad weather to which their small craft was hardly suited, they had completed the 2,500-mile course in a very fast

Beat, a mainstay of the crew.

time. At each stop they had been cheerful and disparaging of the fearful discomforts they had suffered, although we knew how wet and cramped they must have been in the bad weather. A remark of Beat's had stuck in my mind. When asked how he had fared in a gale off the Shetlands he had replied with a shrug, 'Ah, fine. No problem. Only now and then we go down a wave and, er, the boat turns sharply and then, er, she goes flat over.' He had thought little of such alarming manoeuvres. Indeed, the most impressive quality about Beat was his calm matter-of-factness. It was difficult to imagine him in a flap about anything, however bad the situation. Beat also had nerve. When he and Albert had been too tired to do any navigation towards the end of the third leg of the Round Britain they had followed another yacht through the shoals off Lowestoft as if glued to its tail. That yacht had been mine and, as I had struggled with pilot books and charts, I had been forced to admire Beat's simple solution to navigation.

Beat was finishing a college course in yacht design and was then going to crew on a Swiss Admiral's Cup entry. As luck would have it he had no plans after that, and when I asked him to join us he had no hesitation in accepting.

Indirectly, we also found another important crew member at the Boat Show. One day the *Golly* was visited by several members of the exuberant Scottish Ogilvy-Wedderburn family, one of whom was married to an old friend of mine. On hearing that we were going to compete in the race, they immediately declared that their youngest sister, Bumble, currently away on some remote Scottish island or other, should be our cook. She had sailed quite a bit, they said, and could cook an excellent meal. More importantly, she had done both simultaneously.

By nature the Ogilvy-Wedderburn family were extroverts with a hilarious, earthy sense of humour. I had only met Bumble twice, but I remembered her as having the same outgoing character. Added to that she also loved being outdoors and visiting unusual places, having spent two summers cooking for visitors on the remote island of St Kilda. In principle, I was very keen to have just one cook rather than having that chore shared between all the crew. Food would be very important for our health and our morale and, if left to a rota system, it might arrive late or badly cooked. A cook who loved to sail sounded ideal. We arranged that I would write to Bumble and set out all the details. This I did, painting a fairly black picture of the conditions so that she would not have any falsely glamorous ideas about the race, and suggesting that, if she was interested, she should come down and see what was involved when we had bought the boat.

It never occurred to me not to have a mixed crew, although I am always the first to admit that there should be a high proportion of men to handle a large boat effectively. But in many respects women can pull their weight just as well as men and, in the case of some jobs, even better. A few of the boats which were to take part in the race were not taking women as a matter of principle, saying it would cause too many problems. I felt that finding a group of people who would mix successfully depended far more on their personalities than their sex. I was looking for relaxed, confident, friendly and able people who would not fall into a 'problem' category. Certainly, those skippers who insisted on all-male crews were probably very wise, for I could think of several characters among the crews who could never have been couped up with a plain girl for a week, let alone an attractive one for six weeks, without propositioning her!

I had a clear idea of what I was searching for in my crew. Compatibility was the most important feature, with sailing ability a close second. Enthusiasm, an easy-going nature and, above all, a sense of humour were vital to survive incarceration in a small space with eleven other people. Pure sailing ability would never be enough. Months later when the crew were assembled I was happy to see that, on the whole, everyone got on very well together. Indeed, many were to forge firm friendships over the months to come. Apart from the odd incident, we were to be a united and happy crew.

I was surprised to find how many people believed I would be taking an all-girl crew, some men because they thought the idea rather 'sweet' (they had obviously never tried handling a large boat without the aid of strong men), and some because they assumed a female skipper would want to prove something about Women's Lib. The idea that the mainspring of able or talented women's achievements is a desire to get even with men, or even to beat them into the ground, is a demeaning notion, promulgated by the popular press with their love of out-of-date clichés. Any mention of Women's Lib was guaranteed to make my blood boil. It would even produce an angry response from Jacques who, like me, was a great believer in individuality rather than Women's or Men's Lib. Sometimes, Jacques would profess an interest in going round the world with eleven women, a sort of all-girl crew with keeper, but would look at me with a grin and admit that it was difficult enough looking after one woman and he didn't think he could manage eleven.

It was now some time since we had been in contact with Robert and Robin, and we arranged to meet them at the show. They were naturally very excited about the sponsorship, although worried about making the grade as crew. They agreed to help with the fitting out and preparations during the summer and, in return, we put them on the short-list for ordinary deck crew or 'winch fodder'. Certainly Robert had the sort of outgoing nature that would be an asset in a large crew; no sooner had he arrived at the show than he was greeting a dozen long-lost friends and propping up the Guinness stand with the help of a decorative blonde. Robin, on the other hand, had a quiet, dependable nature that would also blend into a group very well. Both Robert and Robin were currently employed, one as 'something in a merchant bank', the other as a chartered accountant. They were confident their firms would give them time off and, even if they didn't, they were so keen to do the race they would take the time anyway. This meant we had a possible six for the crew out of the total twelve we needed.

The next essential was a boat. From the Swan 65s available, Jacques and I felt that only two looked promising. One was lying in Malta and the other in the West Indies. Malta being nearer, we went there first but found the boat badly neglected and over-priced. Then quite suddenly, we heard of a third Swan near Rome. I flew out there the next day and by the afternoon had bought the boat. Inevitably it wasn't quite as simple as that – there was a tremendous amount of to-ing and fro-ing before the matter was tied up. But eventually the paperwork was complete and we could start the serious planning.

First, I had to organise the delivery of the boat from Antibes, where she was lying at the termination of the sale, to Lymington, where we would keep her until the race. This meant finding a crew, organising ship's papers, flights, insurance, equipment, charts and a dozen other things, quite apart from putting the plans for the race itself into motion. Life at the farm took on a frantic pace as the office work started to build up. I disappeared under a mound of paper which included the race rules and the regulations concerning equipment and safety, as issued by the organising body, the Royal Naval Sailing Association or RNSA; manufacturers' brochures for everything from winches to unbreakable plastic plates; information on the radio frequencies throughout the world; sail plans; deck plans; and a thousand and one matters that would have to be considered as soon as possible.

To add to the work, Jacques and I chose this moment to come to two momentous and long-overdue decisions. Despite our long seven-month absence on the race, we decided to try and buy a house of our own before we left, preferably in Lymington, the place where we planned to keep the Swan, and also the town where we had the most roots. Here, one cold winter, we had lived aboard our own small boat, *Gulliver G,* which had been an excellent exercise in how to live in cramped conditions. Here, too, we had prepared the *Golly* for the Transatlantic Race. If we moved, it would mean some commuting for Jacques to get to work in Basingstoke but, if it meant having our own house, it would be a small price to pay. The decision was partly logistical – it was difficult arranging a voyage when based a long way from the boat – and partly because we loved the idea of having somewhere to come home to at the end of the race. We started the tiring business of house-hunting in February, hoping to move by Easter.

The second decision was one which everyone, particularly our families and close friends, considered even longer overdue. Jacques and I had been inseparable for nearly three years but, although we had made noises about it from time to time and even mentioned dates now and then, we had never got round to actually getting married. Much of the problem had been lack of time – or so we said. In fact, lack of nerve had been much nearer the truth. Having been free spirits for thirty-four and thirty-one years respectively, Jacques and I had seen no urgency in going through a legal ceremony we had so successfully avoided for so long. However, we had to admit that the time had come when this situation could go on no longer. Having taken the decision, we were thrilled by it and could not imagine why we had put it off so long.

The wedding was to be in early July, six weeks before the start of the race. We resolved to keep the ceremony very quiet, to the extent of total secrecy. This was one occasion when we did not want any publicity whatsoever. It was a naïve hope and we were to be sadly disappointed. Indeed, had we realised how much the press were to make of our wedding and forthcoming 'round-the-world honeymoon' – as if it were all champagne and romance on the afterdeck – and the number of remarks along the lines of 'Clare will take her

new husband along in the crew' – as if I had just invited him – we might have run away to Gretna Green and married under the names of Mr and Mrs Winch-part of no fixed abode, and done a better job at keeping it a secret.

Had I been a pessimistic person, the delivery trip from Antibes to Lymington might have depressed me considerably. As it was, it merely left me perplexed and worried about the incredible number of jobs that would have to be done in the five short months before the start of the race.

When I first saw the boat again, she looked beautiful, lying gleaming in the hot Mediterranean sun. She also looked frighteningly large and powerful and I was sorry it was the middle of term-time and Jacques was not there to help me sort out the intricacies of the boat's equipment. I had two days to discover how everything worked before the crew arrived and we left for England. Beat and his Round Britain crew, Albert, were coming from Switzerland, Robert and Robin were coming from England, and Bumble was coming from Scotland. With another three friends, we would be nine in all.

My attempts to get to know the boat started well enough, for I got the engine to work. But thereafter I suffered several setbacks. The fridge compressor appeared to function, but did not actually cool, the MF radio appeared to function but did not readily transmit, and the bilge and sump pumps had severe electrical troubles. Worst of all, it was obvious there was something unpleasantly wrong with two of the loo outlets. However, I consoled myself with the knowledge that failed gear is the norm on every type of boat. Unless it is coaxed and cajoled nothing, particularly electrics, will ever work.

The boat herself looked as beautiful as she had in Italy, her flush teak decks white in the sun and her varnished interior warm and cosy. She was divided into five main cabins with three loo compartments leading off the sleeping cabins, and a galley off the saloon. She could sleep two in each of the two forward cabins and three in the aft cabin. There were also two pilot berths in the saloon, giving a total sleeping capacity of nine at any one time.

The boat was ketch rigged, having a main mast 75 feet high and a mizzen 50 feet high. She had a wardrobe of twenty-three sails and about half a mile of sheets, halyards and warps. Most of these would have to be renewed before the race.

Having made sure that there was enough gear to sail the boat to England, I organised some repairs and waited for the rest of the crew to arrive. Beat and Albert were the first, although they were uncharacteristically agitated, having had their camera equipment stolen during the train journey through Italy. The others, who arrived by air at Nice, fared little better; some of their luggage was lost and was rumoured to be on its way to Turkey.

As soon as she stepped on board Bumble leapt into action, examining every corner of the galley and planning her stores according to the room in the fridge, freezer and lockers. After half an hour of concentrated study, she declared, 'Well, I think it's a really smashing kitchen!'

'It's a galley, Bumble,' someone whispered.

'Oh, of course!' she replied.

OPPOSITE
ADC Accutrac under
reduced sail.

23

Interior of ADC Accutrac

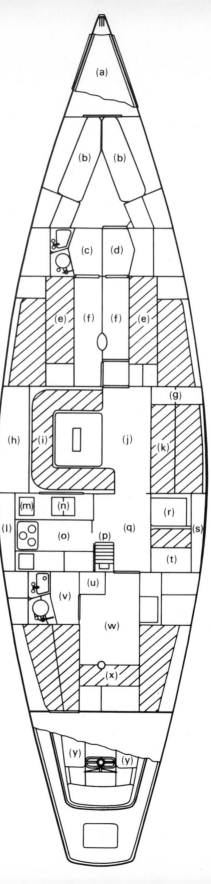

Berths or seats

(a)	—	Anchor locker (sealed off)
(b)	—	Sail bins
(c)	—	For'ard loo
(d)	—	Workshop
(e)	—	Tins stowed under berth
(f)	—	Water tanks under
(g)	—	Lockers
(h)	—	Fruit and vegetable stowage
(i)	—	Fuel tanks under seats
(j)	—	Saloon (engine under)
(k)	—	Fuel under seat
(l)	—	Lockers
(m)	—	Freezer
(n)	—	Fridge
(o)	—	Galley
(p)	—	Companion way
(q)	—	Water tanks under
(r)	—	Chart table
(s)	—	Radio and instruments
(t)	—	Locker
(u)	—	Radio
(v)	—	Aft loo
(w)	—	Aft cabin
(x)	—	Seat
(y)	—	Sail bins

Length overall: 65 ft. or 19·812 metres

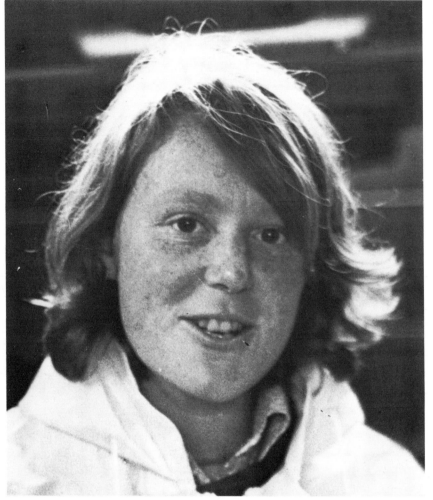

Bumble, a cook in a million.

Later, on examining the aft cabin which she was to share with me, Bumble was heard to say, 'Really a very comfortable bedroom.' We soon gave up correcting Bumble's unnautical vocabulary and began to appreciate her many other qualities. Bumble was friendly, funny and outspoken. She was also, as we had hoped, a first-class cook. In a very short time, the boys had decided she was marvellous.

We had planned to leave on the Saturday at midday but, by the time we had loaded the last of the provisions and waited for the fridge man to finish fixing the compressor, it was five o'clock. Normally this would not have mattered, but we soon discovered that the local diver charged quadruple rate for cutting ropes free from propeller shafts after five on Saturday evenings.

'Your anchor's bound to be fouled,' said the cheerful soul on the boat next door, settling back to watch the fun as we tried to leave the dock. What this delightful character refrained from mentioning was that he had dropped his anchor over ours, and had attached a tripping line to it. This tripping line was floating just below the surface and was lying successfully in wait for our propeller. Two hours later we finally motored out of Antibes harbour having been relieved of several hundred francs by the diver. As circumstances would have it, we had been forced to cut our friend's line and drop his anchor where we could, just under his bow.

As soon as we hit the swell beyond the harbour we had our first panic. The mizzen mast started to whip backwards and forwards in a frightening fashion. We tightened the backstay as much as we could but on raising a headsail we saw that the problem was more general. There was virtually no tension in any of the fore and aft rigging and the main forestay was sagging away in a great curve. 'Just like my grandmother's knickers,' someone murmured.

There was little we could do about this problem while under way. Indeed, we gave it almost no thought that first night, for the Mediterranean produced one of its strong head-winds and short, steep seas. As the boat leapt from wave to wave the motion could only be described as fantastic. Soon Robin had turned pale, then sheet-white and rushed to the side of the boat to roost in misery. 'So sorry . . . .' he murmured between heaves. 'Pretty useless . . . so sorry.' Poor Bumble also followed suit, creeping quietly to the stern and looking dejectedly out into the night between ignominious bouts of sickness. However, she had managed to produce a pan of hot soup and some stew before rushing on deck. This meant that, in the boys' eyes, Bumble was definitely an okay girl. Few of us felt exactly well that night and we were glad when the weather improved for the rest of the trip to Gibraltar.

In those few days many of the boat's vices were revealed. There was a drum winch called Killer which specialised in spinning back under load and trying to break your wrist. Its smaller, equally dangerous, brother on the mizzen mast succeeded in spraining Albert's hand. Worse, we put up the spinnaker one day and nearly lost Beat. Pulled by the full spinnaker, the pole flew out of its cup on the mast – into which it was supposedly locked – and started beating around the foredeck. It smashed a Plexiglass hatch, then hit Beat a hard blow on the shoulder. Luckily for him he fell to the deck just as the great pole swung viciously back across the deck, missing his head by inches. We later discovered that the lock on the mast cup was faulty and thenceforth treated it with necessary caution. These incidents were an early warning of the dangers inherent in sailing large, powerful boats. From then on we were particularly careful to treat all the heavy gear with respect.

We had an interesting time with the sails, too. Most of them had been made by the Mediterranean loft of a well-known sailmaker who would, I'm sure, prefer to remain nameless. The sails were Mediterranean in temperament; they were good and strong to look at, but proved disappointing on further acquaintance. Like the boat herself, the sails were only two years old, yet a small headsail split in a moderate breeze and the reefing cringles pulled out of the mainsail. To be fair, you don't expect sails to last very long on a large boat but, when you find an apparently new and unused sail still in its plastic wrapping, it is reasonable to think it will stand up to the purpose for which it was designed. We kept this sail – a storm jib – and many months later found that it not only let us down, but at a critical moment in the race.

We also encountered troubles of our own making. As we sailed along the Spanish coast we left a sail tied down to the rail to discover that a large wave had carried it through the flimsy netting on the guard wires and into the sea, tearing the sail, bending a stanchion, breaking another and forcing the pulpit over at a drunken angle. Later, as we approached Coruña in north-west Spain, we got carried away with the thrill of surfing downwind for the first time and, as we hit thirteen knots, blew out the spinnaker. Owing to a slight misunderstanding we had been carrying the light spinnaker in what could only be described as a 'frisky breeze'.

The engine was also something of a problem. Every night in the Med. the wind died and we were forced to motor for hours at a time. The engine worked well, but we soon realised that it was eating oil at a terrifying rate. Only by squeezing the last drops of oil from the can and praying did we make the last few miles to Gibraltar.

The electrics were also troublesome. One of the crew became known as the Human Fuse, due to his talent for disappearing into the bilge, holding two wires together and forming a human connection – or, if he was off-form, for creating sparks and blowing the main fuse. Upside-down in the bilge was a favourite position for applying our own special shaft brake as well. Not only did the original brake not work, but it did not exist, though the fittings and controls were there. To stop the shaft spinning, we jammed a broom-handle against the brake disc until the handle burst into flames or the shaft ground to a halt, then leapt down and secured the shaft with some mole grips. Sailing the Swan was becoming a test of ingenuity and inventiveness.

However, life on board was great fun, despite some appalling red wine that Albert had found in an Antibes supermarket. Not only did it stain our lips and doubtless our stomachs, but it tasted of vinegar and old socks. (Albert excused himself by saying he didn't think the English knew one wine from another, a remark which brought a storm of indignation.) I was particularly pleased to see that Bumble was enjoying herself and hoped that she would agree to join us on the race. Apart from the first night the sailing had been warm and pleasant – enough to convert anyone to the delights of boating. To balance the picture, I would try to paint a black portrait of the Southern Ocean, emphasising the bitter cold, the damp, the danger and the discomforts. Bumble would nod gravely, remark that it sounded like Scotland in winter and go happily back to the cooking.

Navigation provided some interesting times too. The radio direction finder did not work – although it had in harbour, of course – and we had no information on the currents through the Straits of Gibraltar, which resulted in our sailing twelve hours to make good thirty miles. But the most interesting aspect of our night in the Straits was the fact that, whichever heading we were on, the compass read the same. Fortunately, it sorted itself out when the boat became upright but we never entirely trusted the instrument until it had been serviced back in England.

We had a long, tedious, windward beat up the coast of Portugal during which we discovered many things that had to be mended, replaced, or simply fitted, while the Bay of Biscay in March gave us a foretaste of how well the

27

Off the coast of Portugal – a taste of things to come?

boat would behave in bad weather. However, moderate conditions in the Channel provided the biggest surprise. As we hoisted a genoa the forestay started stranding at the top terminal and then broke with a loud ping. Fortunately we had a headsail up and the inner forestay set, so we didn't lose the mast, but nonetheless it was an unnerving experience.

'My God,' said Bumble, 'all this on a 1,000 mile trip. What will it be like doing 27,000 miles?'

'Probably terrible,' said Robert cheerfully, adding in the warm tone he always assumed when prompted by cupboard love, 'But if we eat food like this all the way round, we won't care!' He gave Bumble one of his most charming smiles, rounded off by a heavy wink.

Bumble remained totally unimpressed. 'Thank you!' she replied, giving him a sickly grin. 'But no, you may not have third helpings, nor lick the mixing bowl, nor pick before meals when we're on the race!'

'You *are* coming with us then, Bumble?' I asked.

'Oh Lord, Yes!' she exclaimed. 'I know it's going to be dreadfully tough and unspeakably gruelling and all that, but I wouldn't miss it for the world!'

CHAPTER 2

Endless Preparations

I arrived back at Lymington with a long list of jobs for the boat. Most important was obviously the re-rigging. The particular terminal which had failed was infamously weak when fitted to 12 mm-gauge wire and several boats had lost their masts as a result. We decided therefore to have all the rigging replaced with heavier-gauge wire and to use swaged terminals. Also, we were unhappy about the way the mizzen was supported by a triatic stay to the main mast. This meant that the two masts could not be tuned independently. Should one mast break, it would almost certainly take the other with it. We agreed therefore to stay the mizzen independently, although this involved fitting chainplates for two new forward shrouds.

Another priority was a stronger but shorter main boom. The existing one was already slightly bent from a dip in the water at some time or another. We needed one which would stand up to any number of broaches and rolls. Luckily, we were offered a suitable boom by a sparmaker for immediate delivery; it had been ordered for another large boat but never picked up. Otherwise we would have had to wait months, so heavy was the demand for booms at the time. The other essentials were, of course, sails. We ordered cautiously to begin with. At £2,000 a sail we wanted to be certain we were spending our budget wisely.

A further consideration was to lighten the boat. She was weighed down with all the extras that rich cruising men like to put on their boats: radar, electric windlass, generator and endless water tanks to provide water for plenty of showers. Since we would be carrying as little water as possible, showers would be out. Neither did we need two large anchors when lighter, smaller ones would do for kedging near starting lines, if necessary.

And so began the great strip-out. Everything non-essential was taken to the store and left in piles – cabin linings, foc's'le bunks and lockers, mast covers, and cabin doors. However, one door was left by common consent – it was the door to the aft loo so that at least one special moment in our day could be passed in glorious isolation. The loos themselves were not sacred; we ripped out two of the four, making more space in the fo'c'sle for sails, and providing a space for a workshop in one of the shower compartments.

When it came to removing the heavy equipment that we didn't need, we found a great ally in Chris Carrington, the proprietor of one of the local boatyards. He gave us many a helping hand at weekends, mainly in the form of disengaging and dismantling almost everything we let him get his hands on.

We had only to point him at something and, rubbing his hands with delight, he would set about it with great vigour until it succumbed.

Chris would have been an ideal candidate for our crew – he was a fine sailor and had a roguish sense of humour. But there were two problems; he had a successful boatbuilding business which could not be neglected, and a family it would be hard to leave behind. However, Chris was still to play an important part in our project. He agreed to become our agent, a sort of Mr Fix-It, while we were away. Inevitably, we would need spares and equipment sent out to the various stops. Chris would know what we wanted and how to get hold of it quickly.

There were others like Chris who would have made ideal crew members but were unable to take the time off. And then there were the people who were so desperate to come that they were willing to pay for the privilege. However, few had much sailing experience and probably thought sailing round the world would be a rather romantic adventure. In reality, it would be a hard slog, often monotonous, usually uncomfortable, and probably boring for those who were not fascinated by the sailing itself. Neither did most of the people who wrote to us have any specialist skills to offer. We were looking for a doctor, an engineer and a sailmaker, all with some sailing experience, but not necessarily a great deal. We received one delightful letter from a woman who modestly pronounced her only skill to be midwifery, a job she trusted would not be necessary during the trip. At least she realised that skills were at a premium. Many others did not. And some were obviously planning to make the sailing their secondary consideration. There was the scientist who wanted to carry out experiments all the way round the world, but would be delighted to help out with the sailing from time to time. And there were the three freaked-out Americans who were very much 'into the sea' and 'experience-sharing' and 'inter-social relations', who felt the race would be a 'mind-stretching phenomenon'. Undoubtedly it would be – for them!

However, we were still managing to build up our crew by other means. In 1974 Eve Bonham and I had become the first all-girl crew to take part in the two-handed Round Britain Race and had managed to do reasonably well. Evey, although not a dedicated sailor, had proved to be a first-class crew, enthusiastic, hard-working, and with an ironic, self-deprecating sense of humour which always delighted me. When we asked Evey if she would join us on the Whitbread Race, typically, her first reaction was one of self-doubt. She was, she declared, not good enough for such a demanding race; she had nothing to contribute. Although . . . in her usual analytical way, she put her mind through a rapid assessment of the possibilities . . . she might be able to sew a sail? Behind her reticence, Evey was very excited about the idea and finally declared in her straightforward way; 'I may not be a brilliant sailor, but I'd never forgive myself if I was left behind!'

The first weekend Evey came down to work on the boat alongside Jacques, Robert, Robin, Chris and the other helpers, she was determined to show that she could contribute as much or more than anyone else. And she did, then and throughout the race. She applied herself heart and soul to learning the job of sail repairing as well as the role of efficient deck crew. Evey was running a

Eve, determined not to let the women down.

number of cottage industries from her home but, by getting an agent to run them in her absence, felt confident she would be able to get away for the necessary eight months.

Financial planning was always difficult for the crew. Like most of the people who were to do the race, *ADC*'s crew would be unpaid. Quite apart from the dent that salaries would make in the budget, I felt that *ADC* would be a happier boat if none of the crew had to justify a salary to me or anyone else. Some of the other yachts in the race were to have one or two paid hands; one boat had an almost fully professional crew. Whether this made them go faster it is difficult to say, but we certainly found the atmosphere on the amateur entries more congenial.

However, I was able to offer the crew their keep on board, instead of asking them for 'food money' as was the custom on some other boats. In port they had to find their own expenses which, unless they had expensive tastes, could be kept reasonably low. Thus the race should not cost them more than £200 or so.

I anticipated some difficulty in finding a doctor for the crew. It wasn't essential to have one, of course, but I felt it would be rather like being uninsured. If I didn't bother, then disaster would strike in mid-ocean in the form of appendicitis. I could not imagine finding a qualified doctor who would

31

want, or could afford, to take eight months off but, more in hope than expectation, I put an advertisement in the *Lancet* and waited for some replies.

Jacques and I had also decided that *ADC* should have a navigator. Although both of us were capable of finding our way across oceans, we wanted an expert who was experienced in star sights, routeing and weather, as well as the normal sun sights. Remembering Jacques' old crew mate from the previous race who was currently skippering another Swan 65 in the West Indies, we wrote to John Tanner and asked him if he would be interested in joining us. Before becoming a yacht skipper, John had been a master mariner in the merchant navy, and navigator on several ocean races, including the Round the World and the Round Britain. I did not know John very well, having only met him a couple of times, so my letter was tentative, suggesting only that he come over and discuss the matter with us. However, there was no doubt in John's mind for we received a telegram by return, saying 'Count me in.' In a letter which arrived soon after, John told us he would be coming to England in a month, which would provide a good opportunity for me to get to know him and decide whether he would fit in with the rest of the crew.

In the midst of all this preparation and paperwork, Jacques and I finally found a lovely house in Lymington. It was old and had distinct character. However the choice was something of a compromise because, to Jacques' disgust, the garden was rather small. But it was near the marina and very convenient for all matters nautical; also, there were plenty of helpful neighbours around to keep an eye on the place while we were away. After a

John signed on as navigator and tactician.

difficult and protracted move – we did it ourselves under the mistaken impression that we possessed only a few sticks of furniture – it was marvellous to settle into our own home at last. I was anxious to get started on the curtains and redecorating but, with a pang of disappointment, realised I would have to leave it until we returned. The work on the boat and the many arrangements for the trip were taking up my days and most of my evenings as well. But now at least we had somewhere to come home to after the race, and the knowledge was warm and comforting.

Jacques was commuting to work at Basingstoke every day but managed to supervise work on the boat at weeekends. I spent most of my time choosing and purchasing equipment. Many manufacturers were generous enough to lend or donate gear, principally Marconi who once again lent me the long-range transmitter that I had taken on my Atlantic trip. They also lent me an emergency radio for the liferafts and a distress watch-keeping radio. Another company who continued to provide tremendous support were Chloride, who took immense pains to ensure that we had the best storage and engine-starting batteries that could be provided.

We decided on a new deck plan, mainly to make the spinnaker work easier, and ordered new winches, lead blocks and eye plates. Killer and Baby Killer, the two drum winches which had given so much trouble on the delivery trip, were removed. All the gear had to be immensely strong and well fitted to withstand the hard, remorseless downwind sailing we would be doing in the Southern Ocean. There were new liferafts to be bought to satisfy the stringent race regulations; crew clothing to be ordered, yardwork to be discussed, a new racing propeller to choose, the rating certificate to be updated, which meant having the boat remeasured, new end-fittings for the spinnaker poles to be organised, still more items to be removed to provide space and weight. It was a never-ending marathon of organisation, telephone calls, discussion and decisions which kept us busy long into the nights.

One of the principal things to organise was, of course, the food. Bumble had returned to work on St Kilda and it was some time before she worked out the list of provisions. When she finally sent it, I nearly fell off my chair. There was enough food to feed the average family for ten years! How could twelve people possibly eat so much – 160 lb of tinned rhubarb! 200 lb of tinned plums! There were 1,500 lb of tinned fruit alone. With visions of the boat at least five inches down on her marks and wallowing at the end of the fleet, I hastily tried to contact Bumble by telephone, not easy when she was on a remote island, but just possible with the help of the Army. When I got through I asked her, in some agitation, if she was planning to feed a platoon for a year. 'Well, that's about it,' she pointed out, 'but perhaps I have overdone it a bit. I could reduce the tins a little . . . and maybe the dried milk. . . .' Like everyone who organises a long ocean passage, I was beginning to wish I had a crew who never ate – nor, for that matter, slept, for then we would need only half the people!

Eventually, Bumble and I came to a compromise, although I was still unhappy about the large number of heavy tins. By this time it was the end of June and, a supermarket chain having offered to supply all our non-perishable stores, there was a terrible last-minute scramble to send the order through and get it sorted into four different piles ready for shipment to the various stops. Inexplicably, the supermarket people were to decide in the middle of the race that they were not receiving enough publicity for their outlay – which had been £1,500, less than the price of a half-page advertisement in a newspaper – and to ask for their money back. This was the only instance of dissatisfaction that we ever met in our dealings with manufacturers.

In May we sailed *ADC* up to London so that BSR could publicise the boat and their new products to the press and the hi-fi trade. During the trips there and back we took the opportunity to ask some crew applicants to come along for a sail. It was an awkward situation, for they well knew that they were on trial, but it was the only way to discover their capabilities. We had to have people competent to steer, both to the wind and to a compass course, people able to understand and carry out orders from the watch leader and, above all, people who were compatible with the rest of the group. Among those who came along was a doctor, whom we found not through my advertisement but through Robert who had 'heard about him from a friend'. His name was Nick Milligan. He was a registrar, soon to take his FRCS in anaesthetics and, he added disarmingly, to fail it. During his present job at a busy accident hospital he hadn't had enough time to do the necessary studying. A year spent sailing round the world would, he felt, give him sufficient time to steel himself for another try.

Nick was basically a dinghy sailor, although he had sailed on larger boats too. But there were few things about sailing on *ADC Accutrac* that his quick mind didn't pick up that first weekend. Also, he had a wickedly dry humour and a deceptively offhand manner that immediately made him popular with the rest of the crew. By the end of the second weekend he had become our doctor, with the smallest number of patients he was likely to have for many years to come. It was a tremendous stroke of luck to have found Nick, because the few doctors who had replied to my advertisement had sounded rather unpromising. We hoped we would be as fortunate in finding the last few crew members we needed.

It was not essential to have a fully-trained engineer to look after the main engine, which we would be using to generate power; we just needed someone who understood diesels and would be able to carry out routine servicing and repairs. Ever since he had written to us the previous December, we had thought Fred Dovaston might fill this job very well. Fred was skipper of one of the Ocean Youth Club's 73-foot ketches, the *Francis Drake*. As such he would be used to doing most of the boat's maintenance himself. He was likely to be a patient, easy-going sort of person too, because the Club boats took a fresh crew of green teenage recruits every week, all of whom would have to be taught the ropes. However, we could not be certain that Fred was ideal until we had met him ourselves and gone sailing with him. It was not his seamanship that was in doubt but, as always, his compatibility and sense of humour.

When we met Fred, we were immediately struck by his size. Fred was a large, strong man, with shoulders as broad as an ox and one had the feeling he could have handled *ADC*'s gear singlehanded. But for all his strength, Fred was a gentle, friendly character, fond of chatting and 'yarning' about his

Nick, doctor and master of dry wit (*left*); Fred, engineer and raconteur.

sailing experiences. Later we were to discover that he had an almost limitless supply of terrible yet hilarious jokes, but on that first meeting we were only aware of his warm sense of humour and remarkable smile, which lit up his whole face like a beacon. Fred was very happy to become our engineer and, having arranged for him to go on a course at Volvo's, his place in the crew was confirmed.

We also decided to confirm Robert and Robin's place in the crew. They had worked hard on preparing the boat and, although they were inexperienced, they were keen and willing, which counted for a lot. Many people had given me advice about choosing crew and they all agreed on one thing – never have too many experts on one boat, otherwise there would be endless arguments and discussions about everything from the course to the number of sails the boat should be carrying. Better, they all agreed, to have a hard core of experts to run the boat, and a majority of 'gorillas' to carry out the orders. Robert and Robin were to be gorillas. Jacques gave them a demonstration of what was involved in this onerous task by ambling off across the deck, trailing his knuckles, and swinging from the rigging, grunting loudly.

Now and then, in that frantic summer of preparation, we saw other yachts which were entered for the race, a sight which always caused my confidence to waver. Inevitably they looked faster, better equipped, and better sailed than we did. We saw *King's Legend,* a sloop-rigged Swan 65, sail effortlessly down the Solent. We saw the smart, custom-built *Flyer* sail into Lymington on her way to do the fully-crewed Transatlantic Race, which she won with ease. We saw the giant *Great Britain II* being refitted in Dartmouth, ready for her crew of seventeen. And we peeped in at Bowman's yard in Emsworth to get a glimpse of the 77-foot *Heath's Condor* being constructed in rapid time to be ready for the start. *Condor* had a special interest for us because she was to be co-skippered by Les Williams, Jacques' skipper on the first Whitbread Race. Many of Jacques' old crew mates would be going with Les again, including Peter Blake who was to be the best man at our wedding in July.

Seeing all these sleek yachts, I wondered what were our chances of success. Around marinas and bars, there are always plenty of people who will tell you what is wrong with your boat, implying that you haven't a chance of winning. Inevitably, some of this had rubbed off on me and I was beginning to wonder if we had even a remote chance of doing well. This would make Jacques furious and he would tell me, quite rightly, to ignore all the self-styled experts and get on with the job.

We knew we had no chance of line honours, that is, of arriving first at each stop, because this depended solely on absolute speed, and therefore size of boat. One of the large maxi-raters like *Condor* or *GB II* would gain those honours. But the real prizes were judged on handicap. In theory, the application of a handicap – in the form of a certain number of hours each competitor was allowed over the scratch boat – would even out all the differences in speed and give every boat an equal chance of winning. In practice, it was apt to give an advantage to the smaller boats because, in many conditions, they went almost as fast as the large boats. Even when they went slower, it was rarely by as much as their handicaps. However, on a long, hard race, it could be argued that the large boats would stand up to bad conditions more easily and have a better chance of escaping damage.

To obtain a good handicap, we needed a good rating. Several friends who were experts on the rating formula gave us many hints as to how we might improve our measurement by altering the sail area, changing the boat's trim and other such means. After two remeasurements, we managed to lower our rating considerably in time for the start of the race. Now we just had to sail the boat fast!

We took the boat out sailing whenever we could, to study the sails, to find out how best to set them, and how to handle the boat generally. There was no limit to the number of sails we were allowed to take on the race, but there was a limit to the number we could physically fit into the boat. Our wardrobe was hovering at the twenty-three mark which, for a ketch, was by no means excessive. We had replaced many old sails with new ones, but it was impossible to be certain of the additional sails we needed without going on a 4,000-mile trip and meeting every kind of weather. John Tanner, who had come to England to see us, thought we should buy a certain two, while Jacques favoured buying two other sails. In the end, we compromised and chose those sails which would be most versatile. Our greatest error was to trust some of the spinnakers from the original wardrobe. Needless to say, we were to discover our error the hard way.

John stayed a week before returning to his skipper's job abroad. During that time I had a chance to get to know him and admire him for his knowledge of the Swan-class boat. He made many helpful suggestions, particularly concerning deck layout and sail plan. At the same time I was a little worried that John might not enjoy being an ordinary crew member after spending

36

years skippering his own boat. Inevitably, he would have developed his own ideas about how the boat should be sailed and might find it difficult to adapt to someone else's. However, John was confident that this would not prove to be a problem. He said he was anxious to fit in with the existing arrangements and to blend into the crew structure. Certainly, his schoolboyish humour and ability to take a joke ensured that he would fit in with the atmosphere that was developing on *ADC*. We soon discovered that John was a great theoretician and was heard to talk about 'slot effects' and 'wind flow round the forestay'. This made him the butt of many jokes, which he always took in good heart. From the beginning, it was apparent that John had some ideas about sailing which did not correspond with Jacques' and mine. However, I did not feel this would necessarily be a bad thing. Differing ideas could lead to better solutions and, as long as there was some give and take, it should not create a problem. John was an experienced navigator and professed a great interest in tactics. As such, he should be an asset to our team.

As the summer rushed on, the boat gradually approached a state that could be called readiness, although there were still many last-minute jobs cropping up. We had entered for three of the major offshore ocean races being held before and during Cowes Week to give us an opportunity to flex our racing

A weekend sail in the Solent (*photo:* Jonathan Eastland).

muscles. Unfortunately we were not ready in time to enter the Deauville Race in June. Nonetheless, we felt that a cross-Channel trip would be useful, and decided to follow the fleet across. It was a grey, rainy weekend, but the atmosphere on the boat was exceptionally bright – Jacques, being near French soil, was sporting a beret, Robert was planning a sortie into the fleshpots of Deauville, such as they were, and Chris was calculating how much wine he could buy without going bankrupt. But the brightest feature of the weekend was a beady, piratical character named Sam. Sam Badrick had been referred to us by the RNSA from their long list of people wanting to crew on the big race. He had sailed on the second leg of the previous Round the World Race on *British Soldier,* the Army entry. Now, as an Army cook (retired), he wanted to do the whole of the race. 'But not, mate, as a bleedin' cook!' he declared forcefully. 'I've cooked enough bleedin' meals to feed a ruddy army and I ain't going to do no more!' Then he added disarmingly, 'But I'll offer to cook a meal this weekend just so's you'll be impressed with my amazin' all-round skill.'

His real name was not Sam but Anthony, although he was rarely called by his proper name. 'You can see why I'm called Sam, of course,' he declared, grinning. 'You can't? Bloomin' heck, I'm the image of the bloke! Sammy Davis, mate, Sammy Davis.' We looked hard at Sam. He certainly wasn't black, nor was his hair fuzzy but, in a strange way, we had to admit there was a remarkable resemblance. At one time Sam's nose had met something (or someone) and broken across the bridge, while one of his eyes looked a little odd, the result of a motorbike accident when a piece of glass had penetrated the iris. Then there was the beard. But this, we felt, was where the similarity ended, for Sam's beard ran riot at a point somewhere under his chin.

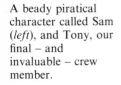

A beady piratical character called Sam (*left*), and Tony, our final – and invaluable – crew member.

Sam brought a new dimension to the boat. His small, wiry frame popped up everywhere and swung monkey-like around the deck, always busy, always helpful, and always with a waggish comment on his tongue. As we left the marina at Deauville, Sam reinforced his monkey-like image by performing one of the most remarkable feats ever seen on a boat. In the confusion of trying to warp the boat off a leeward quay I was suddenly aware, as we finally pulled away, that Sam had not had time to clamber on board after letting go the lines. With the gap between the boat and the dock widening all the time, I started looking for another quay where we might pick Sam up on the way out. But at the sound of a yell, I looked back to see Sam accelerating down the quay, heading straight for the ever-widening gap. With a great leap he launched himself into the air, hung in space for a moment, and then disappeared from view. I waited for the splash but astonishingly there was none. Instead, a battered but still cheerful Sam slowly pulled himself up over the side of the boat – where he had been crouching like a frog since landing – and rolled on to the deck. Sam assured us that he was fine, apart from two broken legs, a crushed chest and a soft head which had made him think it was a good idea in the first place. Later, we discovered that he had grazed his shins quite badly.

'We would have come back for you, Sam,' I assured him.

'Well, I thought you might,' Sam conceded. 'But then I thought I'd better show willin' and chalk up some Brownie points.'

By the end of the weekend several of the crew had come up to me and suggested that Sam should join us, an unusual occurrence because of the awesome responsibilities of making recommendations about fellow crew members. With such a popular choice, there was little doubt in the matter and we offered Sam his place soon after.

Our trip to Deauville also brought us into contact with Tony Bertram for the first time. Tony was the paid hand on one of the top ocean racers and was introduced to us by mutual friends who knew he was interested in doing the Whitbread Race. Tony had all the qualities we were looking for in our final crew member. We needed another sail trimmer and first-rate deck hand, and Tony would fill that bill admirably. Some time later, when he had been sailing on *ADC* a couple of times, we began to realise just what a remarkable person we had found. Not only was Tony an excellent sailor, but he was a good helmsman and first-rate bosun too. To cap it all, Tony was also the kindest and gentlest person one could hope to meet, quite incapable of a mean or ungenerous thought.

With the addition of Tony the crew was now complete and one of my main worries was over. Most of the twelve would have to keep their jobs until two or three weeks before the start of the race on 27th August, but those who were not abroad or working at weekends came down to help us with the work every Saturday and Sunday. Crew training, such as we would have time for, would have to wait until early August.

Meanwhile, the organisational work kept me fully occupied. I had to get hold of the crew's measurements which, with half of them dispersed over Britain and Europe, was no easy matter. I then had to order oilskins, boots, sweaters and polar wear, some of which arrived in the wrong quantities or sizes and had to be sent back. Suppliers of boat equipment had to be chased, gear had to be picked up, letters had to be replied to.

In the middle of all this we tried to make wedding plans, or rather my poor family tried to find out what sort of a wedding we wanted. One day we would decide we wanted to slip away to a registry office, much to the dismay of the family who were secretly hoping we would choose an enormous white wedding. The next moment we would settle for a church wedding, but with only the family present. When my mother and sister were almost on the point of despair, we finally committed ourselves to a small church wedding with a large dance afterwards. This actually burdened my family with twice as much work, for not only did they have to arrange the wedding and the dance, but also accommodation for half the guests afterwards. Typically, they did not complain but leapt into the arrangements without a word of reproach.

Thinking everything was in hand, we were then surprised to find that we would need a special licence to marry in the tiny village church near my parents' house, because it was outside the ecclesiastical boundary and I was being unusual enough to marry a foreigner ('And a Frenchman at that!' said Jacques). This created panic because birth certificates had to be found and, incredibly, we had to obtain the written permission of our parents although, goodness knows, we were well over eighteen. Father made an almost indecent rush to scribble the necessary lines, saying it wasn't every day you found a chap to take your last daughter off your hands and that he wasn't going to hold things up. Finally, about three weeks before the wedding, all the difficulties seemed to have been sorted out. There was only one worrying moment on the occasion of Jacques' stag party, when he nearly got arrested for leaving a restaurant reclining on a table and then dancing down the street wearing little more than a bowler hat and a Union Jack umbrella. Fortunately I did not have to bail him out, although the police would not have had much difficulty in guessing where the culprit lived for, prior to passing out on the boat, Jacques' cronies – including Nick, Robert, Robin and Chris – left his trousers, vest and a sock hanging from the flower box outside my bedroom window.

We were married the following Friday, the 8th July, amid what we fondly believed to be great secrecy, only to find a dozen pressmen waiting for us outside the church. Jacques, whose feelings about the press are not always very kind, had to be restrained from punching several on the nose, particularly when they tried to ask us questions. However, nothing could really spoil the occasion and, after a brief two-day honeymoon, we returned to work delighted with our new status. To Jacques I was now 'the missus'. To me he was, as always, 'monsieur' or 'the frog'.

As wedding presents to each other, we made wild promises. Jacques would give up smoking and I would improve my French to the point of fluency. Within a week, Jacques was smoking his pipe at the bottom of the garden and I was still eyeing the French Grammar where it sat on the bookshelf. 'Never mind,' said Jacques. 'I'll have no problem in giving up smoking once we're on the race. And there'll be lots of time for us to study French together. Just wait and see!' Of course, three months later Jacques was to deny this conversation

OPPOSITE
'Monsieur' and 'the Missus' on our wedding day (*photo: Daily Mail*, London).

40

ever took place and, although I reminded him about it from time to time, he even had difficulty in recalling the original idea. His loss of memory usually coincided with the enjoyment of a good pipe.

In late July and early August we took part in three ocean races, the Cowes-Dinard, the Channel and the Fastnet. By this time all the crew had joined the boat, except for Beat who was crewing in the Swiss Admiral's Cup team. However, the races gave us little opportunity to try out our handling techniques over a wide range of conditions. The wind was light most of the time, even falling to a flat calm on the Fastnet. But on that race at least we could match ourselves against some of the other yachts entered for the Whitbread – *King's Legend, Condor, GB II* and *Disque d'Or*. The flat calm and our abandonment of the race made the outcome indecisive but, just before retiring after a hundred and seventy miles of racing, we found ourselves level with our twin, the other Swan 65 ketch, *Disque d'Or*. It was an encouraging result and we settled down to the final preparations with optimism and enthusiasm.

As time went on, each crew member acquired special jobs that were his or her individual responsibility. In addition to looking after the stowage, Evey was one of our two sail repairers. Sam was the other, having 'strung a few sails together on *British Soldier*'. Fred was now our fully-fledged engineer, after taking a course at Volvo and then servicing every moving part of the boat's engine – or at least all those he could get his hands on. Robin was our winch expert, who would be responsible for servicing and repairing the twenty-three winches. Robert, having readily agreed to become our entertainments officer – he would have to ensure we had enough books, games and party entertainments for the race, as well as making arrangements for birthdays – also agreed, to his eternal credit, to become our loo expert. If he was reluctant to take on this vital task, he did not show it and without a grumble went off to Blake's in Gosport to learn the secrets of marine installations. Nick was, of course, to be our doctor, a job which would fill his spare time well enough, allowing for the usual number of scrapes, scratches and headaches on a long race. Tony and Beat would be our two bosuns, that is, in charge of all the deck gear – the ropes, blocks, running and standing rigging, the cleats, eyes, shackles and splices. As navigator, John would have enough to do without being given another job; so too would Bumble, although in the months to come she was to be a great help with the sail repairs. I was to be the radio operator, with the task of getting through to England every day, while Jacques, with his special skills, would be a general fixer and mender of miscellaneous pieces of gear. He was something of a carpenter, fitter, electrician and maintenance man; someone who was rarely stuck for a solution to a repair problem.

There was another job that Jacques, Fred and I were to do, and that was to make a film for the BBC. Like the programme I had helped make on the Singlehanded Transatlantic Race, this film was to be directed by Bob Saunders and shown in *The World About Us* series. Although I had moaned about the difficulties of using the complex camera and sound equipment when singlehanded, I felt it would be much easier when there were three of us responsible for doing the filming. Also, we would have nineteen weeks instead of just four in which to take the necessary footage for a fifty-minute programme, which should give us plenty of scope.

During the Singlehanded Race I had sent back reports to the *Daily Express,* an arrangement which had worked very happily, and which I understood they wanted to continue into the Round the World Race. Then, in the rapidly changing manner of Fleet Street, the editor and executive editor suddenly 'moved on' and the *Express* found itself with an editor who loved football – but hated sailing. He too 'moved on' some months later in favour of another yacht-loving editor, but by that time I had agreed to send reports back to Capital Radio and write articles for *The Observer.* I was to enjoy writing for *The Observer* very much indeed, but I was to find the transmitting of live radio reports to millions of Capital listeners a terrifying experience, like standing on a platform and speaking to a large audience on a different subject every day for a year.

Just when you think everything might be running smoothly, a dozen last-minute problems turn up. A week before we were due to sail for Portsmouth for the start of the race, we took the boat out of the water for a last antifoul, to discover that the Italian antifouling paint was incompatible with any and every type of British paint. Chris quickly located the only supplier of the Italian paint in the UK, and had their last few tins delivered to us in rapid time. Our fancy new racing propeller finally arrived from Italy, but could not be fitted without extensive modifications to the shaft, which took another few days of our precious last week. Mother, who had steadfastly been visiting every mountaineering, sailing and arctic-wear emporium, sent down a large parcel of what was known as her thermo-nuclear underwear, to add to the large pile of clothing I was trying to sort into essential and non-essential categories. At the best of times I am notorious for packing clothes for every occasion from a full-dress ball to a fishing expedition and was having the usual difficulty in deciding what to leave behind. Jacques was the opposite, feeling that a pair of jeans, a sweater and some warm underwear were about all you needed to circle the world. Everything would have balanced out all right except that I smuggled loads of clothes aboard for Jacques, and remained as indecisive as usual about what I should take. In the end, yet again, I took too much. Having gone to so much trouble to lighten ship I was sufficiently ashamed about this excess of clothing to hide most of it away under my bunk.

There were also many last-minute arrangements to be made about money. Our bills had to be paid while we were away, and cash had to be available in the various stops to provide supplies and repairs for the boat. Fortunately, my father agreed to carry out these thankless tasks and for the next eight months he battled away with the accounts, the invoices and the correspondence while we sailed around the world. At the last minute we also decided that we should have some superior American spinnaker pole-ends and snap shackles, and arrangements had to be made for these to be flown to Cape Town where we would fit them for the second leg.

Probably no departure would be complete without these last-minute panics; somehow chaos and confusion are all part of the scene. Neither would a departure have its usual colour without the other necessity of leave-taking, the parties. Capital Radio gave one, friends gave them, family gave them and Joe Sanders of the Lymington Sail and Tent Co. gave a large one. Joe had supplied me with rope, covers, and endless bits and pieces ever since I had been sailing from Lymington, while Sanders Sails, under his son Peter, had supplied us with two new sails for *ADC* as well as carrying out most of our sail repairs. They were giving us the party, they announced, in celebration of seeing the last of our large sails cluttering up all their loft space.

After a week of good living we were all feeling a little liverish and it was hard to imagine another seven days' hard hospitality in Portsmouth. I have long suspected that race organisers plan parties in proportion to the length of a race. If you have enough of a hangover, you'll be glad to leave on an eight-year trip, let alone an eight-month one.

On our last day in Lymington, as Jacques and I picked up our bags and prepared to leave the house which we had barely lived in, I almost shed a tear. Closing the front door for the last time, I couldn't help looking forward to the time we would return to its warmth and comfort, seven months hence. After a last glance, we turned quickly away and walked down the hill to where the large white boat and our ten companions waited to begin the big adventure.

CHAPTER 3

A Slow Start

'Wow!' said the boys, eyeing the scene at HMS *Vernon*, the naval shore station where we were to spend the week before the race. I was not sure whether they were referring to the crowds lining the quay, to the high proportion of pretty girls among them, or to the fourteen other yachts tied up to the pontoons. Certainly Jacques and I had eyes only for our competitors. There was the smallest yacht, the 55-feet *Traité de Rome*, representing the Common Market; there were the two ultra-light, narrow French yachts *Gauloises II* and *33 Export;* there was the British *King's Legend,* a sloop-rigged Swan 65 with a mostly professional crew; and there was *Flyer,* the Dutch yacht tipped to win the race. *Flyer* had been designed and built specially for the race at a reputed cost of well over half a million pounds. She was owned and skippered by the millionaire Cornelius van Rietschoten. The two large boats who would be fighting it out for line honours were the 80-foot *GB II* with her crew of seventeen, each of whom had paid £4,000 towards the costs of the trip, and the

The fifteen yachts gather at HMS *Vernon*, Portsmouth.

77-foot *Heath's Condor*, co-skippered by Robin Knox-Johnston and Leslie Williams.

Lying just ahead of us as we came alongside was the boat that particularly interested us. This was our twin, the Swiss-entered *Disque d'Or*, also a Swan 65 ketch. Racing against her should be exciting for we would be able to compete on a boat-for-boat basis without worrying about handicap. Or so we thought. In the next couple of days we discovered that *Disque d'Or* had a better rating than us and therefore a time advantage. We looked into this but, although the rating experts and the designer himself reckoned that something strange had happened at the measuring stage, there was nothing we could do short of having both boats remeasured, difficult if not impossible at this late stage. Sadly, we had to leave things as they were, at a psychological disadvantage to us.

Beat was particularly interested in *Disque d'Or* – he was a German-speaking Swiss, while the skipper and entire crew of *Disque d'Or* were French-speaking. We gathered that there was some feeling of rivalry between the two factions, for Beat almost bristled at the mention of the other boat's name, his normally kind features taking on a hard, determined look.

All the yachts that were gathered there in Portsmouth had one thing in common; they were going to be raced very hard indeed. Whatever awe and respect the competitors in the first race had felt for the magnitude and scope of the event, whatever measures they had taken to save their gear or spare their crews, these would be absent now. The pioneering atmosphere of the first event had been replaced by out-and-out competitiveness. Just one look at the professional crew on *King's Legend* would convince anyone of that.

Our week in Portsmouth was going to be a busy one. Between them, the Royal Naval Sailing Association and Whitbread had organised a party for almost every night. Each yacht had been adopted by a Whitbread pub in Portsmouth and one of the most memorable parties was the one thrown for us by the Duke of Buckingham in the High Street. There was no party organised for the night before the start but BSR, as thoughtful sponsors, filled the gap and provided a magnificent evening for us and our families. In the middle of this alcoholic week BUPA, who were providing free medical insurance for all the British boats, gave the crews an examination. Most of us were feeling quite weak by this time and our blood pressure must have been inordinately high, but since the examining doctors had looked in at most of the parties they must have realised the cause of the symptoms.

ADC was always full of visiting friends, family and journalists so that the stowing of clothing, food and equipment was even more chaotic than usual. All the available locker space seemed to be full, although piles of stuff still lay around waiting to find a home. Eve and Bumble eventually solved the problem by rigging up netting above the bunks and across the saloon roof, which they filled to bulging point with cabbages, fruit and personal gear, while six of the largest salamis we had ever seen hung from the grab rails over the saloon table. One morning I saw Bumble carrying a long, unwieldy bundle on to the boat in an exceedingly furtive manner. Having been caught red-handed, she admitted it was a complete set of fishing gear: rods, lines, hooks and weights. Weights

46

The fresh provisions
arrive last – but
where are they to go?

being a word guaranteed to make me blanch, Bumble hurriedly added, 'Think! We can have fresh fish for breakfast every morning.' Thus persuaded, I left her to find a stowage place for it, by far the greatest problem. Some hours later Nick appeared with a bundle that looked long, thin and familiar. 'Fresh fish every morning?' I asked. 'Absolutely!' he replied, 'and very large ones at that.' I later found the fishing gear lashed to a post in the aft cabin. When on the starboard tack the rods were to make a good hook for hanging towels, jackets and wet hats.

One of our more delightful stowage problems was the four cases of Famous Grouse Scotch whisky presented to us by the distillers – a happy event that Bumble, through her extensive Scottish and drinking connections, had arranged. However, I was not so happy at the idea of carrying forty-eight bottles – as opposed to their contents – when we were so desperately trying to save weight. Robert, as entertainments officer, was given the job of finding a solution and came up with two small plastic barrels used in home beer-making, and two plastic sacks with stoppers. Most of this fine whisky was ignominiously decanted into these containers and stowed in the bilge alongside the many cans of beer provided by Whitbread. However, we kept some of the Grouse in bottles just in case a disaster, such as a puncture, should occur.

47

Finally, there was the BBC film equipment to be housed – eight cameras, four tape recorders, three waterproof cases, one hundred film cassettes, two clapper boards, and eight lengths of cable. Most of this equipment was similar to that I had taken on the Transatlantic Race, but there were two additional items which were new and exciting. One was a spray deflector, a kind of spinning disc which kept water off the lenses, and the other was a helmet which sported a camera. Jacques eyed the helmet with delight and was soon modelling it for the benefit of the others. This strange hat had a fitting for a camera on one side and a counterbalancing weight on the other which, everyone was quick to remark, looked just like the bolt going through Frankenstein's monster's head. The strangeness of the headgear was completed by a wire viewfinder which was worn jauntily over the right eye. The helmet should enable us to take action film while leaving our hands free to handle ropes and winches. This and the rest of the equipment were placed in specially built wooden boxes (more weight again!) and put in the aft cabin which Jacques and I were to share with Bumble – if we could ever find the room.

The week passed quickly in a flurry of activity and leave-taking. My parents arrived two days before the start loaded with parcels and packages, bringing back memories of so many other starts. My father took over the boat's accounts and the hundred and one matters that would have to be seen to while we were away. Rates and electricity bills would have to be paid because unfortunately they would appear just the same as ever. Mother brought along a last few pieces of thermo-nuclear underwear to ensure we did not catch pneumonia. She also brought along a new creation – a Comfort Box. In this large plastic container were all the useful and luxurious articles for keeping the body beautiful – talcum powder, toilet water, toothbrush, flannel and soap. There were also items called baby wipes, 'just in case you don't get a chance to wash every day', breathed Mother conspiratorially, and forty pairs of paper knickers, 'in case you run out of the ordinary kind'. Mother knew I was a great believer in paper knickers at sea, although they did have one disadvantage; when a large wave got through one's oilskins, they were apt to disintegrate in a matter of minutes.

'Now, darling, is there anything else you need?' Mother continued worriedly. 'What about food? Are you getting enough to eat?'

I thought of the tons of stores on board and assured her I would be doing my best to eat very well indeed.

'And are you sure you'll be warm enough? And do be careful, won't you? Remember to clip on! . . . You're sure you've got enough warm underwear?'

All of us took some time and trouble to reassure our families during those last few days, not an easy task when we would be away so long and going so far. However, as the Saturday drew near, everyone became bound up in the excitement of the start and forgot their worries to give us a warm and cheerful send-off.

When Saturday, 27th August, finally arrived it had an unreal quality about it. The rush to load the frozen food and last-minute purchases was over. Tony and Beat had finished the numerous odd jobs on deck. Jacques, John and I had

pored over the charts and the weather information to determine our tactics for the first few days of the leg. Also, not unnoticed by me, Jacques had loaded two hundred cigarettes and a dozen tins of pipe tobacco. In good faith, I had brought a fourth-year French course and a French dictionary so that, time permitting, I could study the language. However, I had the feeling that, however much my French improved, it would never be fluent enough to persuade Jacques to stub out his last cigarette!

Finally, it was time to draw away from the dock. Somehow all twelve of us were on board with all our gear, our stores and our equipment. By that time I had given up worrying how much it all weighed.

It was a grey, gloomy day with a curtain of constant drizzle blotting out the higher reaches of the harbour and the shadowy hills of the Isle of Wight. The weather did not improve our spirits as we made our last goodbyes and pulled away from the dock, to the sound of the shouts and cheers of the crowds. It was difficult to imagine what it would be like to return to this same wharf the following spring, after 27,000 miles and every kind of weather. At that

49

Ready to set sail and all twelve aboard (*photo: The Observer*).

moment, the distance we were to travel appeared vast. Cape Town, less than a quarter of the way round the world, seemed a million miles away.

The drizzle turned to rain as we left the harbour and headed for the starting line off Southsea. Low, heavy clouds were scudding across the sky, turning the sea and land the colour of lead. Yet despite the miserable conditions we were all very grateful to the gusty, fitful wind because it was northerly. This would give us an easy run down-Channel, a lucky change from the usual westerly slog which would have been hard on us in our over-excited and slightly hungover state.

The Solent was already thick with spectator boats as we arrived near the line and began our preparations for the start. Some loud screams and yells marked the arrival of one of 'our' boats, a champagne-special loaded with family which provoked much dancing and shouting from Bumble, Eve and the rest of us. Eventually, I spotted my parents looking very wet and miserable in an open boat. But they cheered as soon as they saw us and they put on a brave smile which brought a lump to my throat.

The start was from west to east, across a line off Southsea. We had to leave the Isle of Wight to starboard but thereafter were free to go to Cape Town by any route we chose.

The last thirty minutes before the start were full of tension and excitement. While trying to avoid the many hundreds of spectator boats, we had to put Sam over the side to make sure our folding propeller was properly closed. Once we knew the prop was closed, we hoisted sail and manoeuvred for the start, no simple business when we were nervous, the boat was doing ten knots and we were trying to dodge all the other craft. When the starting gun finally fired, it was almost a relief.

50

It was a downwind start with all the attendant confusion that spinnakers, mizzen spinnakers and big boys bring. Although we were late on the line because I had been over-cautious, we soon had our spinnaker drawing well and were well up in the fleet. With thousands of miles of racing ahead it may have seemed strange that we were all so keen to make a good start. But it was very important to us; it was our chance to show what we could do against the other boats while still in sight of them. Also, we were keen to set a cracking pace from the very beginning. There were many competitive boats and crews in the race and none was going to give or take any quarter. To get ahead and stay ahead we would have to race hard every moment of every day.

From the moment the gun had fired, a subtle feeling of exhilaration came over the crew, a feeling of release from the months of preparation. As we careered along surrounded by the spectator craft, we whooped and cheered and waved and laughed. Jacques came and gave me a big hug at the wheel. 'We're on our way, love,' he smiled. 'Just gotta go fast now.' I mustered a faint smile. My relief at having started was tinged with the weight of the responsibility of the long voyage ahead. If we had forgotten anything important it was ultimately my failure. If I were to make bad decisions in the months ahead, I would be letting the crew down. It was a sobering thought.

Evey grinned broadly at me. 'Don't worry, love! If we've forgotten anything, it's too late now!'

'Goodbye. Goodbye,' yelled Sam at England in general. 'Don't cry – I'll be back!'

'Look over there!' Jacques shouted. Following his outstretched finger, I saw the unmistakable shape of the *Golly,* motoring flat out some yards away. On one bow was a banner which read 'Good Luck, Jacques' and on the other 'Good Luck, Clare.' As usual the *Golly*'s owners, Ron and Joan Green, had gone to a lot of trouble to give us a memorable send-off.

I was also very touched to see some of the Seaview Mermaids there to wave us goodbye. Seaview was the small village on the Isle of Wight, just opposite Southsea, where both Evey and I learnt to sail as children. It was in the Mermaids that I had first gained experience in keel boats, before going on to larger boats and longer trips. I was happy that *ADC* was racing under the Sea View Yacht Club burgee which fluttered from the rigging as we waved to the intrepid and extremely wet club members who had sailed out to wave goodbye.

The only mark of the course in our sailing instructions for the first leg was Bembridge Ledge Buoy, just two miles from the start line. We had to leave this, and therefore the Isle of Wight, to starboard. As we steamed toward the place where we thought the buoy should be – we could not see it for spectator craft – we prepared to gybe, a manoeuvre we would rather not have carried out in full view of several hundred people. However, to our delight and even our surprise, it went extremely smoothly and, having been neck and neck with *Disque d'Or,* we found ourselves clear ahead. We hoped it was a good omen of things to come.

'Perhaps we'd better give them a chance and slow down,' murmured Nick, looking over his shoulder.

ADC and *Disque d'Or* racing for Bembridge Ledge Buoy (*photo: The Observer*).

Now the spectator boats started to thin out. For the first time I spotted the large motor cruiser with my sister and her family aboard, my little nephew and nieces waving vaguely, still too young to understand what the fuss was about. Bumble's family and friends also steamed up again, making us laugh by producing a long riding whip which they lashed through the air, urging us on. Bob Saunders, the director of our film, gave us a last wave of encouragement from his launch, cheering at the sight of Fred avidly filming despite the wet and grey conditions. There, too, were my parents in their small open boat, doubtless suffering from the wet and cold, but determined not to show it.

One by one, the boats started to turn back. One by one, it was the turn of each of us to give a last wave and a last cheerful smile to our families as they disappeared towards the rainy, grey outline of Portsmouth, already miles behind.

'How about some lunch?' said Bumble, suddenly breaking the silence. 'Now you're talking, Bumble!' cried several voices. And we started to busy ourselves around the boat, suddenly aware that there was still much to be sorted out before we could settle down into the routine of shipboard life.

It is 5,800 miles from Portsmouth to Cape Town by the most direct route. For the first half of the leg it should be possible for us to follow a direct course, past Ushant and across the Bay of Biscay to north-west Spain and on to the Canary Islands. If we met sou'westerlies in the Bay of Biscay we would have to beat out to clear Spain, but once off the coast of Portugal we should, with luck, pick up some northerlies and have a fast run into the north-east trades which blow down the coast of Africa and across to the West Indies.

52

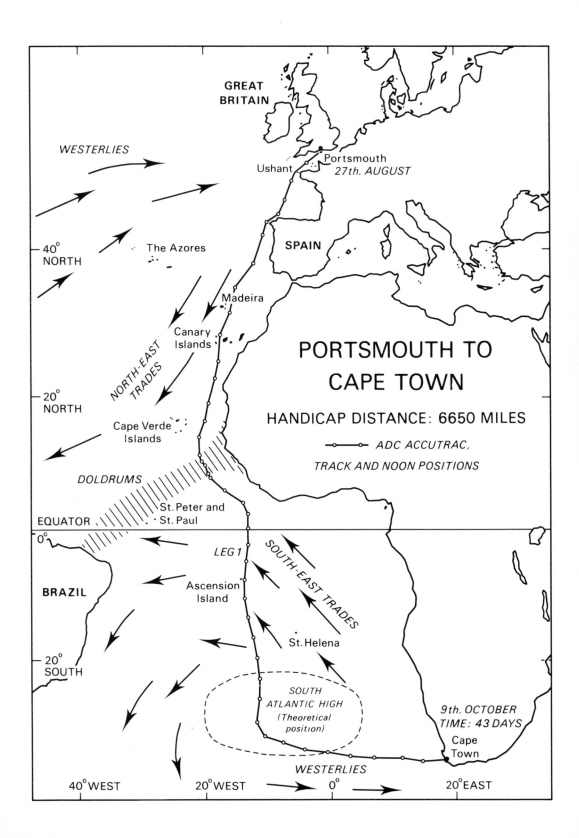

WESTERLIES

GREAT
BRITAIN

Ushant   Portsmouth
          27th. AUGUST

SPAIN

40°
NORTH

The Azores

Madeira

*Canary
Islands*

NORTH-EAST
TRADES

20°
NORTH

*Cape Verde
Islands*

**PORTSMOUTH TO
CAPE TOWN**

HANDICAP DISTANCE: 6650 MILES

—o—o— *ADC ACCUTRAC,*

TRACK AND NOON POSITIONS

DOLDRUMS

St.Peter and
St.Paul

EQUATOR

0°

LEG 1

SOUTH-EAST TRADES

BRAZIL

*Ascension
Island*

St.Helena

20°
SOUTH

*SOUTH
ATLANTIC HIGH
(Theoretical
position)*

*9th. OCTOBER
TIME: 43 DAYS*
Cape
Town

WESTERLIES

40° WEST   20° WEST   0°   20° EAST

The South Atlantic, on the other hand, is characterised by the south-east trades, winds which would be blowing against us, straight from Cape Town. Thus the second half of the leg would consist of a long windward beat. In between the north-east and the south-east trades is that belt of windless sea called the Doldrums which we, like all round-the-world voyagers, would have to cross.

We expected the first leg to take us about six weeks, a long time for the distance, but not so much when one considered the amount of calms and headwinds we were likely to meet on the way. The organisers, when fixing the handicap distance, had anticipated that we would travel 6,650 miles to make good 5,800. If this was so, we would have to average 158 miles a day to arrive in six weeks.

Our first night in the Channel was memorable, although not for the happiest of reasons. To start with, we went the wrong way. To keep up speed we reached up the middle of the Channel instead of heading downwind to Ushant. I thought it would be wise to keep clear of Ushant in case the south-westerly that the radio was forecasting came up, and John was keen to reach up and carry the mizzen staysail for the added speed. In the event, we were both wrong; the boats that headed straight for Ushant got round the corner before the south-westerly arrived, and on a fair tide. We, on the other hand, gained little speed if any by reaching up, then lost the wind for a while, and finally picked up a headwind which forced us close to Ushant, where we met a foul tide. It was not a good start to our race.

Worse still, we had a series of spinnaker disasters. In the gusty north wind that first night we changed spinnakers a dozen times. At dusk we were carrying a brand new light triradial in a small breeze when there was a dreadful ripping sound and the whole sail fell into two sections. Dismayed, we quickly pulled it down to discover that both the side tapes had broken, probably at the point where the sail had been altered.

'Right!' said Eve, moving into action. 'All we have to do is to patch across here. . . then up here. . . .' She sorted through the gigantic sail with dedicated resolution. 'What do you think, Sam?'

'Ye. . .e. . .es,' murmured Sam, studying the problem. 'Or. . . we could just join it. . . here.'

As Eve and Sam settled down to the enormous task of repairing the yards and yards of torn sail, the rest of us hoisted the medium spinnaker. Ten minutes later, Jacques' head appeared down the hatch into the saloon where I was trying to help Sam and Eve. 'You'll never believe this,' he said 'but the medium's got a small rip in it. From the zip on the bag, I think.' There was a loud groan from the direction of the sewing machine.

Later, as the moon came up, the wind freshened and we had to lower the medium spinnaker to put up the heavy. Quickly, Eve put a piece of sticky tape over the small split and returned to the repair of the badly damaged light spinnaker.

Up on deck, we had just settled the boat down, tidied everything away and started to enjoy the beautiful sailing again when another heart-stopping ripping sound rent the air. In the moonlight we could see the scene as if it were

54

day: the sail ripped up one side, up the other, and then across the bottom. . . . Hardly believing our eyes, we then saw the top tear right across, leaving only a skeleton of tapes hanging there in a triangular shape all on its own. The entire centre section had blown out ahead, fallen in the water and was now floating past the boat. As we sped by I nearly leaned over and grabbed the material but, fortunately, did not, a good decision for my arm would have been wrenched out of its socket. We all stared at each other, aghast. Our first night out and one spinnaker torn and another lost!

'I don't think it's our night,' commented Nick.

'This could be true,' added Robert. Then, putting a large cheerful smile on his face, 'Still, we've got plenty more spinnakers to put up.'

'I don't know if I'm going to let you, you spinnaker-rippers, you!' declared Sam, coming up through the hatch. 'But at least there ain't nothing to repair on this last one, so I can't complain.'

Although we had several other spinnakers, the loss of the heavy spinnaker would create a large gap in our wardrobe and, depressed at the thought of not having given the sail a better check before the race, I decided to order a new, much heavier sail that would be virtually indestructible. Two days later I contacted Chris on the radio and arranged for a new heavy spinnaker to be made to my own specifications and sent to Cape Town. Later, we heard that several other boats had blown their spinnakers that night. But, since we were sure no-one else could have blown two in such a small space of time, the news did little to assuage our crestfallen feelings.

After the excitement of the evening had died down, we settled into our watch-keeping routine. We had two watches of five led by two watch-leaders, Jacques and John. Bumble did not keep watch, although she was always available to help with sail changes, should she be needed. I, too, did not keep to a fixed working and sleeping routine, but was available whenever decisions about sail changes and tactics had to be taken. Otherwise I went on deck at odd times, and took the wheel or helped with the deck work when another hand was needed.

We had three four-hour watches at night, from supper-time at eight until midnight, from midnight to four, and from four to breakfast at eight. In the day we chose to have two six-hour watches, the first until lunch at two, the second until supper at eight. In this way the watches automatically rotated their hours every day. Also, a six-hour stretch off-watch in the daytime gave everyone long enough to catch up on their sleep, as well as read and generally relax.

It took us two painful days to fight our way past Ushant and out of the Channel. When we met the light headwinds we were forced to head towards Ushant, although it was surrounded by strong tides which were to set us back many long hours. However, blissfully ignorant of our position – the yachts had not yet started to exchange positions over the radio – we became engrossed in the sail repairs and the problems of settling down into our new environment. By the second day our morale had recovered from the disastrous first night and spirits were high. Bumble had a headache due, she admitted, to being far too excited and Eve, in her keenness to repair the light spinnaker, had run a sewing needle into her finger. But otherwise there was an air of gaiety and cheerfulness.

'I'm going to be a famous round-the-world-yachtsman,' someone sang.

'No, not to me you ain't,' floated up the melodious reply.

Small notices started appearing around the boat – MUSHROOMS ONLY BEYOND THIS POINT was fastened to the bulkhead aft of the main sleeping quarters where the eight crew who 'hot-bunked', or alternated, between four berths slept. Mushrooms was the name given to deck crew on ocean racers because, they maintained, they were fed on manure and kept in the dark.

There was also a sign over the galley which brought a shriek of 'Oh yeah,' from Eve. This one read WOMEN ARE GREAT ON BOATS – AS LONG AS THEY STAY IN HERE. Eve, a great believer in individuality, if not actually feminism, had little difficulty in guessing the brain that had thought up this immortal statement and, going over to John Tanner at the chart table, told him how funny she thought he was. Indeed, John soon became the butt of many jokes. Whenever we were discussing sail handling, John would always refer to the way things were done on *Tangaroa,* the boat he usually skippered. This led to many facetious questions such as 'How would you do it on *Tangaroa,* John?' or 'Now, now! That wouldn't be good enough if this were *Tangaroa.'*

Another favourite subject of John's was the theory of sailing. We listened and learned from John in quiet, obedient silence, and then ribbed him unmercifully about it. However, it had little effect, for John had the hide of a rhino and a blind belief in the power of knowledge, and merely smiled delightedly at our apparent interest in all he was saying.

Our second day was also ear-marked by the first of many occasions when we would have to send someone up the mast. The all-important radio aerial had broken away from its connection at the top of the main mast as we slopped around in a large swell. Sam volunteered to go up and put it back in place, although it would be a long and very tiring job. The boat's rolling and pitching would be magnified ten times at the masthead, with an added whipping motion that would make it difficult for a man to hold on. However, the wind might get up soon and stay up for days, so it was better to get the job done while we had the chance. In the event, it took Sam twenty minutes to reeve a new line between the insulator and the mast and make it secure. By the time we eased him down to the deck he was in such a state of exhaustion that he lay there shaking and panting for ten minutes. Gripping the mast with his thighs, holding on with one hand and working with the other had taken a supreme effort.

Beat, too, went up the mast that day, this time to free a spinnaker which had wrapped around the forestay in the light wind and large, rolling sea. Fortunately he managed to unravel it in a matter of minutes and was down quickly. However, we resolved to design a more efficient anti-wrap netting system to prevent it happening again.

On the second night, we finally managed to pass Ushant and to head south-west towards Cape Finisterre and north-west Spain. The wind had settled in the west, although it was very light. We were faced with the choice of squeezing up to windward and laying Cape Finisterre, or reaching off for

OPPOSITE
Light winds down
the Channel.

56

speed in the hope of finding a freeing wind later. John was very keen to reach off for speed and, bowing to his experience, we put up a reacher and headed below our desired course.

At this time the immense strain of the past few months suddenly hit me and, with the difficulty of adjusting to a strange new routine, I felt terribly tired and weak. This deep fatigue effectively put me out of action for a couple of days and, while I tried my best to pull myself out of it, John and Jacques ran the boat. As watch-leaders, they were in charge of the deck and the sail-handling anyway but, while I was feeling so grim, they were also dealing with most of the tactical decisions. Unfortunately this was just the time when there was a basic disagreement about tactics. John believed in ramping off for speed, while Jacques wanted to make a better course. Finally I joined the discussion, groggy and not very decisive, and we bowed to John's recommendation to ramp off.

A day or so later, I was feeling much better and fitter. I was glad to see that the rest of the crew had also settled in well, and were plainly enjoying the shipboard routine. At first everyone was very willing and keen to do the chores. We had no strict rota system, but asked vaguely who thought they were due to do the washing up or clean the floors. While the weather was fine there was no shortage of volunteers – on the contrary, everyone was anxious to do as much as possible. It was only later, when the weather changed, that we had to organise some kind of rota because of the sudden lack of interest or, more seriously, the disagreements as to who had done the most stints at the washing-up bowl. Diary-writing was also a popular activity and the majority of the crew scribbled away assiduously three or four times a day. Later, only a few of us kept diaries going and frequently had to ask each other what had happened over the previous few days in order to catch up.

In a way we were grateful for those first few days of light winds. Not only could we become acclimatised to life afloat without seasickness, damp and the other products of rough weather, but we could carry out the many odd jobs and repairs that had turned up.

One major event was the operation on Eve's finger. When she ran her hand under the sewing machine and the needle punctured her finger, she never found the end of the needle. Nick now decided that it must still be in there, which meant it must be removed. With ghoulish interest we encircled the saloon table and watched as Nick gave her a local anaesthetic and delved down into the flesh beside the nail.

'Ughhh! It's all rampant flesh, Evey,' said a voice.

'Looks like gangrene to me.'

'How long do you give her, Nick?'

Finally, the needle tip was pulled out in triumph, to a great cheer from the onlookers.

'That didn't hurt, did it?' asked Nick, binding the finger.

'Oh no,' cried Evey, 'I'm just in bloody agony!'

'That's fine, then,' said Nick, smiling in his best bedside manner.

It had been arranged that all yachts would talk to each other on the radio at a fixed time every day. This was known as Chat Hour or Children's Hour and,

Nick operates on Eve, our first casualty.

during the first leg, it took place in the afternoons. For the first couple of days no-one bothered to talk but now, as we sailed down the Bay of Biscay in a fitful westerly breeze, curiosity about each other's positions brought all the boats on the air. We took down everyone's positions and then plotted them on the chart to discover, for the first time, the extent of our mistake in the Channel. We were almost the last boat! A small saving grace was that we appeared to be not too far down to leeward of the other yachts. However, even that consolation was lost to us when John's estimated position turned out to be very optimistic and, on taking some sun sights, we discovered we were well down to leeward without a hope of weathering Cape Finisterre.

More calms and fluky winds off the coast of Spain did nothing to help our position and, when we finally rounded the Cape on the fifth day out, we were sixty miles behind *Disque d'Or* and the other large boats. Our gamble in ramping off at Ushant had not paid off. Now we would have to make up the distance. Strangely this difficult proposition did not depress us. Despite all the downs of the race so far, our morale was still high. In the flat calm we now experienced off Finisterre, we never doubted that the wind would return and give us the chance to catch up.

While we drifted back and forth within sight of the craggy coast, the sun blazed down from a cloudless sky and gave us our first taste of hot sunshine. Immediately, as if at a given signal, the rails became festooned with clothing and bedding while the decks were covered with oilskins and inverted boots. Off-watch bodies lay on sail bags, starting suntans, while the on-watch positioned themselves to face the sun. At lunchtime, a fresh salad was eaten on deck and cold beer drunk to quench the beginnings of thirst. I took the opportunity to do a job that I had been promising Jacques I would do for months. I cut the wild mop of straw he called hair that had long given him the

59

appearance of a friendly sheepdog. Meanwhile Sam, in anticipation of hotter days to come, made himself a colourful sarong out of a sheet. He also indulged in one of his favourite hobbies. Armed with a sheet of paper, a pencil and much mental arithmetic, he calculated that, at our present average speed, it would take us 49·2 days to reach Cape Town – by which time we would have run out of water and, despite the amount of stores, probably food too.

'Thanks, Sam!' someone said. 'Next time we want cheering up, we'll call you.'

John, too, started to indulge his favourite hobby. Without a word, he stripped off and wandered around the deck naked. Later, he suddenly looked up from his sunbathing position and asked, 'I'm not bothering anyone, am I?'

'What if we said yes, John?' Eve asked.

'Well, you'll get used to it!' John replied confidently. 'We all do it in the West Indies, you know.'

'Yes, but there are a thousand other things to look at in the West Indies,' Evey pointed out. 'As it is, every time I look up at the sails I see *you* and, frankly, I'd rather not!'

John, impervious to criticism, went back to sleep and, far from covering himself up, thenceforth appeared naked at every opportunity. However, we did ask him to draw the line at getting out of his bunk naked, for he slept in the pilot berth in the saloon and would swing himself out over people's heads as they were reading, or even worse, trying to concentrate on eating their food.

Another of John's exotic habits was to disappear up on to the bow and enjoy his morning constitutional in the open air, balanced over the pulpit. Whenever he appeared on deck with a roll of loo paper in hand, loud groans and ribald comments would be heard from the cockpit crew. Always quick to join in a joke, John would laugh, tell them what delights they were missing by using the loo, and saunter off up the deck. One morning John appeared as usual, slipped off his trousers and left them by the companion-way as he went up to the pulpit. A minute later Bumble came up on deck, saw the trousers, muttered something about people leaving their clothes about, and took them carefully below. She never made the same mistake again – the sight of John appearing naked in the galley in search of his trousers was enough to make her far less fussy about keeping the boat tidy.

After two days of calms, we finally picked up a light north-westerly wind and roared off on a fast reach for the Canaries. While we had been tacking back and forth in the light airs, we had kept seeing a white ketch on the horizon which we finally identified as *Debenhams,* the British entry skippered by John Ridgway. According to form we should have been well ahead of the smaller, slower *Debenhams,* so her presence was a constant reminder that our position was far from good. But now with the freshening breeze, we were pulling away from her fast. Better still, the afternoon exchange of positions with the other yachts showed that we had gained a few miles on some of the boats ahead. This news was met with an offhand acceptance by the crew. 'No problem,' they said. 'We'll be up there in no time.'

'*Disque d'Or.* . . .' Beat muttered, looking into the distance and throwing his arm forward, as if to say, 'Let's go.'

As we sailed down the coast of Portugal the sea came alive with dolphins, pilot whales and, one exciting day, two large rorqual whales. Phosphorescence lit our wake at night and the skies became clear and sparkling with stars. It was a magical time aboard *ADC* – the wind was beginning to swing to the north-east and to steady, marking the beginning of the trade winds; the sailing was interesting but not too demanding and, most important of all, we were catching up the other boats slowly but steadily. Life aboard fell into a happy routine of keeping watch, eating and sleeping, with enough time to enjoy the delights of sailing under near-perfect conditions. Shoals of flying fish started to appear and each morning John would collect one or two from the scuppers and cook them for breakfast. Nick and Bumble trailed fishing lines hopefully behind the boat but, as they ruefully remarked, we were going too fast to catch anything. However, Nick almost caught a flying fish one night, although hardly in the normal way. He was steering when there was a loud smack and we turned to see him cowering behind the wheel. The flying fish had hit his shoulder then, to his disgust, slithered into the scuppers and over the side. Eve thought this very funny and roared with laughter but Nick got his revenge later by choosing a still, quiet moment in the middle of the night watch suddenly to slap Evey hard on the back yelling, 'Flying fish!' From then on hardly a night went by without the two of them slapping each other on the back when the other was least expecting it.

Robert, as entertainments officer, had arranged a party to celebrate our first

The One Week Out Party; Sam (*left*) introduces two mystery guests.

week at sea. The invitation went up on the notice board in the saloon: 6.00 FOR 6.30 EVENING DRESS. BRING A GUEST. NUMBERS MUST BE RESTRICTED TO 12 DUE TO LACK OF SPACE. This party was anticipated with much eagerness because everyone was in such good spirits. Not only were we making fast speed, but that very day we had sighted no fewer than four other yachts, a tangible sign that we were catching up lost ground. By nightfall we had lost sight of three of them astern, giving us more reason to celebrate. We had two 'guests' that evening. One, a friend of Sam's, had very bright lipstick, two large bosoms, and a very saucy manner; she also had a nose that looked remarkably similar to Robert's. I, too brought a guest, a chap who looked very unwell indeed. His face was bright green and, when we threw him across the saloon, he fell to pieces to reveal a body stuffed with sweaters and a head made out of one of my famous hats. The party invitation had promised the Dance of the Seven Army Blankets, the Singing Doctor, and a Recitation on Ornithology but, by the time the lady with the large bosoms had been deflated by the assembled company and the wine finished, the promised entertainments were forgotten.

As the trade winds strengthened, so the sailing became more exhilarating. Often there would be just enough wind to start the boat surfing and whenever the boat speed went over thirteen knots, there would be a loud cry of 'Coconut' from the helmsman. As the wind gusted and moderated, so we would change spinnaker, put up a big boy, or take it down, or change the mizzen spinnaker for a staysail. In the saloon, there were always spinnakers in the process of being stopped with elastic bands before being packed, or spinnakers waiting to be stopped. Sometimes a backlog of three would build up so that it was a battle to fight your way through the mounds of sail cloth. To accentuate the problem there were always several headsails lying in their sausage-shaped bags on the saloon floor and along the passageways. There was never enough room for all the sails in the bins at the two extreme ends of the boat and we preferred to keep the heavy ones where their weight would be least felt, on the cabin floors.

We had no difficulty in filling our time. If we weren't packing a spinnaker or bagging a sail, we would be involved in our own special jobs or hobbies. Fred cared for the engine with such dedication and thoroughness that hardly a day went by without him dipping the oil, changing a filter, or tightening a belt. He ran the engine for an hour or so a day, enough to generate sufficient power to run the radio, the lights and, most voracious of all, the deep freeze. We became familiar with the sight of Fred's large frame upside -down in the bilge while he chattered away to anyone who would listen about the relative merits of alternators versus dynamos. Fred had also taken a great liking to filming and, whenever anything interesting was happening on the boat, Fred would be there, camera in hand and tape recorder in pocket.

Jacques, too, was very keen to get some good film. One day we heard a commotion of banging and cursing at the bottom of the companion-way. Some noisy moments later Jacques' helmeted head appeared, looking far from pleased. Seconds later the rest of him followed, festooned in wires, recorders, remote switches, camera and clapper board. 'I'll get the hang of this if it kills me,' announced Jacques, tripping over a wire and dropping the clapper board to the deck. With the Frankenstein helmet, his Bermuda shorts which ended somewhere round his knees, and his Brighton beach shoes and socks, Jacques was unanimously voted the best dressed man aboard, if not exactly the best co-ordinated. However, he soon came to terms with the BBC equipment, and between them Fred and Jacques were to take some very commendable footage.

My spare time was easily absorbed by the radio. Every day I made a call to Capital Radio through the long -range station at Portishead near Bristol. At this stage communications were reasonably clear, although far from easy. Portishead was such a popular station that there were always numerous ships booking calls, and they always drowned me out. Sometimes I had to wait for two or three hours before it was possible to get through. However, once contact had been established it was merely a matter of waiting my turn, and then I would find myself going through the terrifying experience of trying to give a live report to Capital Radio. It had been brave of Capital to try the experiment of taking live reports from a yacht and, I often reflected, even braver of me to agree to send them. Somehow or other there were always technical difficulties. Either I could not hear the disc jockey's questions, or they could not hear me, or Russian voices would come drifting in over the air. When reception was really bad I usually shouted a few general comments down the line, hoped they had heard me, and then signed off. At the end of each session I felt like a wet rag.

Radio contact with the other yachts was, however, good. As we approached Madeira two major items of news came through. *33 Export* told us that she was putting in to Madeira for rigging repairs and *GB II* told us that *Condor*'s radio was broken and that she was putting in to the Canaries for a new one. *Condor* had been off the air for some days and it was a relief to discover that nothing was wrong apart from the radio. Already, an atmosphere of mutual dependence was springing up between the boats, in anticipation of our passage through the Southern Ocean when we would be quite alone and far from conventional assistance. If a boat was off the air, we wanted to know she was safe. The Italian racing yacht *Guia* had been sunk by whales in the Atlantic and had gone down in minutes, so we had reason to stay in touch, even at this early stage.

During our passage down to the Canaries, we did not have to worry too much about tactics for it was just a matter of getting there as fast as possible. However, downwind sailing is never as straightforward as you hope and, time and time again, we found our desired course lying dead downwind. Usually, one gybe was more favourable than the other yet Sod's Law would always operate by putting islands in the way. We had to gybe clear of Madeira and later, the Salvage Islands. However, we must have been taking the right decisions for, as we passed Madeira, we found ourselves only twenty miles behind *Disque d'Or,* and further to the west, which we considered a better position.

Most of the time we were making good runs of over 200 miles a day, but I was not entirely happy. I was worried about the way the boat was handling downwind. She had an unpleasant tendency to pull to leeward, roll, and then

FACING PAGE
Above: Off to a
flying start, heading
for Bembridge Ledge
(*photo:* Francis
Redon).

Below left: Gathering
in the light
spinnaker.

Below right: A
spinnaker repairing
party.

try to broach. Jacques, who had often steered *Burton Cutter* downwind, found her hard to handle. Tony and Beat, both excellent helmsmen, also found it difficult to keep the boat going in a straight line. If we trimmed the spinnaker to make her pull to windward, it helped, but only as long as there wasn't too much wind, for then the boat would become almost unmanageable. The answer, we slowly discovered, was to trim the spinnaker with great care so as to pull the boat very slightly to windward, but not so much that she couldn't be pulled back from a windward broach. The Swan 65 was a heavy boat to sail downwind and her keel was too far back to give her the directional stability that modern designs have. But we knew we would have to learn to live with it, and the run to the Canaries gave us the opportunity to get used to the boat's habits before meeting the large seas of the Southern Ocean. (See Appendix A for notes on spinnaker handling and broaching.)

John had different ideas about spinnaker trim. He felt the boat should be balanced in such a way that she could be steered with the lightest touch of the fingers. But, since this seemed to result in the boat zigzagging downwind and trying to pull off to leeward and broach, I considered it neither safe nor efficient. It was difficult to compromise over this because John complained that the safer way of trimming pulled the boat up to windward and involved too much effort at the helm. Without the possibility of a compromise solution, there was nothing I could do but state that I favoured the other method of trimming and leave it at that.

However, there was no room for two different approaches to navigation and watch-leadership. One night I came on deck during John's watch to find the wind had shifted and we were 60° off course on the wrong gybe. When I asked John about this, I discovered that he did not know what the course was meant to be. He believed that speed rather than course was important on a long passage and that a delayed gybe did not matter one way or the other; as long as one was heading in the general direction of the objective, then all was well. It took five minutes at the chart to work out that the delayed gybe had probably lost us ten miles and, when we looked at our position against the other yachts, so it proved. From then on I made sure both watches knew exactly when they must gybe, to avoid any more unnecessary zigzagging and loss of valuable ground.

After ten days at sea we sighted the misty outline of Palma Island on the western edge of the Canaries group and, picking up our skirts in a fresh following wind, we shot towards the channel between Palma and Tenerife. With a bit of luck, we would keep a fresh breeze as we sailed between the islands. And if we were really fortunate we might even pick up a little distance on our competitors ahead.

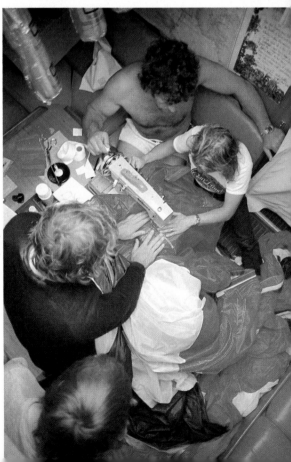

CHAPTER 4

Down in the Doldrums

The sky was black velvet and covered with a carpet of tiny, twinkling stars. Over to starboard we could see the faint lights of the island of Hierro, the most south-westerly of the Canary Islands. We had worried about sailing into the wind shadow of the mountainous Tenerife to the east but, although we were now in its lee, the wind was steady and showing no signs of dropping away.

'What a night!' I exclaimed.

Tony, at the wheel beside me, nodded and smiled with delight. We looked around us once more, bewitched by the magical night, enjoying the speed and the ease of the endless spinnaker run.

'If sailing was always like this, I could sail for ever. . . .'

Hardly had Tony uttered the words than the squall hit us. It came without warning from a clear sky, created by the turbulent airs around the faraway mountain of Tenerife. The wind-speed indicator shot up from ten to twenty knots. The boat stiffened and fled into the night, Tony working hard to steady her erratic course. Immediately our thoughts turned to the overburdened spinnaker but, taken by surprise, we were too slow. With a great ripping sound which brought dread to our hearts, the brand-new working spinnaker tore across the bottom, up one side and halfway across the top. Luckily it ripped no further and we were able to retrieve the whole sail, ripped section and all.

Eve climbed from her bunk and eyed the ruins stoically. 'If we're going to repair it, we might as well do it properly!' she declared, her mouth set with determination. And so began the most intricate and time-consuming repair we were ever to carry out. It took three days and nights of continuous work during which seventy patches were measured, heat-sealed and sewn into place. Taking it in shifts, we worked in twos or threes until we were too tired to carry on. We were determined to do the best possible repair, to have a strog, working spinnaker we could trust again. Only Sam failed to see the point of doing such a fastidious job. 'I'd just bung it together,' he said. 'We'll only blow it again anyway.' At the time, we regarded Sam's prophecies of doom as rank pessimism. Later, we were to see his point of view only too clearly.

As the great repair job started, I reflected on how easily the blow-out could have been avoided. If only we'd been quicker getting the sail down! Full of remorse, I tuned into Chat Hour in a depressed mood, certain that everything must be running smoothly with the other yachts. I was very much mistaken. Three yachts blew spinnakers that same night including *Disque d'Or*. Two days later we heard *Debenhams* and *Adventure* commiserating over their spinnaker losses; one had lost the centre of her spinnaker, the other the tapes

FACING PAGE
Above: Whistling for the wind in the Doldrums.

Below left: One way of cooling off – Fred takes a bath.

Below right: Wet foredeck while beating into the south-east trades.

and corners. Perhaps, one suggested, they should get together and see if they could make anything useful out of the two pieces. As the yachts began to pass more and more information over the radio, we realised we were not the only ones to make mistakes or to break gear and we found the knowledge immensely cheering. Absurdly, we had begun to imagine that the other boats were immune to such commonplace events. As time went on the sharing of news, particularly when it involved admitting a 'nonsense', forged a strong link of comradeship between the boats.

Apart from ripping our best spinnaker, our passage through the western channel of the Canaries was a great success. Once clear of the islands, we discovered we had drawn level with *Disque d'Or*. The leading boats, *Condor, GB II, King's Legend* and *Flyer*,were still between a half and a full day's run ahead but, with so much of the leg yet to race, anything could happen. The important point was that we had caught up.

We now had three to four more days in the trade winds before we would sail into the Doldrums somewhere off Portuguese Guinea. This belt of calms was normally much wider near the African coast, so we aimed to pass some 250 miles off. There we would have another chance of improving our position for, if luck was with us, we might catch the wind before the other boats.

As we left the Canaries behind and headed towards the Doldrums, we enjoyed the last downwind sailing we would have for quite a while. Nick, sensitive to our observations about the lack of fresh fish, began to take his fishing very seriously. One day he was seen sitting astride the coaming, holding a rod and line and, much to our delight, wearing a harness. 'This harness makes you catch larger fish,' said Nick in the expressionless voice he used when giving misleading information. 'If I catch a shark, it can't drag me into the water, you see. Instead, I drag it into the cockpit and kill it.' Since not a single fish had yet been caught, this statement met with some degree of disbelief. Some hours later, long after Nick had abandoned holding the rod in favour of tying a simple line on to the stern, we were all surprised to hear the cry of 'Fish!'.

'All right, all right,' said Nick, 'very funny, ha ha.'

'But there *is* a fish,' someone yelled.

Nick, trying not to look surprised, leapt on deck and found himself grappling with a healthy four-foot fish which he soon subdued and cut into steaks. One hour later, when there was another cry of 'Fish!', Nick was almost beside himself with joy. He hauled in the line and, peering into the gathering darkness, tried to guess what type of fish it might be. 'Probably a tuna,' he decided, pulling in the last section of line, then the weight, and finally the fish itself on to the deck. 'What on earth?' he murmured, bending down to examine the object. Around him, the crew gathered to peer closely at the strange creature. Suddenly, there was a spurt of water and a rapid movement. Laughing and shrieking, everyone leapt for safety as the creature, a lively squid, gave a final squirt and disappeared neatly over the side. 'Ah well,' said Nick, 'you can't win 'em all.'

Nick also had an impressive-looking speargun which he would dangle over the bow in hopeful pursuit of the tempting tuna which swam in the shadow of

66

We catch a fish – it was to be a rare event (*photo:* Fred Dovaston).

the boat. However, the speargun only drew blood once, when Bumble put it in the passageway while clearing out a locker. Fred stepped on one end of it, causing the sharp end to spring up and stab him in the foot.

As the weather became warmer, washing became popular with even the most reluctant members of the crew. Jacques who had put his head in a bucket of sea water some days before and quickly withdrawn it because of the 'freezing temperature', now declared that the water might just be bearable if the bucket was left in the sun all day. At four in the afternoon he proudly emerged, towel and shampoo in hand, claimed his bucket of water and padded off to wash in the privacy of the foredeck. Everyone listened, not saying a word. They all knew that Jacques' hot water had accidentally been used to swab the decks. The water he was about to pour over his head had only just been collected and was quite cold. When the shriek floated down the deck, everyone exchanged guilty glances and waited nervously. But Jacques confounded us all by dancing into view, full of good humour. 'Nothing like a good wash!' he exclaimed. 'You dirty lot should try it some time!'

Sam held out the longest against a cold seawater wash – the only kind there was since fresh water and gas were strictly rationed. He held out even longer than me, famous for my preference for Mother's baby wipes and talcum powder rather than cold water. But finally, one hot day, Sam appeared armed for a thorough wash, wearing a sarong (I don't know where the wind's comin' from wearing this thing, but I know where it's goin'), bearing shampoo which was the only type of soap that would lather in salt water, and sporting his white sun hat on his head. This bore the legend SAM on the front and was adjusted to Sam's head size by a clothes peg on the back. 'Right,' he said, 'I'd like to announce that I won't be havin' a wash the whole of the second leg, so I'm havin' a bath four months early!' We gave a weak cheer then decided, on reflection, that the announcement probably constituted very bad news.

The warmer weather created extra work for Bumble when the fruit and vegetables started to ripen fast. It became necessary for her to sort through the netting and the fridge almost every day to weed out the bad ones. The vegetables were stowed in numerous places throughout the boat and it was only when a sticky liquid started dripping from the roof of the aft loo that Bumble remembered some forgotten cucumbers stowed in the netting there.

After two weeks at sea, Bumble was also having difficulty in finding out who was due to do the chores, particularly the washing-up. In the end she resorted to base tactics. 'Have you ever ridden a penny farthing?' she asked Tony one day.

'No,' replied Tony, smiling innocently.

'Have you ever seen one?' persisted Bumble.

'Er, yes.'

'Right, then it's your turn for the washing up,' Bumble finished triumphantly.

Seeing how successful this ploy was, I used it to find someone to clean the loos, not exactly a popular job. 'Don't you think the loos smell lovely?' I asked one day. 'No,' some unsuspecting soul replied. 'Well, you wouldn't like to go and clean them, would you?' I inquired.

While the wind blew, the heat was bearable. Even two days from the Doldrums the trade winds were fresh enough to keep us cool, as well as busy. Sometimes they came in strong gusts and we hurried to lower the spinnaker before we lost it. Other times the trades seemed to be dying, blowing only fitfully between long, light patches, and our speed dropped below ten knots for the first time since we had left the coast of Portugal. Once, as the wind freshened and we hurried to lower the mizzen spinnaker, the helmsman let the boat run by the lee and Sam, who was hanging on to the tack of the sail ready to pull it in, was suddenly pulled over the rail until only his feet remained inboard. 'Oi,' said Sam, more annoyed than alarmed, 'would you mind sortin' yer arms out, 'ooever's on the wheel.' The boat yawed back and Sam swung gracefully back inboard as the mizzen spinnaker refilled the proper side. Then, indulging her habit to roll, the boat pulled to leeward again. 'Bloody 'ell,' remarked Sam as he found himself over the water again. 'What's the problem, mate? Yer got lock-arm or something?'

As we neared the Doldrums we managed to hold our position level with *Disque d'Or*, a fact of which there was little doubt for, in front of our disbelieving eyes, she appeared over the horizon one day and crossed just behind us on the opposite gybe. Later we crossed each other again. It was extraordinary to see another yacht so close after thirteen days at sea and it cheered us enormously. Here, visible and tangible, was the opposition. We had caught her and now we would beat her! It was an exciting moment, full of optimism and hope for the future. We needed little encouragement next day to enter into the spirit of our Two Week Out Party. The highlight of the celebration was a limerick competition which produced some bawdy, some passable and some simply terrible rhymes, all of which reflected our downhill slide into schoolboy humour. Robin, not sure of how to write a limerick, wrote a sonnet, Bumble, with her earthy humour, composed a rhyme about loos. Eve, the literary star, produced the only limerick with the correct metre. While Jacques quite unashamedly recited some lines without the slightest suggestion of rhyme, which easily won him the worst limerick prize. Unperturbed by such an unpromising start, Jacques became quite bitten by the limerick bug and composed limericks the rest of the way round the world. However, much to our entertainment, he always managed to produce a last line at least ten words too long and never, to my certain knowledge, one that rhymed.

There was only one cloud over the party. We had discovered that all the whisky in the plastic sacks had become tainted by an unpleasant scent. At first Robert was mortified and apologetic but, after an inspection of the more solid plastic containers, declared that all was not lost. Nearly all the Grouse was still pure and that which had been spoilt would, Robert was certain, pass muster in a good punch.

The day after the party the wind dropped to a faint breeze and the heat became humid and oppressive. Although we were still cheerful and high-spirited, the heat began to wear us down until we became tired and lethargic. On Nick's suggestion we took salt tablets which helped overcome the tiredness, but it was still an effort to do much work under the midday sun. So hot was the deck that the helmsman steered with one foot in a bucket of water, and for once it was considered a friendly gesture to throw water at each other. Fred, resourceful as ever, managed to rig up a hose to the deck pump so that we could spray ourselves with water and fill up the children's paddling pool which Robert had brought in lieu of a canvas bath tub, which he had been unable to find. The pool, although small, did provide a cool sitting-place and became very popular with everyone. Even Fred took to bathing in it although, by the time he had lowered himself into it, most of the water had overflowed.

In the searing heat we counted ourselves lucky that *ADC* was fibreglass. The aluminium and steel boats would be very much hotter below. The crew of *Traité de Rome* complained of the tremendous heat inside their 'tin can' boat, a situation not improved by the severe water shortage on board. To save weight they had taken on the bare minimum of fresh water before the start and now, if there was no rain soon, they would be extremely thirsty until they arrived in Cape Town.

Fresh water was rationed on every boat, but we had taken enough for drinking and cooking as long as we were sensible about it. Cups of tea and chocolate at night, prepared to pass the time rather than to quench our thirst,

I take a bath with a
view.

were cut out. Instead people helped themselves to water from a five-gallon
jerry can at the galley door, which would have to last us all day. Pouring the
water from the can was enough of a nuisance to ensure that no-one took a
drink lightly. Bumble used as much salt water in the cooking as possible but
still had to use about two gallons of fresh a day – to make up milk from
powder, to mix with salt water for cooking vegetables, and to reconstitute
dried meat which she used to augment the frozen meat. Teeth were cleaned in
salt water, and there were many sour faces pulled until people got used to the
habit.

Sam was in charge of the water supply and monitored our consumption
very carefully. Each of the three tanks was used in turn and there were four full
jerry cans for emergencies. Sam came to me after ten days, worried that we had
already run through a quarter of our supply when probably not a quarter of
the time out. Thereafter we introduced the jerry can system and found it
reduced our consumption sufficiently to make full rationing unnecessary.

The heat made Bumble's work in the galley extremely uncomfortable as she
sweated over a hot stove. She prepared cold lunches during the worst of the
heat, but always made a hot dinner for the 'growing boys'.

'Trouble is, Bumble, we're growing in the wrong directions!' Nick declared.

'That's because you're pigs,' replied Bumble, never one to mince words.

Bumble catered for the hungry crew effortlessly despite the small three-burner cooker and the generally cramped conditions, no mean feat when the crew expected and received meat, two veg, and pudding every evening. As if the cooking of one meal wasn't enough, Bumble usually managed to produce a non-meat dish for me as well. As a vegetarian, I was nothing but a nuisance yet Bumble would make soya stew, vegetable curry and all kinds of delicious dishes for me. I insisted that it was not necessary, yet I so appreciated her efforts that my insistence was probably not very convincing.

As the wind became lighter we daily expected to find ourselves entering the Doldrums, and anxiously searched the horizon for signs of the characteristic black clouds and heavy sky. Suddenly on the sixteenth day our waiting was over. We had been ghosting along under spinnaker when Jacques suddenly called everyone up to lower the sail. A dark cloud with heavy rain was fast approaching from dead ahead, in the opposite direction to the wind. Being at the wheel, I quickly turned the boat to port just as the wind swung round 180° and blew from the south. Two minutes later we found ourselves beating into a light headwind as rain poured down out of a leaden sky. Ten minutes later the wind swung to the west, then to the east. It was the unmistakably confused pattern of the Doldrums.

Beat helming in the Doldrums – it required much concentration for little progress.

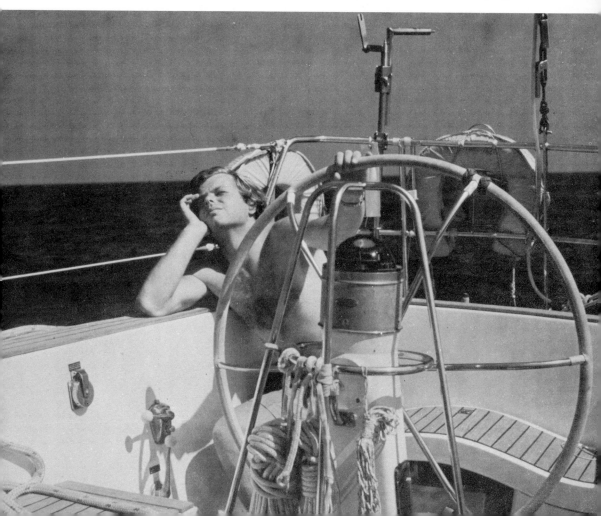

While it poured with rain we rushed around catching water off the booms, or stood soaking ourselves, or shampooing our bodies. Dirty washing was brought out for a hasty wash and rinse. Nick, now at the wheel, had his hair shampooed by Evey until the suds ran down into his eyes and he couldn't see the compass. Jacques, who was wearing his bright green Bermuda shorts from the West Indies, suddenly discovered that the dye had run and his legs had turned bright yellow. Muttering '*Merde alors*', he tore the shorts off and wandered around naked until his legs looked a little less jaundiced. Nearly all the boys stripped off to wash in the heavy downpour and Bumble, coming up suddenly through the hatch and seeing a naked body, said 'Oh!' and averted her eyes, only to see yet another. Retiring below, she came up later when the sun was out to find that some of the men were still naked, drying off in the sun. 'Goodness!' Bumble declared, 'I've never seen so many toggles in my life!'

Later most of us tacitly agreed that nude bodies were not nearly as pretty as the sea and that nudity should be restricted to sunbathing on secluded parts of the foredeck. John, being without any personal modesty at all and even possessing some vanity about his all-over tan, did not feel there was any need to cover up and wandered about naked nearly all the time.

To sail through the Doldrums one needs patience and perseverance. A modern yacht can do a reasonable daily mileage with only a breath of wind, by using large ghosting sails and paying constant attention to their trim. Under each large black cloud that hovered threateningly overhead, there was usually a breeze which would send us scurrying along at six or eight knots for a few minutes. Then the breeze would die away and we would have to nurse the boat along to manage as much as one knot.

Our position was, however, good. According to the radio information, we were holding *Disque d'Or* and had gained on *King's Legend* and *Flyer*, both still in the Doldrums. Since the belt of Doldrums could and often did suddenly move 200 miles north or south, it was possible we might pick up the wind at the same time as the leading boats. Alternatively, we might be delayed in the calms much longer – a thought we preferred not to dwell on. Whatever happened, we knew that there was a tremendous amount of luck involved. Theoretically, we were in the right place and should pass through the Doldrums as quickly as possible, in two days or so. But, since nothing ever runs true to form at sea, it could take four. Whatever happened, we were glad to know that *Disque d'Or* was still close by. If we were delayed, then she would be too. Or so we innocently believed.

It is still difficult to understand how the unbelievable happened, but it did. In our second day in the Doldrums a plane of French journalists flew over us and confirmed by radio that *Disque d'Or* was exactly ten miles away to the west, totally becalmed like us. Not suspecting what was to happen a few hours later, we believed this information to be good news, and settled down to enjoy the rare event – even for the Doldrums – of a calm so complete that the boat was motionless, her sails hanging like clothes drying on a still, summer day. We kept diving in the water every time the plane flew over, pretending to abandon ship. We swam, although not for too long in case of sharks. We cooled off by aiming the hose at each other and bathing in the paddling pool.

We also enjoyed the company of four new travelling companions, a group of tired and very small swallows who arrived panting for breath and quite worn out. These creatures, having investigated the rigging, masts and deck, decided that none of these places offered a comfortable place to sleep and that, like us, they would make a home below. One sat on the chart table beside John, seeing how far there was to go, while the others sat on a headphone cable stretched across the corner of the saloon, in front of a map of the world. Come nightfall, when we turned on the saloon light, three huddled in some netting, while the tiniest, most delicate of the birds hid beside the radio receiver, almost out of sight.

Visitors in the Doldrums; a plane of journalists and some exhausted swallows.

However, the birds were soon forgotten when we heard the incredible news on Chat Hour. *Disque d'Or* gave a position sixty miles ahead. Worse, she reported she was doing a steady five knots. Without bothering to look on deck I knew we were doing less than a knot, and my heart sank. It seemed incredible that we could be almost motionless while *Disque d'Or* steamed off ahead. For a moment I wondered if the other boat might be playing a joke on us. But, even as I thought it, I knew it wasn't true. Somehow or another *Disque d'Or* had got away – and from just beside us.

The next day was as deadly as the last. The sun hung like a great red tomato in the hazy, windless sky. The sea, as unrippled and glassy as oil, undulated slowly in the slight swell. For hour after hour the boat was motionless, just swaying slightly from side to side, the halyards slapping against the masts and the cutlery rattling in the galley. We found the small swallow by the radio had died in the night, while his companions seemed more frail and tired than before. They made short sorties out over the sea only to flop back on deck, panting and dejected. One tried to take off but failed and flopped pathetically into the water. Unable to watch the poor thing struggling, Jacques dived in after it and put the damp little object back on deck. However his heroism was in vain, for the swallow died a few hours later.

73

By evening, we were all feeling rather dejected. There was still no sign of wind, the heat and humidity had been particularly oppressive and our swallows were dying. I decided it was time for a party. I announced, moreover, that it was to be a Rite to the God of Wind.

'No problem,' said someone, 'just give Fred some baked beans.'

'Ha!' exclaimed Fred. 'You're not exactly roses yourself, old mate. And as for your socks . . . .'

The rite was to be a good noisy affair. All the pots and pans were brought up from the galley while Robert managed to produce some plastic whistles that made a variety of extraordinary noises. As the red sun slid into the oily sea, we sent up the most terrible commotion that must have been heard for miles. We beat the pans, we clanged the pots, we blew the whistles. At the end of it, we all felt immeasurably better, if only because we had let off some of the pent-up steam and frustration of those long, windless days. As a final offering to the powers that be, I poured a tot of whisky carefully into the sea, and added another for good measure. Bumble and the rest of the whisky connoisseurs were horrified at the waste but Jacques and Fred, mariners of long standing and therefore superstitious like me, took the matter very seriously.

Our efforts brought no result. Throughout the long, frustrating night and the next morning there was hardly a breath of wind. By now the tension was almost unbearable. Our position had looked so promising and now it was slipping away with the whims of the wind. A full-blown storm would have been preferable to that calm – at least we could have battled our way through it. As it was, we were quite helpless to do anything to improve the situation. Some of the crew covered their disappointment by talking and joking a little louder than usual, others went quiet, and I repaired to my bunk to read. I did not trust myself to go up on deck without shaking my fist at the elements – and that would have been bad luck. Not superstitious, us modern mariners!

By this time there was only one swallow left, but to our joy he took a drop of water at last. Even better he then ate a tiny morsel of raw mince. Two days before, I had asked Capital Radio about the swallows, what they ate, where they were going. They told us that worms were their natural diet although, during their long migration to South Africa, they would not need much food. South Africa! It seemed extraordinary that this tiny bird – we had christened him Gilbert – should also be on his way to the southern tip of Africa. We decided that Gilbert would have to be fattened up if he was to make the trip successfully. Fred and I spent hours tempting the little bird with pieces of mince until, to our delight, he developed a taste for it and ate so voraciously that we feared he might die from overeating. There was a tense moment when Gilbert disappeared in a sudden squally shower which arrived under a black cloud. But when the squall had passed Gilbert was back again, eager for more mince and plodding around the deck as if he owned the place.

'Where's Gilbert?' I asked an hour or so later, as I brought up fresh supplies of mince.

OPPOSITE

Off-watch activities in the Doldrums.

'He's here,' said five people simultaneously. There, indeed, were five Gilberts. And looking up the mast we spotted another five. Eleven Gilberts were not so endearing as one, particularly when all of them wanted to roost

74

Is that you, Gilbert?

below and leave droppings in our clothes and bedding. We rigged netting over all the hatches and spent hours chasing the little birds out of the boat. Eventually, when darkness fell, they gave up their attempts to get below and huddled miserably on the deck so that we had to step carefully to avoid crushing them.

Another terrible night of fitful winds and a boat speed of two or three knots heralded our fourth day in the Doldrums. By now, nothing could mitigate our situation. When a south-westerly breeze finally sprang up and steadied through the day, we did not particularly welcome it. It had come too late for us. *Disque d'Or* was now 250 miles ahead, while *King's Legend* and *Flyer* were over 400 miles ahead. In the past four days we had been so miserable about our daily positions that we had not passed them to the other boats but now, finally, we gave our position to *GB II*. Immediately, *Disque d'Or* came on the air. She could not believe what she had heard and asked *GB II* to repeat it three times. When our position was confirmed we could imagine only too clearly the scene of rejoicing around *Disque d'Or*'s radio.

As the wind strengthened, the swallows flew off one by one until only four remained. 'Gilbert? Gilbert?' Fred called, holding some mince in the tweezers. 'Gilbert? Is that you? Ah!' he exclaimed as one bird leapt for the mince. 'Gilbert, I think that's you!'

Finally, as the boat started to heel and pitch in the first firm breaths of the south-east trade winds, Gilbert too flexed his wings, circled the boat a few times and was gone. To reach South Africa he, like *ADC*, had a long windward passage ahead of him.

As far as 40° south, the South Atlantic weather is dominated by a large high-pressure area. To the south of it are the westerlies and the Roaring Forties, and to the north are the south-east trades through which we now had to sail. In the middle of the high there is little or no wind at all. We had the choice of freeing off and sailing around the high to find the westerlies, a route which would add a good many miles to the trip, or of trying to squeeze to the east of the high, a shorter route but also a windward one which would reduce our speed substantially. To make the choice really difficult the high, like all highs, was unstable. Its size, pressure and, worst of all, its position, could change dramatically within half a day. Thus we might think we were passing well clear of it only to find it had moved several hundred miles and was sitting right on top of us.

To help us decide on our route, we gathered all the weather information we could find. To begin with we spent hours trying to decipher weather synopses in Morse and other codes, using a tape recorder with a special slow playback. However, after many hours of toil we would usually end up with, at best, scrappy information. Much better was the brilliantly simple and highly informative system developed by the French yachts. They merely made contact with a large French oil tanker on the radio and asked its radio operator to decipher the synopses and forecasts and pass them on in plain language. The yachts would then pass the information on to the rest of the fleet, as they were bound to do under the rules (no yacht was permitted a

76

private source of weather information). When one tanker got out of radio range, its radio operator would arrange for another tanker to take over the service, and so on.

Although this system provided us with excellent weather maps we, like the other yachts, soon concluded that it was not as helpful with decision-making as we had hoped. It became clear that the movements of the high were so rapid and unpredictable that no amount of information could help us guess which way it would move next.

In the end, we decided on the windward route to the east of the high. It was not an easy decision. John felt, as before, that we should go for speed and, although he never actually recommended the longer route, I felt that it was the one he preferred. Jacques, on the other hand, pressed for the windward route. It was a difficult decision, but I was encouraged to agree with Jacques because, firstly, the wind was southerly for the first few days, enabling us to make good easting on the starboard tack; secondly, *King's Legend* and *Flyer*, now about three days ahead, were doing well on this route; and thirdly, we didn't want to follow along behind *Disque d'Or* on the long route. John accepted the decision quite happily, agreeing that either route could be the right one.

So began the long windward slog. After the four disastrous days in the Doldrums, everyone made a great effort to restore morale and cheer each other up. Jacques appeared in stunning garb of Bermuda shorts, pyjama top, a tie tied in a large bow, straw hat and large sunglasses. For our further entertainment, he did his keep fit exercises which were so perfunctory as to involve a few twitches and a couple of half-hearted skips leading to immediate collapse on the deck. Sam, too, always made us smile. 'Mornin', guv,' he would say to me at breakfast, as he passed the cereal. ''Ere, bash yer gums on this!' Sam had a mode of expression all his own, which never failed to startle and enthrall us. 'You French git,' he yelled at Jacques, 'This washin'-up ain't done at all. You've bin lyin' like a Naafi clock!'

As a reminder that our problems, though disheartening, were relatively small, we heard that *Condor*, who had been in the lead, had lost her mast and was making for Monrovia to fit a new one that was being flown out from England. *Japy-Hermès*, a French yacht, was also facing a serious problem. One of her crew was suffering badly from kidney stones and was in great pain. This boat, too, was making for port, to Recife in Brazil. Compared to this, losing about five places did not seem so bad.

But despite this news and the crew's efforts to cheer each other up, our Halfway to Cape Town Party was not a jolly affair. The invitation reflected the atmosphere on the boat: ARE YOU FEELING HALF-BAKED, HALF-HEARTED AND HALF-WITTED? COME TO A HALF-WAY PARTY AT HALF-SIX. HALF-DRESSED. HALF-CUT? We were now beating hard to windward and the incredible bumpy motion was having its effect. Robin and Eve became seasick and the rest of us felt off colour. I lost my appetite and got diarrhoea, leaving me weak and tired, while the others suffered lethargy. The boat was permanently heeled at an angle of 20–30° and, once the wind swung round to the south-east, we settled on the port tack for ten days without respite.

Life below had to be lived at a difficult angle: nothing could be left on the

Into the south-east trades and the spray flies.

table or in the galley without sliding across. All movement was an uphill climb or a downhill slide. Spray started to fly over the deck and we were forced to close all the hatches, making the air below hot, humid and none too pleasant. We never minded getting wet on the foredeck while changing a sail – the water was warm and we enjoyed the exercise. But below decks the wet atmosphere made everything sticky and damp and clothes never really dried. The South Atlantic was not a particularly sunny place – there was usually a layer of cloud covering the sun and this seemed to make the atmosphere humid and sultry, despite the fresh wind.

It was also very noisy below as *ADC* leapt from wave to wave and crashed into the occasional steep one. For the mushrooms who slept up forward the noise was often accompanied by violent descents of the bow and they would find themselves lifted clear above their bunks. In the aft cabin Jacques, Bumble and I were accustomed to ear-splitting din – all the sheet winches were situated just over our heads. It was like trying to sleep in the works of Big Ben, such was the thunderous racket of grinding cogs and wheeling winch barrels. The crashes of the bow made us jump to begin with but, like the other noises, we soon got used to them. As Tony remarked, we would need to hire a tribe of dustmen to empty bins outside our doors in Cape Town if we were ever to get to sleep there.

In the middle of this settling-down period, when we were a little seasick and uncomfortable, we experienced two gear failures. One of the two hydraulic backstay tensioners, which regulated the fore-and-aft tension of the main

78

mast rigging, started to leak and lose pressure. This meant that the forestay started to sag and we lost much of our windward efficiency. As the days passed, the problem got worse until we had to abandon the hydraulics altogether. We took up what tension we could on the bottlescrews, but it made little difference – the forestay had a bad sag, we could not point high, and so the situation would have to remain until we reached Cape Town. Having chosen the windward route this was a real blow. By this time it was too late to change tactics and take the longer route – we would merely lose more time. Instead we would have to make the best of the situation, unsatisfactory though it was.

Despite all Fred's tender care, the engine was the next to fail. After many hours down in the bilges, Fred emerged with the news that a fuel pump had broken and that he could not repair it. This meant we would have a shortage of power for the remainder of the leg. We had a small portable generator, just enough to produce power for the essential radio and navigation instruments. But the freezer was another matter. This gadget ate power at an enormous rate, especially in the warm weather, and there was no question of keeping it going for long. There was only one problem – it was still half full of meat. Bumble took the news with equanimity and declared that everyone would have to eat a lot of meat, wouldn't they? And eat they did. Steaks for breakfast, cutlets for lunch and roasts for dinner, a menu which was the envy of the rest of the fleet.

One good thing resulted from the engine's failure. We no longer had to endure it running for two hours every day. This had long been an unpopular event. For some reason we never quite understood, Fred always chose to start the engine at meal times, and as the telltale buzz of the ignition came on a loud groan would go up from the saloon table, and we would prepare ourselves for two hours of noise and extra heat. Now we would only have to listen to the quiet buzz of the little generator up on deck. With the shortage of power the boat took on an eerie, mysterious air during the hours of darkness. The nights were long and, in order to read or find clothes, we carried small torches with us everywhere. Bumble suspended two torches from the roof of the galley to see what she was cooking, while two more were suspended in the netting above the saloon table so that we could see what we were eating. People lay in their bunks resting torches under their chins to read books, then balanced them on their knees to pull on their sea boots. Fortunately we had plenty of torches and batteries.

On the 20th September we crossed the Equator. This event had long been viewed with some anxiety by many of the crew – and especially by me – for, apart from Jacques, John and Eve, none of us had crossed the line before. This meant we were in for a hard time at the hands of Neptune. On the other hand we were nine against three as I pointed out to the other first-timers, and if we banded together there would be little that the minority of initiates could do in the way of dunkings, wettings and other ceremonials.

Evey threw herself into the arrangements with great enthusiasm, preparing costumes, a trident for Neptune, and various nasty dishes of mixed foods to be forced down unwilling throats. However, it was all for nothing. Come the great moment, the crew were either mending the hydraulics, trying to fix the engine or feeling sick. Eve rushed around trying to muster support for the ceremony but finally gave up in despair. Indeed we were a sorry lot and, even if the party had got off the ground, it would have been rather half-hearted.

The sailing itself was the key to the boat's happiness. As long as the sailing was enjoyable and challenging, everyone was cheerful and full of verve. We liked lots of activity in the form of sail-changing, tacking and trimming. Sitting on the same tack, bashing into a short head sea for day after day was not particularly demanding and, since it was also extremely wet and uncomfortable, the crew's spirits were not at their highest.

Some days we would be reasonably busy taking in reefs then shaking them out again, but on other days a whole watch would go by with no more than a few sail trims to keep the deck crew busy. As a result we tried to occupy ourselves in other ways. I busied myself with the radio, which was taking up more and more time as it became increasingly difficult to get through to England. Bumble studied the bird life and told us the names of the seabirds that swooped around the boat – the sooty shearwater, the gannet, the booby and the stormy petrel. Fred tried to exhaust his repertoire of good, mediocre and excruciating jokes during the long night watches, and eventually succeeded – whereupon I suggested he change to the other watch so that he could tell them all again. At least once a watch John, Tony, Beat or Sam would make a careful inspection of all the gear. If they found anything amiss, they would almost leap on it, so eager were they to repair it and occupy themselves for a few hours. Through the gaps in the clouds at dusk, Jacques would take sights of stars that did not seem to exist in the Almanac. This led to the discovery of the 'Redon Star', the name for any star that Jacques could not immediately identify although, on several nights at least, it was suspected to be Aldebaran. On deck we would often play word games to pass the time. Down below, I picked up my French book and got so engrossed in improving my grammar and vocabulary that I hounded Jacques with questions. However, my sudden enthusiasm did not seem to help Jacques in his battle to give up smoking – every time I asked him a difficult question, he would reach for his pipe and light up to help his concentration.

Conversation sank to discussion of 'spotty botties' – a common ailment when our skins were always damp and salty – and to wondering how many times Tony's nose could peel without running out of skin. Poor Tony had a nose which peeled in the sun, out of the sun and, he was to discover, in the freezing cold as well. We examined my feet every day for 'Blue Foot Disease', an affliction caused by buying a not inexpensive pair of blue deck shoes and actually wearing them on deck in the wet, not an unusual place to wear a deck shoe, one might think, but obviously not a place the manufacturers had designed them for. I spent many happy hours composing an imaginary letter of complaint and even tried to photograph my bright blue feet.

For those of the crew who were neither deeply involved in the technicalities of the sailing nor particularly interested in the tactical considerations of the race, the time passed more slowly. Evey, who liked nothing better than to be frantically busy, found the long, windward passage particularly hard. The

80

Above: Hard on the wind. A rare sunny day in the South Atlantic.

Below: Scrubbing off, with Table Mountain behind.

When the wind fluctuated, we were kept busy reefing.

lack of mental stimulation and the eternal discomfort slowly wore her down. One day, after getting soaked twice, enduring two days without sleep because of the wild motion, and trying to struggle into oilskins that had been made too small to fit over her hips, Evey announced that it was all too much and she would rather be almost anywhere else but on a boat. From time to time we all felt like that but, seeing Eve was really feeling low, I tried to snap her out of it by telling her the next leg would almost certainly be worse – probably not the best thing to say. After some days Eve pulled herself out of the depression, but she still found those two weeks hard to bear.

Everyone found something to complain about. I was always rambling on about the lack of communication up and down the deck. Often one would see something going wrong on the foredeck from a position on the wheel and be unable to communicate this fact to the people up forward. The middle deck crew would stand and stare, quite unaware of the importance of passing on messages, and thought the helmsman was shouting to exercise his lungs. In the end I persuaded everyone that they must yell messages up the deck or use sign language – it didn't matter which. But it took a long time for people to realise the importance of communication on a large boat.

Damp bedding, dirt and squalor, clothing lying around – everyone had a small grouse about something. Music cassettes left out of their boxes and not put away was a favourite, a dirty galley was another, and of course, the state of the loos. The loos were not bad by most standards, but the pumps gave trouble from time to time, making it extremely difficult to keep them clean and sweet all day long. The forward loo was the most temperamental, and everyone started using the aft one, another cause for complaint because of the long queue that formed in the morning and the far from rosy aroma that began to pervade the aft cabin all day long.

Normally, grouses were aired straight away and, after the aggrieved person had made a small public complaint, the problem would disappear for a while. Human nature being what it is, the same thing would start happening again a few days later, until another complaint was made. But all in all everyone made a great effort to make life as comfortable and bearable as possible, not only for themselves but for everyone else. Apart from the odd time when one person would snap at another, we were able to live together in harmony and grumbles were rarely made or taken personally. When we complained, we were really complaining about the conditions, not each other. With the possible exception of Tony, who loved sailing however uncomfortable it was, everyone was worn down by the long, relentless slog against the south-east trades. Day after day, we pushed *ADC* on into the short wet seas, the boat always heeled well over and the deck covered in spray.

Doubtless the long windward passage would have been more enjoyable if our position had been better but, although it was disappointing enough already, we now discovered it was slipping even further. Ahead of us *King's Legend* and *Flyer* were having an exciting duel to be the first yacht to reach Cape Town. *GB II*, who had taken the lead after the ill-fated *Condor* lost her mast, had taken the longer route and fallen into the centre of the high where she now sat becalmed and helpless, watching the two smaller boats squeeze to

the east of the calms and head straight for Cape Town. For those three yachts, the direct route was proving to be the better route by a significant margin. However, for us on the direct route just three days behind, it was proving to be very far from the better route. From their daily positions we had seen how *Flyer* and *King's Legend* had been slowly freed, enabling them to make up to the east until they were clear of the high. But, although we expected the wind to free us almost daily, we waited in vain and it never did. The route which was being so generous to the leading boats was to be unkind to us. As a result, we were forced to squeeze up and lose speed to stay east of the high. John felt we should crack off to gain speed, but this would send us due south and straight into the calms. As it turned out the idea would have proved a good one, for the high was to make an enormous and sudden move straight across our path. But there was no way of foreseeing this and, rather than change tactics at this late stage, I felt it would be best to plug on.

Ten days on the port tack and we became used to climbing uphill.

To be sure of doing well on this first leg luck, more than anything, was what was needed and luck had been conspicuously absent for *ADC*. Perhaps we had taken some bad decisions too. But when one route could be extremely favourable one day, and disastrous the next, it was hard to decide anything on a reasoned basis.

Now we had to make the best of the situation. We had been overtaken by three or four boats on the longer route but we might yet make up one or two places. All we needed was some of that elusive luck.

83

CHAPTER 5

Windward Passage

The log entry read, 'The other watch is a drag on the rations cos' they ain't pulling there wieght' (*sic*). In fact inter-watch rivalry was friendly and far from fierce. For one thing, we regularly moved people from one watch to the other. Not only did this give them a chance to see the members of the opposite watch, whom they might not have talked to for weeks, but it prevented one watch from growing apart from the other in terms of effort and ideas. It also had a very favourable effect on morale. A change of watch members would lead to more comments in the log: 'Eve changed watches and joined the best watch in the whole ship,' and 'Robin changed also – he joined the fastest one!'

While we ploughed on through the trades and the sail-handling remained undemanding, we learnt to use our time to better effect. We took to playing word games in the cockpit. Off-watch, letter-writing became a very popular pastime and some letters became 100-page epistles by the time we reached Cape Town. Food was also immensely popular, although somewhat difficult to eat when the motion of the boat was always doing its best to throw everything on the floor. Many was the time we picked food off the sail bags which covered the saloon floor or, seeing a morsel fly into an inaccessible corner, looked the other way and left it there. One day the boat lurched just as I was manoeuvring across the saloon with a full bowl of porridge, and the contents flew out and hit one of Robin's boots which was lying on the floor. Before I could get there, the porridge slid slowly down into the boot to congeal in the sole. I asked Robin whether he preferred a sticky boot or a soaking wet one without porridge. He said he didn't particularly mind, so he got a soaking wet one.

One day I took over the wheel from Jacques while he went below to have lunch. Someone pointed out that the centre hatch was open a crack and shouldn't we close it. 'No, don't worry,' said Jacques, 'me missus is at the wheel. We won't get wet!'

A few minutes later I let my attention wander for a moment and allowed the boat to take a wave badly. A shot of green water came up over the deck and covered the centre hatch. There was a loud yell and general commotion from below, and I tried to look suitably repentant as a dripping Jacques appeared at the companion-way. 'Oi!', he said in a noticeably cool manner. 'I thought you of all people could drive this thing! Me lunch is swimming in seawater and there's a drip running down me spine. . . .' At that point words failed him and he went down to change into some dry clothes. From then on we thought it wiser to keep the hatch closed all the time.

The team of helmsman and sail trimmer, always looking for more speed.

Our table manners had deteriorated over four weeks, not only because we had to hold the bowls right up to our chins to be sure of getting the food into our mouths, but because we wanted to save on washing-up. At the beginning of the race we had been wildly extravagant with dishes, using a plate for the main course, a bowl for pudding and separate knives, forks and spoons. A little mathematics and we calculated there were seventy-two dishes to wash each day and about 120 pieces of cutlery. Washing-up was never very popular at the best of times, but when the water was salty and cold it was even more of a chore. When some of the crew started licking their plates after the main course so they could be re-used for pudding, the idea spread like wildfire. Forks and spoons were well licked too, ready for the fruit and custard.

The only drawback to plate-licking was that most of the boys were now adorned with long, scraggy beards which accumulated almost as much food as their tongues picked up. Thus a cry of, 'Tongue to the right!' would be the cue for the offender to lick the right side of his beard and pick up stray morsels. Sometimes someone would cry, 'Ah, yesterday's baked beans!' as they cleared up the shrubbery around their mouths. Feeding-time was not a very refined affair.

However, food itself remained one of our great joys, always eagerly looked forward to. When Bumble went into the galley to start preparing a meal a head would appear through the door, sniff, peer over Bumble's shoulder, and ask what was on the menu. Sometimes she told them, sometimes she didn't. Going

85

A difficult time for Bumble as food would regularly fly across the galley.

to windward was a very difficult time for Bumble. The boat was heeled hard over to starboard so that the cooker was uphill and Bumble had to lean against a strap to support herself. When the boat pitched and shuddered, anything not properly wedged would fly across the galley or spill down into a locker. 'Hell!' Bumble would cry from time to time, a moderate reaction considering the difficulties she was dealing with.

Sometimes Bumble would give the boys a hard time when she found the washing-up half done or the galley dirty. Hands on hips, she would stand in

86

the saloon and ask, in mock rage, 'Who is reponsible for *this* mess? Unless they come and clear it up there won't be any custard for supper!' Since a custardless supper was about the worst fate the boys could imagine, the work would usually get done.

On the 24th September it was Bumble's birthday, a really splendid affair. Before the start, Robert had collected dozens of cards and some presents from Bumble's family and friends and now produced them like a rabbit from a hat. Among the presents were children's games and a home-recorded cassette, full of funny songs and family jokes. Sam had made a birthday cake, which Bumble cut with great ceremony after blowing out some tiny candles. Bumble was overwhelmed by it all and suffered a bout of homesickness the next day. She had come on the race shortly after the death of her father, and it had been very hard to leave her family at such a time. She added, crying quietly, that she also felt useless on the boat – all she could do was tail and wind winches. I persuaded Bumble that this was a very useful contribution to the boat, as was the amount of work she did on the sail repairs. It was ironic that Bumble, of all people, should feel she was not contributing enough when she spent so much time helping on deck as well as cooking in the hot, hard conditions of the galley. Being a very cheerful and optimistic person by nature, Bumble was soon her old self again. It was the only time we ever saw her at a low ebb.

After the queasiness most of us had felt during the first few days to windward, our stomachs and appetites soon returned to normal. However there was one appetite that never failed to astound us. Robin had a slim build and no bulk to feed, yet he ate for two. He was rather embarrassed by his appetite and whenever Bumble asked who wanted second helpings, Robin would feign disinterest and stare intently at the table or into space, without saying a word. After a while he would look round the table in a sheepish manner, say, 'Well, if no-one else is going to . . .', and pass his plate into the galley. Sometimes he would say, 'Er . . . only if there's some going', or, 'If you want to have it finished . . . .' Once, when Robin had a third helping of pudding after making feeble protestations of, 'No, I couldn't really,' Sam eyed him with a grin and said, 'Robin, me old mate, let's face it – you've got the breaking strain of a Kit-Kat!'

Robin never survived a night watch without going below to finish off the leftovers or make himself a jam sandwich. He would slip into the galley in a shifty manner and would eat quietly and unobtrusively. If someone disturbed him he would jump guiltily and almost hide the food behind his back. Since anyone was free to eat anything whenever they wanted, poor Robin's guilt must have been a leftover from boarding-school. The fact that we all laughed and joked about it couldn't have helped either. Many months later Robin became inured to our comments and ate second helpings without self-reproach. However, he would still say, as he passed his plate, 'Only if there's some going . . . .'

Lack of privacy did not prove to be a problem during the six weeks we were at sea. Although the boat was going to be very crowded in port when twelve of us would be keeping the same hours, it was never a problem at sea. There would usually be four to six people on deck, four people asleep or reading in their bunks, and the rest reading or writing letters in the saloon. At mealtimes it became quite crowded when six were seated round the saloon table at once, but otherwise there was always plenty of room. If you wanted to be on your own, you flopped into your bunk and no-one would disturb you.

We were fortunate enough to have a stereo cassette system installed in the boat, which had been a generous gift from a kind benefactor, Charles Williams. The system ran through all the cabins and each bunk had its own set of headphones, so that each of us could listen to music when we chose. This was just as well because our tastes in music were as different as chalk from cheese. Robert and Robin were the teeny-boppers who liked rock, punk rock and various other kinds of agonised moaning with a rhythmic background. One of the funniest sights was to see Robin washing up with the headphones on, eyes closed in rapture, as he swayed and 'Ooah-Oooed' to music no-one else could hear. Sometimes when Robin was in his bunk, we would hear a loud 'Wa-wa, babay', followed by the sound of a rhythmic tattoo drummed on the leeboard. The rest of the crew liked everything from light to classical music and opera, so in the evenings when everyone enjoyed listening we tried to play as great a variety as possible.

In the second week of that long windward beat, we really began to settle down, just as one can settle down to anything given enough time. We became houseproud again and made more effort to keep the saloon clean. Eve had a blitz one day and tidied away all John's girlie magazines which regularly littered the seats and, after a bumpy wave, the floor. These magazines were slowly disintegrating from being on the floor so often and, of course, from the number of people who read them. As Eve picked up the pages and pieced them together she roared with laughter and cried, 'Good Lord! You don't actually find these ladies *fanciable*, do you boys? They look physically distorted to me!'

We took it in turns to clean up the food, odd bits of clothing and general gunk which got behind the sailbags on the cabin sole, and now and then someone, usually Fred, would clean behind the cooker in the galley, another unpleasant spot. We would keep most of the large, heavy sails below. We usually kept three of the long sail bags snaking through the saloon, another two in the forward cabins, and one in the workshop. The spinnakers, however, were round and bulky when packed, and they lived in the after cabin. Sometimes we had to climb up two sails and then duck our heads to get out through the doorway. If we thought we might need to change a headsail, we would pull the new sail up through the main companion-way and snake it up along the deck to the foredeck. If the change was imminent, we would hank the new sail on, ready to be raised as soon as the old one was down and unhanked. If the change was uncertain, we would tie the sail down to the side deck, still in its bag.

As we progressed south, the wind became more variable in speed, ranging from fifteen to thirty knots in the space of a few minutes. It was not feasible to adjust the headsail area that frequently, so we relied on reefing and unreefing the mainsail most of the time. Some days, the reefing and unreefing was so frequent that the deck crew could no longer complain of having nothing to do.

Hanking on a jib, ready for a sail change.

For two days the wind oscillated between fifteen and forty knots and they were so busy they were almost wishing for the quiet times again.

It was a job to get the boat to feel well balanced while she was driving hard on the wind, and the wheel would often feel dead in our hands – or as Jacques would say, 'It's got Dead 'Elm disease.' Later we were to make more use of the

89

mizzen for balancing the boat. We never ceased to be amazed by the amount we were always learning about the boat. Tony, who had sailed on a number of hot racing machines, remarked on it particularly. And he was to remark on it again 20,000 miles later.

At 25° south we began to wonder if the south-east trades would ever relent. Far from freeing us as it should, the wind forced us to head slightly west of south – a disastrous course – and then it blew up to a very uncomfortable and wet Force 7. Almost in despair, we wondered what the weather could possibly produce next.

We did not have long to wait. Within two days the barometer was high and after two long, hard weeks of wet, windward sailing we found ourselves becalmed. 'Oh no,' I groaned, 'we've sailed into the middle of the high!'

Looking on the bright side of things the boat was at least upright for the first time in weeks. We could walk around the boat without holding on, we could work without oilskins, and Bumble could cook in comfort. Looking on the bad side, we might be stuck there for days.

There was only one thing to do. I took a bottle of burgundy and, without even opening it, dropped it neatly over the side. Giving Neptune Scotch in the Doldrums had not been a success but he might just like red wine. In truth, it was not very good red wine – it had not travelled very well, as they say – and resembled vinegar and citric acid. However, I felt I had done all I could and, not being overfond of staring at a windless sea, I repaired to my horizontal bunk for a relaxed sleep. For the first time in many days it would not be necessary to wedge myself against the leeboard to stop myself rolling out.

Some hours later, Jacques came to the side of my bunk and shook me awake. 'There's some wind,' he said. 'From the north! And it's going round to the west all the time.' I sat up, trying to take it in. We had been virtually becalmed for most of the day. Now I could feel the boat starting to trickle along. A westerly wind? If only it would hold. . . .

It did. It came in fits and starts, blew and faded, veered and backed, but held sufficiently to take us into Cape Town a week later. The high must have passed straight over us, then stopped. *Traité de Rome* and *Adventure* were both caught in its calms for very much longer than us, so we were fortunate. Our change of luck was not enough to catch the boats who had passed us by on the other route – *GB II, Disque d'Or, Tielsa,* and *Gauloises*. They were miles ahead. But by that time we counted ourselves lucky just to maintain our position.

The downwind sailing had an immediate and remarkable effect on us all. There was laughter, noise and vitality once more. Jacques found his Redon star again and renamed it Aldebaran. Bumble kept jumping up and down as she identified several species of albatross, as well as the famous Cape pigeons. Eve suddenly found a dozen interesting topics of conversation. The boat was upright again, the hatches could be opened for air, everything dried out below and there was plenty of fast, demanding sailing, with many sail changes to keep us fully occupied. Beat started dreaming about the 'crispy chicks' he was going to meet in Cape Town, while Robert stretched our credulity to the limit by saying, in a suitably grave manner, that he was looking forward to visiting all the art galleries and museums. Robin undoubtedly started imagining his first large meal, while Bumble became what we could only describe as bumptious. Cape Town was in for a very hard time.

Being under the influence of the westerlies, it was not long before a frontal system came through. As rain and cloud developed we knew the wind was likely to veer, but we were totally unprepared for the rapidity with which it finally did so. It took only thirty seconds for the wind to swing round 60°, so that we suddenly found ourselves sailing at right-angles to the swell, rolling so far and so violently that the main boom was dipping in the water. If this was a foretaste of the Southern Ocean we were going to be in for an exciting time – and we looked forward to it eagerly.

Shortly after the front had passed through and we were under spinnaker again, we also had a foretaste of an experience that was to become so familiar that it was almost part of our lives – the starcut spinnaker fell down. On this first occasion, it fell down because we exerted too much pressure on the luff as we tried to lower it. It parted across the top and down one side, a trick it was to perform many times in the future. Unhappily for the sailmakers, it was never to prove quite beyond repair.

Spinnaker rip apart, we had a smooth, fast and uneventful run into Cape Town. Eve was finally persuaded that she had seen a 'green flash' above the setting sun, a phenomenon that everyone had been remarking on for weeks but that Eve had been quite unable to see. She was still doubtful that the flash existed but, more to quiet those who taunted her with being unable to spot it, she suddenly yelled 'green flash' and dared anyone to deny it.

Triumphantly, Evey also located a piece of leather needed for sail repairs, that she had been searching for since the Equator. Originally she had asked John to look under a floorboard while she looked elsewhere. He had reported no luck, but now she looked there herself, Eve found the leather straight away. She left the leather in a prominent position on John's bunk. However, a day later it was Eve's turn to find something in her bunk. Moreover, it was a large, slimy salami. Eve had long been saying how tired she was of having the salamis swinging endlessly over our heads in the saloon and, salami not being her favourite food, had suggested throwing them over the side or using them for fenders. No-one owned up to putting the sausage in Eve's bunk but we all noticed that Nick was grinning like a Cheshire cat.

Two days from Cape Town there was tremendous excitement, for we suddenly saw another yacht. It was the French *Neptune,* who had sailed by the longer route. It was to be an interesting meeting for, in the two days it took us to reach port, we were to take fifteen hours out of *Neptune.* This cheered us no end because, although we did not beat *Neptune* on handicap, it made us realise what we could achieve given similar conditions and a bit of that elusive luck.

The prospect of land, civilisation and entertainment brought a change to everyone's appearance. Scruffy beards and stubble disappeared, hair got washed, and clean clothes, hitherto unseen, were shaken out ready for arrival. We had been at sea for six weeks and, although the first weeks had passed quickly, the last three had stretched out to such an extent that we could hardly believe we were about to arrive.

After a long sea passage, the first sight of land is always magical and none was more so than our first glimpse of Table Mountain, a small grey outline on the far, clear horizon.

'I say, John, well done!' said Robin, very much impressed by the exactitude of sextant navigation. 'Looks as though Cape Town's actually dead ahead.'

As we neared port we used our last few pints of fresh water for washing and arrived with no more than a few drops in the tanks. We had been uncomfortably close to running out altogether. In fact, the only thing we had run out of in all that time was tomato ketchup, due to Beat's insatiable appetite for the stuff. We had all watched in wonderment as he had consumed it with breakfast, lunch and dinner. He would probably have eaten it for tea as well, except that it didn't go with honey, his other favourite food.

To entertain the boats already in – and we had the feeling there would be at least six – we dug out the remnants of the heavy spinnaker that we had lost in the Channel and composed a slogan to be written across the last remaining panel. The suggestions for the slogan included FOR SAIL – ONE CAREFUL OWNER, ONLY 43 PANELS MISSING and EASY REEF SPINNAKER, but in the end we chose WATCH THIS SPACE. When we were towed into the yacht basin we hoisted the skeleton of the spinnaker with the slogan printed across the last remaining panel.

We were seventh boat in, and ninth on handicap. *Flyer* had won the leg by just two hours from *King's Legend* but, because of their remarkably fast passage around the high, the two boats were days ahead of the rest of the fleet and in an almost unassailable position to keep their lead for the remainder of the race.

The times that the fleet achieved were magnificent. *Flyer* had done the leg in just under thirty-nine days, three days faster than *Burton Cutter,* first home in the first race and a much larger boat. We ourselves were only one day behind *Burton Cutter*'s time, and a full day ahead of *Sayula*'s time. *Sayula,* a Swan 65, had been the handicap winner of the previous race.

These times reflected how very competitive this second event was proving to be. There was no room for cruising or taking it easy if you wanted to do well. The fact that we would be heading into the Southern Ocean would make no difference. All the boats would push as hard or even harder than before.

Despite being only seventh boat in, our arrival in Cape Town was euphoric. The other boats gave us a traditional welcome by sounding their fog horns and waving, then gave three cheers for our ridiculous spinnaker. As soon as the formalities were completed, we were free to enjoy the hospitality of Cape Town. Robert, never one to hold back, leapt on to the quay, strode up to the first pretty girl he saw, affirmed she was South African, and gave her a large kiss. We could see he wasn't going to have much time for the art galleries and museums.

Our stay in Cape Town was expected to last about two and a half weeks (the restart date was never fixed until most of the fleet were in) and we were going to need every moment of it. After moving into a hotel and enjoying the longest, hottest, most enjoyable bath in the world, Jacques and I started to plan the work. The new pole ends, safely arrived from California, had to be fitted by a boat yard. The hydraulic backstay pumps would have to be repaired. There was welding work to be done on the stanchions. The new fuel pump for the engine, which should have arrived from England, would have to be fitted by the local Volvo agent. The compass, which was again sticking when the boat heeled, would have to be repaired. The sails would have to be overhauled and some sent to a professional loft. In addition there were many smaller jobs which we would have to do ourselves.

Our first difficulty occurred when we discovered that the fuel pump, ordered by radio three weeks before, had not arrived from England. I contacted my father, who had been dealing with the matter, to find that he had put the order through, confirmed it twice and had thought the part safely in South Africa. After many more phone calls it transpired that Volvo, unimpressed by any sense of urgency, had never sent the part. Moreover they suddenly announced that they wanted cash in advance before despatch. This was their final mistake, for they incurred the full flood of my father's wrath and must, I think, have regretted their inefficiency and lack of co-operation.

We experienced minor difficulties with some of the other jobs but, after four or five days of hard work, there was a good chance of everything being finished on time.

One of the more enjoyable distractions of working on board was the number of visitors who asked to be shown over the boat, giving us the excuse to stop whatever we were doing. Sam would give some of the more colourful tours pointing out such spots as 'Tanner's Hell-Hole' and 'Bumble's Bistro', while warning people from entering the stuffy port cabin because 'There're a pair of rampant socks guarding the door.'

Our hosts, the Royal Cape Yacht Club, were extremely hospitable. Knowing the priorities of visiting yachtsmen, they had arranged for outside caterers to provide the most lavish food at a very reasonable cost, morning, noon and night, and, because the yacht basin and club premises were some way from the centre of town, they had also arranged for transport in and out of the city several times a day. Fortunately for our crew, General Motors had arranged to lend us a car or two at each stop, a tremendous help when there was so much rushing about to be done and a limited budget. Several club members gave barbecues, swimming parties or dinners for us, until the surfeit of good food and easy living changed our shapes dramatically. I put on all the weight I had lost since the Doldrums – and probably a lot more.

Prompted by Bob Saunders of the BBC, Jacques and I abandoned work for a couple of days to go sightseeing and visited a vineyard, an old farm, and a lush natural forest of exotic flowers and shrubs. Another day, we slipped away to visit the Cape of Good Hope itself, curious to see such a famous place at close quarters. It was a wild, beautiful place, a nature reserve where baboon, ostrich and zebra roam free. The Cape is the meeting place of the Atlantic and Indian Oceans and it is said that the water on the Indian side of the promontory is warm and blue, while the Atlantic water is cold and green. Some days, the legend continues, you can see a clear dividing line of colour stretching away to the south. We looked but could see nothing but greeny-blue, white-capped sea. We remembered the other name for the Cape – the

Cape of Storms, and hoped it would be kind to us when we left on the long leg to New Zealand.

The stopover was also an opportunity to exchange gossip and ideas with the other boats. We learnt that they too had found the leg long and, at times, tedious. Some had got caught in the high for twice as long as others. *33 Export*, by going too near the African coast where the winds were light, had been delayed by several days. *Condor*, having fitted her new mast in Monrovia with the help of a ship's crane, arrived in Cape Town a week before the re-start, which gave her just enough time to prepare for the next leg. The seventeen crew of *GB II* said they had been cramped and more than a little damp during the leg. One of the sleeping cabins was known as Virginia Water because of the constant streams that ran down the bulkheads, while the aft cabin was called St George's Hill because it was so exclusive. The other two cabins were known as Coronation Street (the bunks were in a row) and The Flats (the bunks were stacked one on top of the other).

We arranged to swop excess stores with the other boats – we had too much flour, jam and dried milk, and exchanged them for pâté, washing-up liquid and breakfast cereal. There was a friendly atmosphere between the great majority of the crews and a real desire to help by lending tools or giving advice. Often people from one boat would go off sightseeing with the crew from another. Having seen their own shipmates for six continuous weeks, it was a pleasant change to meet some of the others.

It did not take much observation to realise that some boats were happier than others. Some crew members were asked to leave their boats while others merely hinted at 'personality problems', but considering there were 170-odd individuals living in cramped conditions on fifteen boats, it was not surprising

In front of Cape Town Yacht Club.

that there were differences of opinion and clashes of personality. As one of the organisers had so rightly observed, the only real problems on the race were likely to be crew problems and gear problems. Almost every boat was to find this painfully true.

It seemed we had only just arrived when it was time to start thinking about leaving again. The non-perishable provisions had to be unpacked and stowed, every tin being marked with waterproof ink and stripped of its label. More film arrived from the BBC, and Bob Saunders gave us another briefing on how to use it. Poor Bob had discovered that during the first leg we had sometimes forgotten to synchronise the sound with the vision – a basic mistake which would give the film editors a time-consuming task trying to fit one to the other. Also, we had failed to keep a film log, making it difficult to fit the sequences into the chain of events. Having made all the amateur's mistakes, we decided we could only improve.

After many telexes and visits to the airport, the fuel pump finally arrived and was fitted. This was a great relief to us all, particularly Bumble who could now bank on having a freezer in which to store the frozen meat. The alternative would have been dried meat or – a thought which filled me with dread – tinned meat in heavy tins. I expected the next leg to take only five weeks, so we could take fewer weighty provisions, but I would have liked to see the boat even lighter.

Our new heavy spinnaker had arrived safely from England and looked a lot stronger than the last. The other sails had all been overhauled and were ready for loading. Also arrived from England were a couple of parcels containing magazines, a wide selection of the latest paperbacks and some warm woolly hats. These had been sent by Charles Williams, our kind benefactor. Charles was a semi-retired businessman and songwriter who had given us the stereo cassette system and now these presents for no other reason than that he thought we might like them. Indeed, he managed to guess the very things that we most appreciated and we were very grateful to him. Another surprise came from Flexlands School in England which had 'adopted' us. Many of the pupils, who were aged between five and nine, sent us marvellously colourful pictures and letters which we pinned up in the saloon.

During the final few days we put the boat into dry dock, removed all the strange goose barnacles which had appeared in the Doldrums, and painted the boat's bottom. Scrubbing, sanding and painting the great overhanging undersides was a tiring and messy job, but with nearly all the crew working together, chatting and joking, it was far from dull. Back in the yacht basin, we put sheepskin round the lower shrouds to try to prevent the mainsail chafing against them during the predominantly downwind sailing of the next leg. The sheepskin looked pretty for a day then suddenly turned jet black. Since we had arrived, we had thought the magnificent old steam engines that shunted back and forth behind the Yacht Club were very quaint and pretty. Now, with the wind in the wrong direction and the rest of the boat fast turning black, we thought them dirty, messy monsters, and not very pretty at all.

As the restart date drew near, our excitement built up. Some of the crew would be sad to leave Cape Town after only two weeks, but most of us were

Skippers' briefing before the second leg.

keen to get going again. Robin, Robert and Beat had been surrounded by pretty girls ever since they arrived but even they were looking forward to getting to sea again. For Nick the moment could not come to soon – he had acquired three parking tickets and had almost been arrested for speeding. The speeding offence would not have been grave except that, when stopped by the police, Nick had got out of his car and left the automatic in 'drive'. Fortunately he had been able to leap for the brake just before demolishing the police car, but it had not made a favourable impression on the officers, who had been glad to hear that he was about to leave the country.

The day before the start Jacques, John and I settled down to finalise our tactics for the next leg. The handicap distance to Auckland was 7,400 miles, although a more direct route would cut the distance by many hundreds of miles. There was a major problem in trying a really direct route; a straight line from Cape Town to Auckland would take us down below 70° south – on to the continent of Antarctica! Even going as far as 60° south, we would risk meeting solid pack ice. Between 50° and 60° south, we were likely to meet a significant number of icebergs, not a problem most of the time, but lethal on a dark night or in fog. It was now late October and spring in the Southern Ocean, but the

96

nights were still long enough for there to be several hours of darkness. Under these circumstances, iceberg-hopping might be rather a risky undertaking. To be sure of staying clear of the bergs, we would have to stay north of 50° south.

Another important consideration was the weather. The Southern Ocean is dominated by powerful low-pressure systems which sweep around the globe from west to east, similar to those which dominate the British weather to the north. However, apart from the tip of South America, there are no large continents to break the force of the systems in the Southern Hemisphere, and they blow round and round the world without restraint, normally moving faster and generating stronger winds than their counterparts in the north. Hence the well-earned name for the area between 40° and 50° south: the Roaring Forties.

The secret of racing through the Southern Ocean was to go as far south as you dared without getting the wrong side of the low pressure systems, where there was a serious risk of headwinds. By staying safely to the north of the lows, we should keep good, strong westerlies and attain long daily runs which should compensate for the extra distance we would be travelling. But the question was, how far north did we have to go to stay in the westerlies? We studied the weather information available through the South African meteorological service but the information was not very comprehensive for the simple reason that little data was available. Apart from the occasional research station on the isolated Southern Ocean islands or the Antarctic continent itself, there was nobody to send in weather reports. Satellite photographs provided some useful pictures of weather systems, but could not give the relative air pressures, and were therefore limited. I felt we should play safe and go no further south than 50°. Jacques thought this route would be satisfactory while John made no recommendation either way. John preferred to play tactics by ear, deciding on the course according to the wind. Certainly, something could be said for this but I felt it was important to have a basic strategy before setting out, otherwise we might weave all over the ocean.

Before the start we had a crew meeting to discuss the coming leg. We were all aware that it would be tougher and more demanding than the first, but I wanted to be sure everyone understood what the greatest dangers would be. No-one needed reminding that falling overboard would be fatal. When sailing fast downwind, it would take as much as five minutes to lower the running sails and turn the yacht round, then another ten to return to the spot where it was thought the person had fallen. The chances of finding anyone in a large sea would be almost nil and, even if the boat managed to return to the right spot, it would be highly likely that the person would have died from exposure in the icy sea. In good conditions, there was a better chance of keeping the person in sight and of turning the boat round faster, but since people usually fell overboard in bad conditions, few had survived such an accident in the Southern Ocean. On the first Whitbread Race, three men had lost their lives.

On *ADC* we were all very keen to avoid such an accident and everyone was determined to wear his safety harness and clip on all the time. Of course it was not to work out that way. Clipping on was a tremendous nuisance, hampering the deck work to such an extent that we were forced to abandon the practice whenever speed and efficiency were required. Only in really bad conditions did we make a real effort to attach ourselves to the boat.

Losing someone overboard was the worst thing we could imagine but losing the boat came a close second because, even if we should climb safely into the liferafts, the chances of being picked up before we froze or starved to death were very small. Most of the things that cause boats to sink could be classed as Acts of God – hitting debris or sleeping whales, or being attacked by killer whales. However, being holed by a fallen mast acting like a battering ram in the water was a fate that was probably avoidable. The important thing was not to lose the mast in the first place. Assuming the rigging was not going to fail, there were just two manoeuvres which might bring the mast down. The first was a capsize, which could conceivably occur in the large seas of the Southern Ocean but which I believed to be avoidable as long as we kept the boat going fast in bad conditions. The second was a leeward broach, and it was this, particularly, which worried Jacques and me. Broaching occurs when the helmsman can no longer control the boat downwind because either there is too large a spinnaker up or the spinnaker is badly trimmed, or both. I tried to impress on the crew how important it was to avoid broaching or, if it was unavoidable, then to broach to windward. In view of what was to happen just a few days later, it was good advice.

Finally, we agreed to try a new watch system. In difficult conditions five people would never be able to lower a spinnaker on their own, so we decided to adopt a standby arrangement. Two people, one from each of the two watches, would take it in turns to have a day off – a proposition which met with great cheers of approval. However, there would be a serious catch. During the twenty-four hours they were off duty the two would be on standby to help with each and every sail change, bringing the deck crew up from four to six and, with Bumble and me, a possible total of eight. The two off-duty crew would also be responsible for doing all the washing-up and the cleaning during those twenty-four hours – an idea which also met with great approval. Jacques was the only one who looked a little unhappy at this suggestion since, as he was always reminding us, he and washing-up really didn't get on – a fact of which I was well aware.

The meeting over and all the fresh provisions loaded, we were ready to motor out to the start. Ahead of us lay the Southern Ocean, according to legend the harshest ocean in the world. There was every possibility we would cross it safely; we had a strong boat, a fine crew and we had made careful preparations. Yet as we left the security of Cape Town harbour there was not one of us who did not feel the thrill and excitement of fear and uncertainty.

CHAPTER 6

Into the Southern Ocean

ADC Accutrac's start from Cape Town was well reported in the popular press, not because we made the best start – although it was a pretty good one – but because of the send-off we received. Bumble and Fred had been adopted by two eccentric South Africans named Reggie and Clive, who appeared in a launch emblazoned with the name *ADC Accutrac*. Having cheered themselves hoarse and drunk several bottles of champagne, they followed behind us, their boat swooping and accelerating, then swerving and slowing down. The grand finale came when Reggie suddenly threw all his clothes off and stood on the cabin roof cheering and waving both arms until he lost his balance and fell overboard. Clive then jumped in and the two of them swam around, still shouting and laughing, waiting for their launch to come and fetch them. What most impressed us was their apparent immunity to the temperature which, though it was springtime, was far from warm.

The wind was kind to us, however. We had a gentle beating start and a series of short tacks down to the Cape of Good Hope. It was not a particularly fast start, but anything was preferable to a stiff breeze on the nose, a situation we dreaded until we regained our sea-legs and worked off the over-indulgences of two weeks' soft living ashore. Nonetheless, we were rather sleepy and not feeling very alert until the next day, when the wind died away and we found ourselves in close company with most of the other yachts. For some time we were almost becalmed. However, this was no hardship as long as everyone else was in the same position. Later a narrow strip of cloud appeared and we discovered that there was a small breeze underneath it. By tacking from one side of the cloud to the other we could stay in the wind and make a little progress. This led to a ludicrous situation. Because the wind was bent and distorted at the edges of the cloud, we found ourselves on the same tack as other boats but pointing in completely opposite directions! For hours we made slow progress backwards and forwards, crossing tacks with one boat then another until, at last, a little more breeze sprang up. Suddenly, more boats appeared over the horizon and we realised that, except for *King's Legend*, the whole fleet was in sight. We had some great racing that day, using the wind shifts to improve our position gradually. Eventually we were pleased to see that we were, if only for a moment, leading the other boats. The larger boats overtook us once the breeze strengthened, but being in the lead gave us a great deal of encouragement while it lasted.

The next day we picked up the first of the westerlies. This was an exciting moment; if everything ran to form, we should keep these westerlies all the way

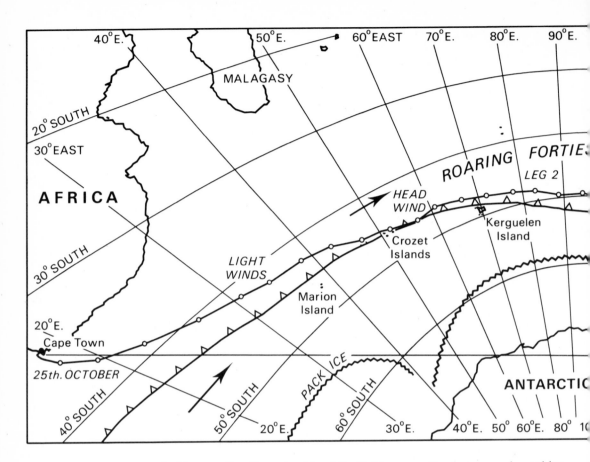

to the Tasman Sea if not Auckland itself. However, the day was coloured by two events. First, John took a bearing of the rising sun and confirmed our suspicion that the compass had a deviation of over 10°. Magnets fitted in Cape Town to correct heeling error were undoubtedly the culprits and we had no hesitation in throwing them over the side. From then on, the compass gave no more trouble.

The other event was more worrying – the large turning blocks on the quarter, through which sheets and guys ran, were lifting slightly off the deck. If these enormous blocks tore out we would be in serious trouble. It took four hours to drill the necessary holes and fix some large bolts through the blocks on to the toe rail, not an ideal solution but all we could manage while the blocks were in use. The stresses and strains that would be put on these blocks and the rest of the spinnaker gear over the next five weeks would be enormous. It would be disastrous if anything were to give way at this early stage.

As we went into our third night, our position was still excellent. We could no longer see any of the other yachts, but according to the radio positions we were right up at the head of the fleet. But we had little time to reflect on this, for the weather was starting to 'get interesting', as Tony put it. A sudden wind shift and a darkening sky heralded some Southern Ocean weather. We were not yet

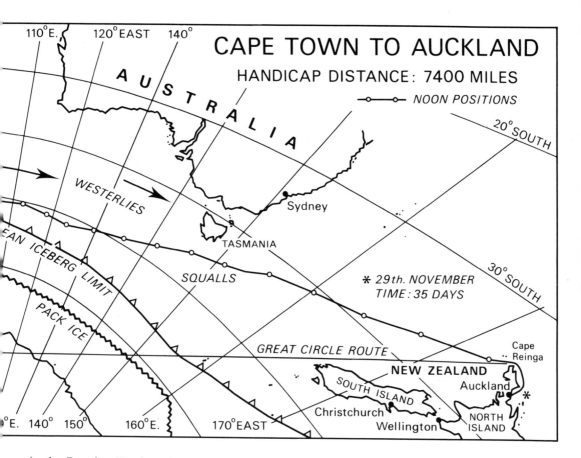

CAPE TOWN TO AUCKLAND

HANDICAP DISTANCE: 7400 MILES

○—○— NOON POSITIONS

110°E. 120°EAST 140°

AUSTRALIA

20°SOUTH

WESTERLIES

Sydney

TASMANIA

30°SOUTH

SQUALLS

AN ICEBERG LIMIT

PACK ICE

✳ 29th. NOVEMBER
TIME: 35 DAYS

GREAT CIRCLE ROUTE

Cape
Reinga

NEW ZEALAND

Auckland

SOUTH ISLAND

Christchurch

NORTH
ISLAND

°E. 140° 150° 160°E. 170°EAST

Wellington

in the Roaring Forties – but as near as made no difference. By three in the morning there was fifteen knots of wind over the deck and we thought it best to put up our new heavy spinnaker for the first time. The spinnaker looked indestructible. It was made of the strongest cloth and solidly built. It was also bright red, which led us to call it the Red Monster. Being the first time we had put the sail up we had to experiment at trimming it. I was at the wheel and John, as watch-keeper, was in charge of the deck.

We raised the sail without any trouble and then started to trim it. To begin with, the sail was set too far to leeward so we reset it with the centre of the sail on the centre line of the boat. However, *ADC* was still tending to roll too much, making her sheer first one way then the other so that steering was very difficult. I suggested flattening the sail. But John insisted on pulling the pole further back, saying it would provide the necessary stability. In fact it did quite the reverse. The boat started to roll hard to windward and I had a struggle to keep the boat on a straight course. At the same moment the wind started to freshen.

'Let's tame this tiger,' I said. I asked the crew to flatten the sail and get the pole back to its original position. But it was too late. As the crew rushed for the winches, the squall hit. With the spinnaker so badly trimmed, we hadn't a hope. If Fred had put his great strength against the wheel, he might have been able to hold her. I could not.

First she started to roll badly. Then, with a sick feeling in my stomach, I felt her start a particularly bad roll to windward. She went over and over, the spinnaker pulling her further and further. Terrified of broaching to leeward, I flung my whole weight on the wheel to stop her from continuing to turn that way. At last, I felt her start to straighten. As the mast whipped upright the spinnaker, being free to flop from one side to the other, immediately swung round and pulled the boat hard over the other way. This time she went right over and nothing could stop her. She kept turning and turning until she was beam on to the seas and held over on her side by the spinnaker. There was chaos. People were clinging on to the deck, trying not to slide down into the sea. There was a fearful noise and commotion as the spinnaker started to flog, and the entire boat started to shiver and shake as if it were in the mouth of a mad dog. The off-watch crew tried to scramble up the companion-way but, the ladder being at an angle of 50° or so, it was not easy.

My first instinct was to get the boat upright again. Evey was just nearby and I called to her to give me a hand. Together we pulled on the wheel for all we were worth. At first nothing happened and then, quite suddenly, the boat responded and started to right herself. With horror, I realised what must inevitably happen. With the spinnaker still too full, the boat would roll right over the other way and broach to leeward. I tried hard to steady her, but it was no good. With a sudden flip, she rolled over again and swerved the other way. This time with the main aback, she went over so far that the water was running along the deck up to the level of the cockpit. With disbelief I saw a long, sausage-shaped bag float past me. It was a sail bag which had been tied down on deck. There was nothing I could do to save it.

Now, all hell broke loose. The spinnaker pole was buried in the sea, under the most terrible strain (we were still doing quite a good speed, even on our side). Fortunately, the foreguy broke and the pole emerged from the water, still in one piece. The mainsail and mizzen were hard aback and the only things stopping them from slamming across were the vangs. Worried that they might break and the booms might smash across, taking the backstays with them, I fought to right the boat once more. When she came upright I was, at last, able to keep her there, for the spinnaker pole was now thrashing about in the air and the spinnaker flying somewhere around the masthead. Tony, as always the one who leapt into action, rushed forward and started pulling the pole down with the lazy sheet. Suddenly the pole dropped of its own accord and, without hesitation, Tony released the spinnaker so that we were able to lower it in the normal way.

With a sigh, we realised that the boat was in more or less one piece. However, I was mortified to find that the sail bag we had lost had contained our best headsail, the Number Two genoa. Otherwise the main damage was to the spinnaker pole which was seriously bent. We would not be able to use it until it could be repaired in Auckland. With only one pole, the numerous gybes in the weeks ahead would be long, time-consuming manoeuvres.

Jacques, Tony and I held a post-mortem. We were severely shaken and very

'Mushrooms' at work.

anxious to make sure the same thing did not happen again. The important thing, we agreed, was to prevent the boat from broaching to leeward at all costs. I described my endeavours to right the boat, which had led to the leeward broach, and we agreed that it would have been better if I had left the boat broached to windward until such time as we could let the spinnaker fly. This could have been dangerous too, if there had been a foul-up, but we agreed it was the lesser of two evils. John did not feel that his method of trimming the spinnaker had contributed to the broach although I felt bound to say that I thought it had. He was not present at the post-mortem but was clearing his bunk which resembled Covent Garden – it had filled up with fruit from the netting on the other side of the saloon.

'It's been a nice outing, but can we go back to Lymington for tea now?' asked Robin the next day. The wind had increased and for a while we were shooting along under storm spinnaker, surfing down the big seas.

OPPOSITE
The big red spinnaker up and still under control.

'This is great!' said Fred. 'Just what I came for.'

'Ya, fantastic,' murmured Nick, 'but I think I'll sleep in the for'ard cockpit lockers.'

Fred gave him a look. 'The ones with the liferafts in?'

'Too right,' replied Nick.

It was a time of adjustment for us all. The broach had given us a bad fright and now the fast downwind sailing was keeping us very busy. Not surprisingly, we were cautious with spinnakers and took them down in good time before the wind became too strong to carry them. However, the starcut outwitted us by falling down twice in two days. The first time the ring at the head pulled out – a quick way to lower the sail – and just a day later we blew it so thoroughly that only the bottom was left attached to the tape. It was becoming increasingly clear that the starcut was past its best.

Despite our caution, the storm spinnaker was also damaged that day, after catching on some wire. In the saloon Sam and Eve were submerged by sail repairs and working day and night to finish them before any more spinnakers were blown. Sam put a plaintive plea in the deck log: 'Will the next watch please look after the spi?'

The most difficult sailing was, as always, at night. Then we had to steer by the instruments and, with a large sea and a fresh wind, it was not an easy task. In the day you could judge which way the boat was veering by looking at the horizon. At night you only had your instincts and the wind direction indicator to tell you how to correct the boat's course. Tony and Beat were natural helmsmen, always able to keep the boat on a straight course, while Nick and Robert were fast coming up to an excellent standard. Fred was very competent too and, whenever the steering was particularly difficult, could bring the boat back on course by brute strength alone. The wheel always looked minute in his hands. Jacques was a good helmsman, but hated steering downwind because of the boat's nasty habits of rolling and broaching, while Evey sometimes lacked the confidence to tackle the job. John always gave us heart failure by letting the boat pull to leeward, due to his manner of trimming the spinnaker. I enjoyed helming but, when the conditions were bad, did not have the strength to stay on the wheel for more than half an hour at a time.

Steering was always physically hard when under spinnaker. *ADC* was a heavy boat and one had to exert a lot of strength to keep her on the straight and narrow. We took it in turns to steer, staying on the wheel until we tired or started to lose concentration. When somebody asked, 'Want a spell?' we would hand the wheel over and take a rest.

Those first few days of fast downwind sailing were tense. Having had one spectacular broach, we feared that each roll of the boat was leading us to another. Doubtless we were over-cautious as a result, but it was frightening to see the incredible power of the boat and to imagine what might happen if something important broke. The force in the sails was brought home to Robin when he was holding the mizzen staysail halyard in readiness to ease it away.

On the radio to the other yachts – while Sam threatens to make fine adjustments to the transmitter! (*photo:* Eve Bonham).

He suddenly yelled in agony as the halyard slipped on the winch and ran out through his hands. His palms and fingers were badly burnt and he was our of action for three days until the wounds were sufficiently healed for him to do some light deck work. Sam too, had an interesting experience on the end of the big boy halyard, which he was pulling in an attempt to get the sail to refill. Refill it did, suddenly hoisting Sam a good fifteen feet up the mast.

All the incidents, large and small, had the effect of slightly unnerving us. We had been at sea only five days and every day some new damage or injury occurred. However, Chat Hour soon revealed we were not the only ones, and the experiences of some of the other boats made ours look pale by comparison. First, *Gauloises* broke her rudder and put back to Port Elizabeth for repairs, then *33 Export* reported having bent her main boom. *King's Legend* had broached, *Tielsa* had blown two principal sails and *GB II* had sailed over her spinnaker losing a guy, sheet and halyard in the process. Later we heard that *Disque d'Or* had also bent a spinnaker boom, and was having trouble with the end fittings. Her skipper kindly warned us that we might have the same problem and, on checking, we found we had. This was a great favour because Jacques was able to repair the ends before any serious damage was done.

This list of damage reflected the fact that the whole fleet was racing flat out. We may have been entering the Southern Ocean but as far as we were concerned we might have been off Cowes. Of course there were some differences. Apart from the seas, the one that struck us most was the speed with which the weather systems came through. One moment it would be blowing north-west twenty knots, the next south-west thirty knots. As a result, we never had any problems about finding enough to do. All day we were

106

changing spinnakers, from medium up to storm and back again. The saloon was always knee-high in thousands of square feet of nylon, waiting to be sorted out and packed into bags, ready for hoisting again. The standby crew were usually busy for most of their twenty-four hours off.

Nevertheless the watch system was a roaring success. The idea of having one day off in every five was very popular because it meant a break in the routine. The two standby crew could read, sleep or relax when not required on deck and, even if they were up changing sails most of the night, they could at least go back to their bunks between each manoeuvre – a great privilege.

Better still, there were no more problems over whose turn it was to do the chores. Not only were the people on standby happy to do the washing-up and cleaning, but they began to take tremendous pride in their work, like newly married housewives. They would fuss about, tut-tutting at the mess left by the others, cleaning and sweeping with great concentration and aplomb. Cleaning the loos was never popular but a bucket of seawater and a strong dash of disinfectant was usually adequate when administered with great panache.

Sam and Evey were on standby together. They were both avid cleaners and tidiers and would spend a long time at their chores. Like everyone else, they were also keen to make up for lost sleep, and to spend much of their spare time snoozing in their bunks. However, they had to forego their leisure and nearly all their sleep because of the amount of sail repair work to be done. 'I don't mind,' said Evey. 'We'll probably have a quiet standby next time.' The two of them were to live in eternal hope.

After a few days at sea, we felt we had hardly stopped in Cape Town at all, so quickly did we slip back into the routine of shipboard life. Despite the fright that the broach had given us and the amount of work that the downwind

Gathering in a spinnaker under the main boom.

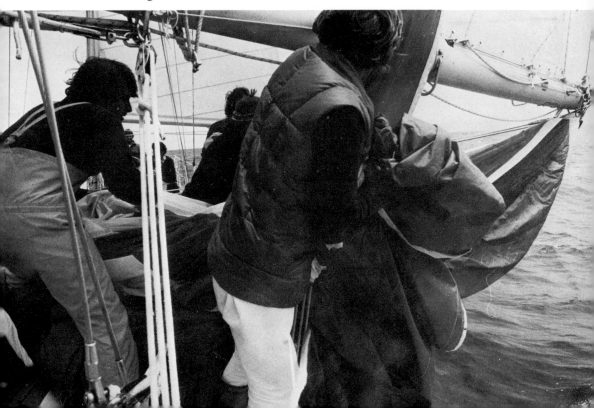

sailing provided, we were enjoying ourselves as we had never done before. The sailing was fast and exciting. Better still, the boat was upright and life below was reasonably comfortable. Everyone was in high spirits. It was not long before all the old jokes reappeared.

'Hey, you murderer of poor innocent frogs,' Sam would yell at Jacques.

'You British git!' would come the reply. 'How you can call yourself civilised when you play cricket and eat Marmite, I don't know!'

However, our enthusiasm for life was a little damped on the sixth day when, at nearly 42° south, the westerlies died away and we found ourselves almost becalmed. 'Sure we're not in the Whispering Forties?' Nick asked. 'No, no, it's the Doldrums extended by 5,000 miles,' Robert replied. In such conditions, we were far from surprised to see the lightweight *33 Export* appear from over the horizon and sail right up to us.

The light winds continued for another two days, and we soon discovered that we were under the influence of a high-pressure area to the north. Only the yachts heading far down to the south avoided it. *Debenhams,* under John Ridgway, was already at 45° south and reporting plenty of wind with a rapidly dropping temperature.

'Where're you off to, John?' one of the boats asked.

'Ah, we're off to see the ice to remind us of home,' replied John, who lived in the far north of Scotland. Indeed, there were to be no half measures in John's search for ice. Day by day, he took *Debenhams* further and further south until we dubbed him 'Ridgway of the Antarctic'.

While the wind was light I took the opportunity to go through the man overboard and liferaft drills with the crew. The man overboard drill was a little depressing, since we knew there was so little chance of picking anyone up in time, but at least we would be doing everything possible. Planning the life-raft drill was much more popular, as we discussed the best makeshift spars and sails for the two rafts, the provisions we should take, and the equipment we would have room for. On the first leg we had kept water and food on one side for the rafts but now, as we entered the cold and isolated Southern Ocean, we would need plenty of warm clothing, much more food, and some good fishing tackle if we were to survive. The other yachts would provide our best chance of rescue in the event of sinking, so we tried to give them an accurate daily position. However, the difficulty of estimating positions was well illustrated by the discrepancies between those given by two yachts when in sight of one another. The day we saw *33 Export* our two 'positions' differed by as much as twenty-five miles, a situation which led to many exchanges over the radio: 'Our navigator's been asleep for a week actually', 'Just turn left at Tasmania and you'll probably find New Zealand', and 'Our position may well be wrong, *mon vieux;* our chart's got a bit of spaghetti bolognese right over the spot.'

Two days later we saw *Disque d'Or,* but this time our positions more or less coincided. After a week at sea, it was extraordinary to meet another yacht, particularly *Disque d'Or* whom we had met in the middle of the first leg. But she was the last sign of life we were to see for another four weeks and, once she had disappeared over the horizon, we had the ocean to ourselves again.

108

Our first week out was celebrated with a Hallowe'en party. Eve came dressed as a white witch, Robert as Dracula – a role into which he threw himself with great gusto by sinking his fangs into ladies' necks – Bumble came as a 'fright', her face black and her hair in a fuzzy mess, while I came as a clown, with red cheeks, blackened eyes and wearing a beret marked 'frog' on my head. It was difficult to set up an apple-bobbing barrel, so we strung Marmite-covered bread from the saloon roof and contented ourselves with trying to catch the swinging morsels with our teeth. It was a messy game.

As we sailed further east we slowly started to escape the influence of the high, but the wind was far from steady. Every day I was in touch with Cape Town Radio, who in their helpful, efficient and courteous way gave me what weather information they had. What we really needed, though, was the full synopsis from Pretoria, which only a qualified Morse radio operator could supply. Without ships nearby it seemed we would have to go without the information. Then one of the isolated islands in the South Indian Ocean, Marion Island, made contact with the fleet and solved our problem by offering to provide weather reports in plain language. At 47° south, Marion Island was by no means the most southerly inhabited island, but it must be one of the most isolated. During the eight days we were in contact with their radio operator we gathered information about their community of fourteen scientists. They were stationed there for thirteen months, with only one visit from a mail ship after six months. They lived in a settlement of twenty huts with cat-walks between because of the marshy ground. Most riveting of all, the fourteen men shared the island with 650,000 penguins. It seemed a pity to be sailing past such an island when we all wanted to visit the place, but such is the ridiculous nature of long-distance racing.

The weather maps from Marion explain the extraordinary weather we continued to experience. One day we had freezing headwinds, the next light, warm tailwinds. To our chagrin the boats who had made off to the south were finding steadier westerlies and our position, which had been so good, was no longer outstanding. The only consolation was that we were in company with *Flyer*. She, too, was beginning to lose out – her great rival, *King's Legend,* was far to the south and increasing her lead all the time.

As everyone continued to push their boats, there was yet more damage and injury. *King's Legend,* who was probably pushing harder than anyone else, reported one crew member with a bad gash in his head which they were trying to stitch up (they had no doctor), and another with aching kidneys after being hit on the back by a boom. *Neptune,* one of the French yachts, broke both her spinnaker poles, while *Adventure* had given themselves a severe shock by running into a whale.

We paid a great deal of attention to the gear, fearing similar breakages or injury. The stresses and strains on blocks, guys, sheets and sails going downwind was far greater than going upwind. Moreover, the continuous rolling created a powerful sawing effect between one piece of gear and another so that the mainsail would chafe on the shrouds, the pole ends would chafe through the guys, and the masthead halyard blocks would chafe against the U-bolts. It was a continuous battle for Tony and Beat to find the chafe points on the gear before the damage was done. Fortunately Jacques checked the pole ends again one day to find they had loosened at yet another point. Sam and Eve never put up a sail without examining it carefully for signs of chafe. Light wind or heavy, everything seemed to get worn just the same.

The tactics themselves were not easy either. Whatever course we wanted, it was always dead downwind. Furthermore, once we were settled on one gybe, the wind would shift slightly and make the other gybe more favourable. We had terrible trouble with the Crozet Islands in this way. One day I announced that we would pass neatly to the north of the islands, and the next that we would pass to the south. Finally, I suggested we should aim straight for the group of rocky islets and then, with a bit of luck, we would miss them! Jacques was delighted at this and asked us if we'd got our passports handy since it was a French possession and they didn't let mere Brits in that easily. 'Tomorrow,' he promised, 'it'll be *escargots* and *pommes frites.'*

'Ughh!' exclaimed Sam. 'What's wrong with good old fish and chips then?'

Each gybe gave us at least half an hour's hard work, often more. With only one pole, we often had to lower the spinnaker, repack it and raise it again on the other side. It took eight people working flat out to complete the operation. The main boom had to come across, requiring at least four people to work the sheet and the vangs. The pole had to be set up on the other side, complete with topping lift and foreguy. The mizzen had to be gybed and the staysail or mizzen spinnaker reset, which involved countless operations to re-reeve the tack lines and sheet, and to change and secure the halyard. By the time we had

110

tidied up the boat again, checked that all was as it should be, and fiddled with the trim of the sails, we were boiling hot and ready for a rest.

At last the wind decided to send us just to the north of the Crozet Islands and we looked forward to having a glimpse of them at dawn next day. Then, choosing the worst possible moment to arrive, thin wisps of fog started to climb across the starlit sky. Soon we were surrounded by a dense, grey blanket. The weather report from Marion did nothing to suggest the situation would improve – the visibility there was down to 150 yards.

We were now faced with the worst possible circumstances. We were approaching some rocky islands at full speed, in bad visibility and carrying sails which were difficult to lower quickly. The depth sounder could give us little warning of approaching danger because the water appeared to be very deep right up to the rocks. There was only one thing to do and that was to alter course to take ourselves even further to the north of the danger. Even so, I spent a sleepless night straining to see through the fog, while the others took it in turns to stand listening and watching on the bows. Jacques continued to entertain us with descriptions of the civilised lifestyle that could be found on even the remotest French possession, but most of the time he, like the others, sat quiet and still, waiting for something to happen. At three I went down to the chart table again to study our position, and to try to estimate the effects of the current, which were largely unknown. I must have dozed off for the next moment I was woken by a voice saying, 'It's clearing!' Up on deck, a dramatic sight met my eyes. The fog was pulling away in long ragged fingers to reveal a livid dawn of fire and flame. First, the dome of sky above us became streaked with colour, then, quite suddenly, the fog rolled away from the southern horizon to expose the dark, jagged shapes of the Crozets, silhouetted against the yellow-pink sky – safely to leeward.

By the 5th November, our eleventh day at sea, we were clear of the Crozets and heading south of east again. But the Forties were still not roaring for us. While the boats in the lower Forties reported strong winds and boat speeds of up to twenty knots when surfing, we and *Flyer* had moderate winds which hardly enabled us to surf at all. Still, we consoled ourselves, those to the south should get headwinds one of these days. It only needed one low-pressure area to pass to the north of them and they would get slowed down.

In the event, as Jacques would say, the laughs were on us. A small wave depression, in the middle of a front, passed over us and gave us headwinds for sixteen wet, uncomfortable hours. After that we no longer believed that the weather was in the slightest degree predictable, and no longer expected a certain pattern to emerge. Nonetheless, we could not help noticing that *Gauloises,* who had just left South Africa with a new rudder, got severely battered by headwinds when she went a long way south a week later. As always one needed an enormous amount of luck to go ocean racing and, if it wasn't coming our way at the moment, we could at least enjoy sailing in the Southern Ocean.

We were now at 47° south, and aiming to go as far as 50° south before turning up towards the Tasman Sea. What surprised us most about this isolated ocean was the amount of life there was to be seen. Bumble, bubbling

111

with excitement, identified four different species of albatross, as well as prions, sooty shearwaters and our old friends the Cape pigeons. ('What, no budgies?' asked Sam.) We saw the most dramatic black and white porpoises, unlike any I had seen before. Someone said they had spotted a penguin, but this met with some scepticism and remarks about wishful thinking. It was not impossible though, for many of the other boats reported penguins further to the south. Beautiful and aloof birds were always with us, the elegant albatrosses gliding high above our wake, hardly moving their enormous wings as they searched and waited for some meal we never saw them catch.

Day by day it became noticeably colder and most of us donned our winter longjohns, woolly vests and balaclavas. Only Bumble, born and bred in cold Scotland, seemed immune to the temperature. The sharp, piercing air penetrated our boots and gloves as we sat in the cockpit on the long night watches and we had to go below and rub the circulation back into our hands and feet. Hot drinks had long been popular during the night watches, both to warm up the body after long periods of immobility and to break the monotony of the long four-hour stints. Now that it was cold, the making of drinks, previously considered a chore, suddenly found no end of recruits, for the galley was warm and the water took at least ten minutes to boil. There were no more complaints either at the strange variety of drinks that people asked for. The order was never five coffees or five teas, it was one coffee, one tea, one chocolate, one Bovril and, Robin's speciality, a hot Rise and Shine.

Below decks it was a little warmer, particularly when we managed to run the heater. This diesel-fed machine blew hot air through the boat and was fairly efficient when it was working. However it had the nasty habit of asphyxiating the helmsman by belching out black smoke through the flue just behind him. On the port gybe, terrible coughing and spluttering and cries of 'Gas masks!' would accompany the starting of the heater. Unkindly, we would take the opportunity to make pointed remarks about the two smokers on board. 'Put Beat on the wheel,' someone would say, 'he'll never know the difference.' Beat, good-natured and cheerful as always, would take the wheel and be overcome with coughing, the same as everyone else. Not surprisingly, we did not run the heater for very long, particularly when the fumes started to seep into the cabins after ten minutes or so. The smell of diesel fuel and smoke made our stomachs unsettled.

However, at our latitude the cold was moderate compared to that which *Debenhams* was experiencing. At 58° south they had entered the area where the south polar chart predicted pack ice. 'Got some huskies, John?' someone asked Ridgway. 'Then you could make it into a polar expedition.'

Ridgway admitted it was a little cold. The shrouds were icing up and the deck was covered in snow. There were plenty of icebergs too, but nothing that they were worried about yet. Some of the other boats had also run into heavy snow and icebergs at 55° south and reported freezing temperatures. *Condor* likened her spinnaker to a venetian blind – it was so frozen it came down in slats.

We were finally beginning to pick up westerlies as strong as the boats to the south but, being on a higher latitude, we had further to travel to make the

OPPOSITE
A moment's respite between spinnaker changes.

113

same amount of longitude. Until we all started to turn north again, there was little chance of our being able to catch the boats ahead. Most galling of all, *Disque d'Or* was now a clear day in front.

But we had little time to worry about our position. The spinnaker work became more and more demanding as the wind began to blow at last, coming in great squalls and fronts, and requiring constant trimming and time-consuming gybes. The standby crew were having a particularly hard time of it, packing and re-packing sometimes four or five spinnakers a night as we changed up and down. 'Nothing like a restful standby,' Nick would say. 'When do we go back on watch?'

Lowering a spinnaker was the most difficult task of all. If the wind suddenly freshened and we found ourselves with too much sail up, down it would have to come. We went through a very tense few minutes as we eased the guy and pole forward, for this was the moment when the boat was at her most unbalanced. While being let forward the pole would also have to be lowered, requiring some co-ordinated work between the three deck crew manning the winches. Once the pole could be reached someone, usually Tony or Beat, would stand on the pulpit and reach out and release the spinnaker, a precarious manoeuvre. However, the release itself was much easier now that we had the new American snap shackles which would release under load when a spike was put against the trigger. Once released the sail had to be pulled in under the main boom and in the lee of the mainsail. When the foot was gathered, the halyard was slowly eased until the sail was down.

The standby crew were kept busy packing spinnakers.

Below, the spinnaker was carefully sorted out and 'stopped' into a long

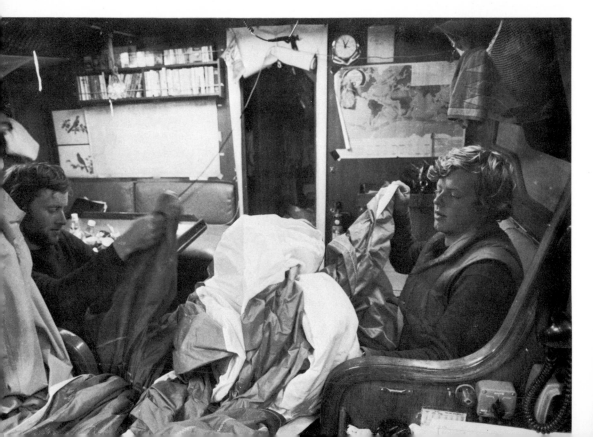

sausage, using elastic bands. In this way it could be rehoisted without filling; only when the halyard was right up to the top of the mast would someone pull on the sheet. This would break some of the bands and allow the wind to get into the sail – the next moment it would open and fill with a great ooomph that sent a tremor through the boat.

The strong westerlies gave us a lot of work to do, and I found that my daily calls to Capital were taking a great deal more time now. Although I had a daily schedule with Cape Town Radio, it was becoming increasingly difficult to make good contact with them. The reason for this soon became clear. For several nights the sky had been crystal clear, a dome of black, dense velvet carpeted with tiny, glittering stars. Phosphorescence sparkled in our wake and around the bow, as the boat cut through the dark water at ten or eleven knots. Then, one particularly clear night, we saw strange lights away to the south. They glowed and glimmered in a halo which hovered, then grew, then diminished like the rays of a searchlight. These were the Southern Lights, the Aurora Australis, tied in some mysterious way to sunspot activity and the South Magnetic Pole. Every night for the next week we were to see a magnificent and dazzling display that held us bewitched and entranced. Sometimes there would be a halo away to the south, sometimes two or three stretching in bands towards us. One memorable night the whole sky was ablaze with glittering curtains which undulated and faded and glowed and glistened over our heads. Wave after wave of silver and blue icicle-like fingers reached down towards us, shimmering and gleaming. On the southern horizon there were whole areas of light in the sky, soft blurred circles of arctic blue or snow white.

We watched silently from the cockpit, not wanting to break the spell of these magical nights. However, as I cast my eyes over the spectacular scene I could not help feeling a little downhearted because, the more dramatic the display, the longer I would have to spend at the radio trying to make contact with Cape Town. When there was heavy sunspot activity it upset the ionosphere, the atmospheric band that we relied on to bounce our high-frequency signals back to earth. Often it would prove impossible to make any contact at all. And sometimes the system was so upset that the range of signals would be doubled or trebled. At first I could not understand why I was picking up Russian stations on Cape Town's frequencies. Later I picked up Rome on Sydney's frequencies. It was all very confusing until I realised that my range had trebled.

For about two weeks I made only spasmodic contact with Capital Radio and then only to say a brief 'All's well.' Not exactly the exciting live radio reports they had been hoping for, but all I could manage while the earth's magnetism was so upset.

It was not until the 10th November, our sixteenth day at sea, that we really felt the Forties were living up to their reputation of roaring. We were at nearly 49° south when the wind finally blew hard enough for us to attain boat speeds of twelve knots, and fifteen to twenty when surfing.

Surfing was the most thrilling experience for the helmsman. Every so often a steeper wave would rise up behind and, as the stern started to lift to it, the

helmsman had to line the boat up, then do nothing but hold on tight as the boat shot down the slope at fantastic speed. A speed of fifteen knots merited a coconut, but a 'real go-go' had to be nearer twenty. It was impossible to judge speeds accurately because the speedometer only went up to fifteen knots. However, we could make a rough guess according to the height of the spray that flew up from the bow. If it hit the main boom, we were doing fifteen or over. If it flew a quarter of the way up the mainsail we were doing eighteen. If there was a total 'white-out' it was twenty or more.

Below decks, the off-watch crew always knew when the boat was surfing; after a breathless moment of suspense as her stern rose, there would be a dull roar as she gathered speed, then a vibrating and shaking like riding on a tube train.

'The take-off was smooth enough,' Sam would say, 'but I'm worried about the landing.'

If the surf was a good one, we would hear a great yell of delight from the helmsman, so gripping and exhilarating was the experience. Beat was particularly addicted to surfing and his normally composed features would break into a great grin of pleasure whenever he achieved 'lift-off'. When the surf was really outstanding – as it often was when Beat was at the wheel – we

OPPOSITE
Preparing to hoist a spinnaker.

Steering became hard but exhilarating (*photo:* Nick Milligan).

would hear all the deck crew shrieking and laughing as they took cover from a white-out, a surf so fast that the spray obliterated everything and flew into the cockpit.

This kind of sailing was exhilarating but also very hard work for the crew. To keep the good speeds, we kept spinnakers up as long as possible, only taking them down when the wind increased to the point where the boat was uncontrollable. It was always difficult to draw the line between competitiveness and foolhardiness. Our first broach had unnerved us, but now we were just beginning to establish the limits of our abilities and those of the boat. She was difficult and heavy to steer downwind and the helmsman had to rest frequently. The wind, which fluctuated and veered and backed with a rapidity peculiar to the Southern Ocean, kept the deck crew busy too. One serious mistake and we could break the mast or the boat, or injure one of our companions.

At almost 50° south we were aware of the special atmosphere of the Southern Ocean, its changeability, its harshness and its isolation. Apart from the other yachts, now spread out over a very wide area, there was no civilisation for thousands of miles. To all intents and purposes we were on our own. As the sea temperature continued to drop, we became more careful about clipping on and moving around the deck. None of us forgot that three men had been lost on the previous race.

One evening I asked Tony to open a bottle of wine and the five of us in the cockpit drank a toast to the three young men, Dominique Guillet, Bernie Hoskins and Paul Waterhouse, swept overboard in separate incidents four years before. Sam was below asleep as we drank and, unaware of our small tribute, appeared on deck one day with a prayer book in his hand. Going to the rail, he faced out over the sea and quietly read a prayer for the three men. Sam was the only one of us to have been on the second leg of the last race and still had vivid memories of the shock and horror the crews had all felt when the news had come through.

A few days later, it seemed that the same dreadful thing had happened again. We heard a rumour on Chat Hour that someone had been lost from *Condor*. After waiting several anxious minutes while the skipper of *B & B Italia* rattled on in interminable Italian to his compatriot on *Traité de Rome*, we finally ascertained that someone had fallen overboard but had been picked up again. Luckily for him the sea had been almost calm, and he had been in the freezing water only a few minutes before the boat returned and scooped him up. We all breathed again and hoped that the race would never be marred by another terrible loss.

CHAPTER 7

The Roaring Forties

Sam came up through the hatch, suddenly gasped and stared at a point high above the head of the helmsman, then cowered and threw his arm protectively across his face. It was Sam's favourite trick. Unless the helmsman looked over his shoulder all the time, he had no idea of what was coming up behind. When it blew hard the odd wave would rear up higher than the others – though never as high as the monsters of Sam's imagination. Waves were rarely a problem, except when they came at us sideways after a rapid windshift. Then they would frequently flop into the cockpit and a look through the aft cabin window

Sam would always survey the conditions before coming up on deck.

FACING PAGE
Above: Visitors in
the Tasman Sea; two
shag cormorants try
to rest.

Below: A fast
downwind run under
boomed-out jib in a
gale.

OVERLEAF
Under storm
spinnaker a wave
breaks over the deck.

into the cockpit was like a view through a goldfish bowl. After a time the beginnings of a yell from the helmsman would bring an automatic response from those in the cockpit and they would simultaneously duck their heads and raise their feet.

Large waves that came up from behind could always be ridden easily while the boat was going fast. I have long suspected that speed is the secret of safe downwind sailing. Not excessive speed so that the boat is uncontrollable, but a speed just below that limit, for it is then that the boat rides the waves rather than the waves slewing and pooping the boat. For this reason – and of course because we were racing – we never slowed the boat down when it blew hard. Particularly important is the need to put on more sail when the wind has dropped but the seas are still large. On the first race *Sayula* had capsized just after a storm, when her crew were on the point of putting up more sail.

Keeping the boat's speed high, but not too high, was difficult to judge and we were always on the point of changing spinnakers. 'Are we going to change?' someone would ask. 'Er . . .maybe,' would come the reply from Jacques or John, as they waited for the wind to make up its mind. So frequently did we consider changing sail and so often did people ask what was happening that the response developed into a standard reply: 'It's a definite maybe.'

The barometer sometimes gave us a good indication of what the wind was about to do. When the glass shot down, we knew it would blow; when it shot up we knew it was going to blow harder. When it levelled off it was going to moderate. However the barometer gave no warning of squalls, nor fronts with their sudden wind shifts nor, indeed, the speed with which the conditions were going to change. It was these things we needed to know to decide which spinnaker to put up.

We abandoned trying to predict the weather more than two hours in advance. One day I boldly stated that the barometer was bound to rise soon, only to watch it continue to plummet. 'There you are,' I said. 'Predictable!'

The average wind strength during our voyage through the Southern Ocean was Force 6 or 7. We were escaping lightly and we knew it. Yet we didn't want to! We longed to have gale-force winds all the time. Then we could have achieved surfing speeds using a boomed-out jib rather than a spinnaker. As it was, we were always fighting spinnakers up and down and always, it seemed, on the point of broaching. This knife-edge situation was terrible for our nerves until we tired of worrying about broaches, breakages, and all things alarming. We became accustomed to the wild motion, the constant rolling and yawing, and learnt to relax and enjoy our moments of leisure below. If the boat took a heavy roll no-one would take any notice. If she rolled badly the other way, someone would count 'two'. If she went over again everyone would chant, 'Three and over we go!' Usually the boat just skidded sideways for a moment until the helmsman got her under control again. After holding tight to the book we were reading, the board game we were playing or, in Bumble's case, the food she was preparing, we would relax and continue as if nothing had happened.

There were many notable occasions when we did a little more than skid. Rather, we broached. The first time, the wind rose during Jacques' watch and,

although he left the storm spinnaker up, he was not happy with the way the boat was handling in the difficult cross-seas. After John had taken over for the midnight-to-four spell, I stayed up for a while but went below to sleep after John had settled at the wheel and told me he was perfectly happy with the handling. Some time later I became wide awake, for the boat was rolling wildly and seemed out of control. I put my head up through the hatch and asked John if he was happy with the situation. On receiving an affirmative reply, I returned below. However I was wide awake again a few minutes later as the rolling became more violent. Jacques was awake too and we found ourselves clinging on to the sides of the bunk for support. Clearly the boat was out of control and the spinnaker would have to come down. I got up and made my way towards the companion-way again, meeting Sam on his way to tell me the spinnaker must come down. I was halfway up the companion-way when we broached. It was a real humdinger. Flat over on our side and complete chaos. Robin fell out of his bunk on to Eve, who had rolled out of the lower bunk on to the floor. Fruit, vegetables, books and assorted gear flew across the saloon into John's bunk, while everyone tried to scramble into their oilskins and up on deck. As soon as I arrived on deck, I yelled, 'Ease the sheet,' and a few moments later we were upright again. Another ten minutes and we had the spinnaker down. It was an unnerving experience, but not half so bad as the first broach which had been so nearly disastrous. No damage had been done and after half an hour's hard work everthing was back to normal.

Two nights later it was Jacques' turn. He was at the wheel when we were hit by a 45-knot squall which no-one had seen coming in the dark. Jacques ordered the sheet to be released to prevent a broach, but in the haste and confusion it was eased too fast and formed a riding turn on the winch, effectively jamming it. As I scrambled up the companion-way, someone yelled for a screwdriver to work the trigger and release the spinnaker from the guy. Normally a spike was kept on deck for this purpose, but I reached for a screwdriver, assuming the spike was lost. As I opened the tool drawer we broached and I abandoned the screwdriver to rush on deck in my night attire of long and baggy woollen underwear. I was freezing after two minutes but it didn't seem to matter while the boat was lying flat on her side. I shouted into the darkness, 'Ease the sheet.'

'It's jammed,' came the reply over the sound of the wind and flogging canvas.

'Let the guy fly, then.' I hoped it was a wise decision.

Fred was at the winch and started to ease the guy a little at a time, safer for him and everyone else in the cockpit, but not so good overall because the spinnaker, having been collapsed, suddenly refilled several yards from the boat and threatened an even worse situation. Fred was quick to react and wisely let the guy go completely. It ran out through the turning block like a bullet, its tail whipping so fast it snaked and cracked through the air.

On another occasion, late at night, we were trying to lower the spinnaker in a lot of wind. I was on the guy and was trying to ease it out. There were five turns on the winch but the rope was soaking wet and, although it would not ease at first, it suddenly shot out of my hands and wham! It was snaking out

FACING PAGE
Above: Following sea in the Roaring Forties – threatening to soak the cockpit crew.

Below left: A Southern Ocean sunset.

Below right: As we near New Zealand, a quiet day for a change.

121

There was no easy way of raising the mizzen staysail – this time it develops a twist.

through the block. This would not have been serious – indeed it was a fast if desperate way of lowering the sail – but with a sound like the twang of a bowstring, the guy came to a shuddering halt, bar-tight. There was a knot in the end which prevented it running through the turning block. Either someone had broken our golden rule and tied a knot (knots were common practice for halyards but never under any circumstances for spinnaker sheets or guys) or, more likely, the guy had tied itself into a knot while snaking and whipping out through the block. Either way, we were in trouble. The spinnaker was filling some twenty yards away from the boat and starting to play around with the boat like a cat with a mouse. Quickly, we let the sheet run and winched the

122

flying spinnaker slowly back towards the boat, using the lazy sheet. Half an hour later, tired and fed up with spinnakers, we had the sail lowered and a jib boomed out in its place.

'How about a cuppa?'

'You bet! What kept you?'

A hot drink was always popular, particularly after an 'interesting experience'. We did not complain if our tea was too strong (a 'spoon-stander') or too weak ('fortnightly tea') or blinking near water ('lighthouse tea').

Despite the hair-raising nature of the broaches, we were now far more philosophical about them. It meant, after all, that we were pushing hard. If we never got caught with too much sail up it would mean we were undercanvassed. Furthermore, we were getting more confident about how to deal with broaches when they occurred. A windward broach could usually be brought under control fairly easily. It was only the feared leeward broach that was difficult to deal with – and we had no intention of repeating that exercise.

For day after day we ran on in the frequently changing weather of the Southern Ocean. Slowly we learnt how to handle the boat in all the varied conditions the Roaring Forties could produce. If the wind came up the crew would automatically move to the winches after calling to me and the standby. When the standby came on deck, they would move to a vacant position, ready to help lower the spinnaker if necessary. We hardly needed to discuss what we were going to do any more and a couple of words of corroboration would suffice. We communicated a lot by sign language and questioning looks. Eyebrows in the air might mean 'We're ready to raise the jib. Are you ready your end?' while a thumbs up would give the reply. Sam had his own shorthand language on deck. When someone asked him something and he didn't hear, he would shout, 'Say again, Over'. And once the message was received would sign off with, 'Roger. Over and out.'

When the wind 'fluctu/ated' – our own description of a variable wind – it was not unusual to change sail three or four times in quick succession and we soon learnt to get on with the job as rapidly as possible. It was no good ruing the fact that we had just raised a sail which was now unsuitable to the conditions. Down it would have to come and up must go another. Having the wrong sail up meant we were either losing speed or out of control – the latter we soon knew about but the former was more difficult to judge. Bumble would always cry, 'More sail, more sail!' and she was a good influence on us. If we could imagine having a larger sail up and not broaching, then up it must go.

During this time of fast and demanding sailing, life on *ADC* was rarely better. We were busy, tired, but happy. The only difficulties between individuals occurred over sailing policy. As before, John's ideas on certain crucial matters differed from Jacques' and mine. John felt that it was a waste of time to gybe on every wind shift since speed was more important than course. Also, he still preferred to steer the boat with the spinnaker pole back, despite the broaching that seemed to result. More worrying, as the leg progressed there had been less and less feedback between the two watches until John's was working independently from – and at odds with – Jacques'. It had reached the point where the sails would be completely retrimmed at the change of watch and a different course sailed. It was Jacques who suggested the solution. To improve continuity, he would move to John's watch, leaving Tony to fill his place. After a general discussion we further agreed that we must all make more effort to improve the flow of information and to be more flexible in our ideas.

These matters apart, life was running very smoothly. Bumble's skill in the galley ensured we were well and happily fed. As always she was a bright and cheerful companion, and only ever complained when there was good cause. Every four or five days she would do the shopping, which involved going into the forward cabins, lifting up the bunks and taking out a supply of tinned food from the lockers beneath. One day, Bumble came stumbling into the saloon, a look of disgust on her face and two very nasty socks held lightly between her fingers. 'This is too much!' she exclaimed. 'The stink in those cabins is bad enough without my nose having to meet *these*!'

As before, the forward cabins were getting a little ripe and some people's sleeping bags and clothing were worse than others. With all the switching around necessitated by the new watch system, people could rarely use the same bunk all the time. Even if they did manage to – Sam was particularly fussy about 'his' bunk – they usually had to share it with different people on the opposite watch. Robert's cast-off clothing gained an evil reputation, mainly because he left it lying around, and his sleeping bag was reputed to be none too pleasant. Although he hotly denied these 'highly imaginative accusations', I noticed no-one was very keen to share a bunk with him! Similarly, Fred's feet were not known for smelling of roses. However, apart from the odd comment, everyone accepted the inevitability of unsavoury scents developing and even admitted they themselves might be at fault. I kept well away, both from the discussions of who was to hot-bunk with whom, and from the cabins themselves. There had to be some privileges in being the skipper and the relatively spacious aft cabin was one of them.

As always, sail repairs were part of our everyday life. The starcut ripped around the edges for the fourth and fifth time. We never bothered to patch the thing but just stitched what was left of it back on to the tapes, so the sail was getting smaller and smaller. Soon we estimated we could use it as a storm spinnaker – except that it would never stay up long enough to merit the name.

One day during a gybe the main split straight across the middle. We were using our old mainsail for the downwind legs and had our new one in reserve for just such an occasion as this. The repair of the old mainsail took days and days of backbreaking work. It was far too thick and bulky to fit through the sewing machine and virtually all of it had to be done by hand, using needle and leather palm. As always, Eve and Sam settled down to this toil without a murmur although it was their day for standby. With a regularity that almost defied coincidence, sails were tearing either during or just before their day off.

The mainsail had split because the seams had chafed. The spinnakers went for different reasons. While you can always get away with being overcanvassed on a small boat, you cannot on a large boat. The sheer weight of wind in almost 3,000 square feet of sail will blow it out if it is carried too

124

Lowering a boomed-out jib.

long. The starcut was always blowing out because it was literally weak in the head. And every time we repaired it the head became a little weaker. Eventually we put in a new head panel, but it was the design of the sail which was really at fault and our efforts did little to improve it. For the rest of the spinnakers, we had learnt the wind speed at which each spinnaker had to be taken down and by this stage most of the repairs were for small snags and rips, rather than full blow-outs.

One marked feature of the cold, wet Southern Ocean was the heavier, denser air. For any given wind speed, the air was more solid and unforgiving. We soon learnt that we had to change down to a smaller or stronger sail much sooner – or rip it.

The news from the other yachts suggested that they too were having an eventful time. The usual broaches and breakages were reported daily. However, in addition to these relatively normal occurrences, there were two pieces of news which were more alarming. *King's Legend,* who were pushing incredibly hard judging by their position just behind the larger *GB II* and *Condor* and by the number of broaches and blown spinnakers they reported daily, now came on the radio and told us they had a worrying leak. Every hour several gallons of water were coming in from a crack above the skeg and just forward of the rudder stock. They were relatively cheerful and calm about the matter, despite being able to see daylight through the crack when the helmsman turned the wheel hard to one side. Clearly the terrific pressures exerted by a strong crew on the steering gear were beginning to weaken a vital section of the boat. It was impossible for them to avoid putting strain on the section – going fast downwind involves using a lot of wheel with a lot of force – and every time they turned the wheel the crack would open due to the lateral pressures on the skeg. But while they were well ahead of *Flyer,* they were not going to slow down unless it was absolutely vital. They arranged a four-hourly radio schedule with two of the other yachts just in case the problem should suddenly get worse, then continued as before.

We did not fully appreciate what had happened on *GB II* for several days after we heard the first shreds of news. We understood someone had been injured, but only later did we realise how serious it had been. When fighting to lower a spinnaker during a squall Rob James, the skipper, and Nick Dunlop had rushed forward and inadvertently stepped into a loop in the guy formed when the spinnaker collapsed. When the spinnaker refilled the guy tightened with enormous force and the two men found themselves caught in a noose which was squeezing them like a vice. Rob was caught round the knees and Nick round the waist. Rob was lucky, in that he suffered only bruising and the effects of lost circulation and was unable to walk for two days. Nick, on the other hand, was lucky to escape with his life. As the rope tightened around his waist his blood was unable to circulate, his tongue shot out and swelled up, his stomach emptied itself, and his eyes came out of their sockets and turned bright red. Fortunately, the crew managed to cut the guy before Nick was killed. He was desperately ill for several days but eventually recovered, having sustained no serious internal injuries. The incident was a salutory lesson to all of us – spinnakers were dangerous and loops in ropes even more so.

The furthest south we reached was 51° after three weeks at sea, then, drawing a great circle course to the northern tip of New Zealand, we started to inch slowly northwards. At this most southerly point it grew very cold. In the night it often hailed or snowed and we donned balaclavas and face masks to guard our faces from the cold, biting wind. Once, the wind came on to the beam and we were able to reach without a spinnaker, a pleasant change but one which made the wind seem colder still. The heater chose that auspicious

Fred does some filming.

moment to give up completely and refused to start. However, body heat and the warmth from the galley kept the interior cosy enough. As before, we found feet and hands difficult to thaw out after hours on deck. I solved the problem by taking an empty whisky bottle, filling it with hot water and putting it in my bunk to defrost my feet.

We all wore plenty of underwear, with wool polar suits and quilted Puffa jackets on top. Sam also wore his motorcycle goggles and a thick woollen hat which made his hair stick out at right-angles from underneath. He looked like a cross between a Hell's Angel and Batman. When we remarked on this, Sam would look injured and reply, 'Have you ever had a sewing machine thrown at yer head?'

The cold and damp had a lethally corrosive effect on the electrics and mechanics. The navigation and flood lights refused to work. The torches we used on deck during the hours of darkness kept seizing up – of our total of twelve only four had switches that actually switched. Cameras positively hated the conditions and Fred spent much of his time oiling and renovating the BBC equipment. Olympus had given Jacques and me two superb Olympus OM2 cameras for the trip (which took most of the pictures in this book). We made every effort to keep them dry but inevitably they got covered in salt spray from time to time and, as everyone knows who tries to maintain mechanical equipment on a boat, there is enough salt in the air to make the finest piece of machinery rust anyway. On opening up the cameras we found water had got inside the body and rusted one small lever. Once this was cleaned and oiled, they never gave any more trouble.

In Fred's servicing programme there was one small piece of equipment he overlooked, which was the BBC clapper board. The BBC must have had a hilarious time when they saw one particular take. I held up the board, said 'Take thirty-four' and attempted to clap the clapper. Nothing. I pressed harder. Nothing. Eventually, I persuaded the clapper arm to descend by standing up and pressing down with all my might. The resultant clap sounded more like a soft thud. The hinge of the arm had corroded like everything else.

Fortunately the Marconi transmitter was still going strong, mainly because it was in one of the driest parts of the boat. South of Australia the radio reception began to improve and I was able to send more reports through to Capital Radio, via Sydney or Perth. We were also able to catch up on more news from the other boats. *Debenhams* had finally run into solid pack ice and had poled herself out of it. Not surprisingly, they were now heading north. *Condor* had seen icebergs at 55° south and *Tielsa* at 53° south. Only days after reporting her leak, *King's Legend* had done a Chinese gybe (presumably from broaching to leeward), wrapped her spinnaker round the forestay, and bent her spinnaker pole.

The race was developing into a tremendous contest between those who had gone south and those, like *Flyer* and ourselves, who had stayed further north. *Flyer,* so fast and light, had drawn away from us because, quite simply, she was the faster boat. She had been specially designed for the race; her light aluminium hull and modern design made her almost unbeatable downwind. Only the much larger *Condor* and *GB II* could keep ahead.

The tactic of staying north had not paid to begin with, but now the tables seemed to be turning. *Flyer* was catching *King's Legend* and it looked all set for another marathon duel between the two yachts. *Disque d'Or* was coming north fast and it was doubtful whether we could actually overtake her, but we would certainly catch her by several hours. With a bit of luck, we might even pick up a couple of positions on our arrival in Auckland. We pressed on hard, eager to make the most of the wind and keen to reach our destination.

Turning north had been a psychological boost and now, with an exciting last couple of thousand miles in view, we were even more encouraged. We experienced none of the depression and monotony we remembered from the second half of the first leg. Our lives involved pleasant routine, sufficient comfort and plenty of variety, the three necessities for an interesting voyage. Before breakfast, as the smell of bacon and eggs floated up from the galley, the off-watch would put their noses up through the hatch, rub the sleep from their eyes, and decide if the weather was fine enough for cleaning teeth on deck without oilskins.

'Not very clement, is it?' Off-watch to cockpit.

'This is true.' Cockpit to off-watch.

'Am I going to get wet if I come up to clean my teeth?'

Long pause. 'Well now, *we're* dry. But on the other hand we wouldn't like to guarantee that *you're* going to be dry. Let me see . . . there was a wave two hours ago . . . very nasty indeed!'

128

'Well, I think I'll risk it anyway.'

Grasping a mug of salt water, toothpaste and toothbrush, a figure would dash to the rail and quickly scrub his teeth, then fly back down the hatch. Sometimes the dasher would get wet, but more often was lucky and stayed dry.

The off-watch had twenty minutes to eat breakfast – or less if they were lazy about getting up. At one minute to eight o'clock, there would be murmurings from the cockpit: 'Nearly ready, you lot?' At eight o'clock, there would be cries of, 'We're dying of cold.' And at one minute past eight, there would be a deafening sound of four whistles being blown. When the new watch eventually scrambled up on deck, there would be great theatrical sighs, exaggerated examinations of wristwatches and many comments to the effect that the other watch not only went more slowly and changed sails more slowly, but were incapable of arriving on deck in anything but slow time.

Normally the changeover of watch was fairly smooth, and at least two or three of the new watch would be on deck by the appointed hour. However, Robert was nearly always late. One night the opposite watch decided to ensure that Robert was up on time for once and called him fifteen minutes early. Half asleep, Robert failed to notice that he was the only one getting up and struggled up on deck a full ten minutes early, to great cheering and laughter, particularly from John. 'Very funny, Tanner!' Robert exclaimed, somewhat peeved. 'How's the boy scout movement? You're *Accutrac*'s answer to Baden-Powell!'

The midday and evening meals coincided with changes of watch and the crew would eat in two sittings, those about to go on deck first, and those

'A figure would dash to the rail and quickly scrub his teeth' (*photo:* Nick Milligan).

coming off watch second. After every meal, the two smokers would zip up on deck for their gasp of tobacco. Beat rarely had trouble lighting his cigarettes, but Jacques would encounter insuperable difficulties in lighting his pipe. He would disappear head-first into corners of the cockpit and run through a dozen matches without success. Cursing roundly in highly expressive French, he would try another corner, contorting himself into a series of strange postures, bottom in the air and head lost to view. Sometimes it was so windy that he would stick his head down the main hatch and try lighting his pipe there. This would meet with some critical comments from those eating in the saloon. 'No smoking below – and certainly not old shoe leather!'

'Ha!' Jacques replied one day. 'You make all this fuss about a bit of tobacco, but it's nothing compared to ————'s farts, and no-one complains about them!' It was a fair point and from then on Jacques was allowed to light his pipe in the companion-way.

John would fix our position once a day, at noon. If the sky was clear he would also take star sights at dawn and dusk. The day's run was calculated from noon to noon which, because we were travelling east at such a high latitude, was considerably less than a full twenty-four-hour day. Nonetheless, we managed to do runs of between 220 and 240 miles every day. So rapid was our easterly progress that we had to put the clocks on every few days to keep up with local time, which differed from Cape Town to Auckland by nine hours.

Sextant in hand, John waits for the sun to appear.

Often, we would try to guess the daily run just before John worked it out and we were rarely more than a few miles out. If someone overestimated by ten

miles or so, it was an opportunity to slip in a provocative comment. 'Of course, I forgot! Nick was on the wheel for three hours last night and driving like a drain. Must have lost us a good ten miles.' The butt of these jokes varied from day to day, depending on who provided the most promising material.

Chat Hour was the other high spot of the day, when those who were up and about would gather round the Marconi transmitter in the aft cabin and listen to the news. Sam would usually take down the yachts' positions while I operated the set. Later we would go and plot the positions on the chart and measure the runs of the other boats. Very often the others gave their wind speed and direction, so that we could plot a primitive weather map. Ever since we had lost contact with Marion Island we had been without weather information, but this did not matter a great deal. Not only was the forecasting very unreliable, but there was little we could do to escape the weather anyway. Even if more favourable conditions existed just 100 miles away, it was rarely worth making a sudden detour because of the extra distance involved. Having chosen your route according to the theoretical weather patterns, you had to sit back and accept whatever turned up.

Jacques often operated the radio, particularly when conversing with the French yachts who sometimes spoke so rapidly and in such colloquial French that only Jacques could unravel it. *33 Export* always had news to tell. Either the entire crew were coming out in boils – not surprising when we saw the state of their galley in Auckland – or the skipper had poured boiling water into his lap, nearly ruining his prospects. They broached at least five times a day, they calmly said, and wrecked so many spinnakers they couldn't count them. Their main boom had broken and had been repaired using metal they had cut out of a bulkhead, a task that had taken days of work with a hacksaw blade. *33* was a small boat and uncomfortable inside, but nothing worried her crew because, unless something went drastically wrong, they were all set to win the handicap prize for the leg.

Halfway 'along' Australia, and 1,000 miles to the south of it, the weather started to become very squally. For over two weeks the wind had been blowing at anything from Force 4 to Force 8, and normally around 6 to 7, mild conditions for the Southern Ocean. Now it appeared that the approaches to the Tasman Sea were to produce more violent weather. One day it blew hard from the north-west, then veered 90° and blew hard from the south-west. Then a large black cloud appeared from over the horizon behind us. We prepared for a gust of wind but, despite the numerous squalls we had already encountered, nothing prepared us for the force of this one. It suddenly blew fifty to sixty knots, a good Force 10 or 11, and we had to hurry to lower some sail. Fortunately we had a jib up at the time and not a spinnaker. Nevertheless we managed to drop the jib over the bow so that the sheet ran under the boat and caught in the rudder. A deft move by the helmsman – actually it was pure luck born of panic – and the sheet freed from the rudder. When we pulled it inboard it was covered in antifouling. 'One less patch of antifouling to be scrubbed in Auckland,' said Tony.

For the next week we ran harum-scarum past Tasmania and across the Tasman Sea, blown along by a series of squalls which whistled across the sky.

'We have lift-off!' – a good surf (*photo:* Beat Güttinger).

We became avid cloud watchers. If a cloud looked dark and forbidding we would have a full spinnaker alert. The standby crew would be called up and the seven of us would wait by our stations until the squall hit or passed safely to one side. The decision as to which sail to carry was more difficult than ever and the cockpit echoed to the cry of, 'It's a definite maybe' whenever a change was mooted.

Between squalls the wind gave us some superb surfing as it hovered around the Force 7 to 8 mark. One night Sam entered in the deck log, 'Storm spi handed as spray from surfs makes steering difficult – helmsman cannot see where he is going.' The next watch treated this comment with derision – it was perhaps a little exaggerated – and suggested that the others had merely been 'chicken'.

When there was too much wind for a spinnaker, we would hoist and pole out a jib. Yet in one important respect this often led to more trouble than raising a spinnaker. However carefully we pulled the jib up, the strain on the hanks was such that they would often break or jam or – worse – rip the sail as it flogged back and forth. This created a lot of work for Sam and Eve although they never complained. However, they were heard to comment that they wouldn't mind going *upwind* again, just to have a rest.

During this downhill run we managed to lose the ends of both the mizzen staysail halyards up the mast. The staysail was always being raised and lowered as the wind speed changed. One day one halyard was lost – 'It sort of sprang out of me hand,' Nick said – and then we lost the other in a terrible mess of ropes and weights when trying to re-reeve the second. Now someone would have to go up the mast. Normally quite willing to stand back and let somebody else do the heroic stuff, I elected myself as the ideal candidate to go up the mizzen on this occasion. I was worried that a heavy person on the top of the mast in the big roll might be sufficient to break a tang and bring the whole thing down. It was an interesting experience. Gripping with my knees and trying not to get thrown around too much, I was soon trembling with the exertion of holding on as the others winched me up. Once I had reeved the halyards I wasted no time in asking to be lowered again. Back on deck I could appreciate why Tony and Beat, the two who usually volunteered to go up the main mast, always needed a rest afterwards. Even when it was moderately calm the top of the main mast shot back and forth like a violent pendulum. I told Tony that I would award him a gold watch on his hundredth visit up the mast. He smiled and said he'd rather make it a few less visits and be awarded a pint of beer in Auckland.

As we shot past Tasmania, 150 miles to the north of us, the seas became larger and the water bluer. The sun came out and slowly began to warm our feet and hands. On the 23rd November we did our best run ever, a distance of 255 miles noon to noon, in the most glorious conditions of sparkling seas and blue, clear skies. Gradually, oddments of clothing appeared on deck for drying and airing. Thick sweaters were taken off and hats removed. We turned our white faces to the sun and stretched ourselves out like cats on a hot roof.

Frontal weather systems were still coming through, producing grey clouds and driving rain, but they only lasted a day or so, and then the sun would reappear. One blustery day two shag cormorants came to visit us, probably young birds who had lost their way. They were a very popular addition to the boat because they provided such rich entertainment when trying to balance on the end of the mizzen boom. With each roll and surge of the boat they counterbalanced the motion by recoiling their long, scraggy necks, then extending them again in rapid, jerky movements. They looked like two rather nervous Turkish contortionists. They even tried to sleep, putting their heads under their wings until the boat rolled, when their heads would shoot out again and jerk backwards and forwards in great agitation. When we surfed and the spray flew up and over the mizzen boom, the two birds would be washed off into the sea, to emerge cross and bothered some distance behind. After a great deal of flapping they would take off and perch once more, only to be washed off again five minutes later. When they flew off a day later we were sorry to see them go. Despite their ugliness, we had become rather attached to them and their funny antics.

'Well, I'm goin' to wave a flannel at meself,' Sam announced one sunny day. 'And Tanner's goin' to change his shirt, ain't you Spanner?'

John's T-shirt was certainly quite a sight. He must have worn it all the way from Cape Town, for it was dark yellow and distinctly grimy round the edges. 'Well, I don't know,' said John, 'I thought it was beginning to look rather good.'

Trimming the spinnaker.

Jacques also emerged from his winter clothing in less than immaculate order. He had a fine beard, but had forgotten to comb his hair for about two weeks – it would have been four except that I had crept up behind him with a hairbrush when he wasn't looking. Now I tried to surprise him again, but it was no easy matter to get a comb through his matted locks and, to the sound of loud protests, I spent half an hour unravelling it by hand.

The crew could almost scent land now. Robin renewed his deck exercises with vigour, keen to be in good shape for the arrival. Puffing and panting, he would do press-ups, knee bends and arm flappings, an intent and serious expression on his face. Robert eyed himself in a mirror and decided that the scruffy beard would have to go, but a rakish moustache might just set the female hearts of Auckland a-flutter. After an hour with a razor and lots of soap, he towelled himself dry and showed us his new upper lip.

'Ugghhh,' was the general reaction. Sam was more specific. 'What's that dirty mark on yer lip, Jackson? Yer eyebrow slipped down for a drink?'

Clothes other than baggy longjohns and polar suits started to appear. Sam put on his best shorts, which had more patches than material, and was forced to admit they might not survive a thirty-knot gust. He was proved right the next day. Eve, who always became depressed after a long time without a wash, spent half an hour in the aft loo with a cup of water and a flannel, and emerged with clean clothes and a totally new attitude to life.

As we steamed across the Tasman, we held a strong following wind. The boats to the south were slowing down, giving us a good chance of beating them on handicap. It was too late for us to overtake *Disque d'Or,* but while our position against the other boats was improving daily, we didn't care. *Disque d'Or* was pushing hard but, sad to hear, had also developed the same trouble as *King's Legend.* She was leaking badly from just behind the skeg. With two of the Swan 65s experiencing serious hull problems around the rudder area we, as the third Swan, were beginning to worry. We had a thorough look at the steering gear, the rudder stock and the hull, but all seemed to be well. We crossed our fingers and hoped it would remain so.

King's Legend and *Flyer* were having a fine battle ahead of us. *Flyer* was now fifty miles behind her rival, with only four days to Auckland. *King's Legend* was still going flat out, determined that her earlier efforts should not be in vain. She reported yet another spinnaker blown out and another major broach. *Flyer,* less prone to broach because of her design, now reported a broach or two as well, although one resulted from breaking her steering cable.

As we dashed for the northern tip of New Zealand, our natural desire to reach Auckland was tinged with a desperate need to get there before the weather baulked us. A powerful high-pressure area was building up over the west Tasman Sea and was expected to spread slowly eastwards. Like most highs it would bring the most dreaded of conditions – no wind. The race was almost forgotten as we watched the barometer start to rise, waiting for the wind to show signs of dropping.

At first the wind was as boisterous as ever, and we experienced the usual excitements of fast spinnaker sailing. At one point we nearly lost Beat over the side. The spinnaker pole had been eased forward and Beat was poised on the pulpit, ready to release it, when for some strange reason the spinnaker collapsed and started flogging. The pole jerked violently backwards and forwards, causing Beat to duck, lose his balance, and disappear over the bow. Fortunately, he was holding on tight to the forestay and was clipped on by his safety harness, but it still gave us a fright to see him disappear so suddenly. He soon hauled himself up and over the pulpit again and, looking rather sheepish, managed to release the sail from the end of the pole.

Even though we were old hands at downwind sailing, we still managed to do the most tremendous nonsenses. The next day we put up a spinnaker to find we had left a sail tie round the middle of it – not surprisingly it wouldn't open. A few moments later we put it up again, only to find that the sail wrapped itself round the forestay. Down it had to come! One hour later, we finally managed

Holding on tight, Beat releases the spinnaker.

to raise a spinnaker and get it to fill. 'Don't find a hot crew like us every day,' said Nick.

The barometer continued to rise, although sufficiently fast to make sure the wind stayed strong and fresh. However, once the pressure neared its peak, we were likely to run out of wind. We still had 800 miles to go, which would normally take us four days but if the high overtook us it could take us twice as long. *Condor* and *GB II* were nearing the finish and there was a danger that they would arrive just before the wind dropped, possibly gaining enough time to beat us on handicap.

In fact, the strong winds held for two more glorious days of surfing and fast sailing. On the Saturday *King's Legend* scraped into Auckland an incredible two and a half miles ahead of *Flyer,* turning the tables on the result of the first leg. *Disque d'Or* would be next, a day later, and we would be sixth boat a day after that – if we were lucky. The barometer was now so high it could hardly go any further, and the wind was dropping all the time. Behind us, the other boats were already reporting the beginnings of a flat calm.

There was now real heat in the sun and we basked in its warm rays whenever we had a moment to spare. Bumble was unanimously awarded a day off cooking, mainly because she was getting cross with us. She was cross with good reason, of course. We were getting more piggish in our habits and, with the proximity of land, more slovenly about the washing-up and cleaning. Bumble's days off were rarely completely relaxed because no-one knew where anything was kept and the stand-in cook would constantly ask for advice. That particular evening I produced something reasonably edible – at least I didn't get any complaints. Jacques was on standby that day so there was the usual furore about the washing-up. French curses echoed from the galley and there were mutterings about throwing the whole lot of plates, forks and spoons over the side.

When Jacques retired to his bunk that night he left firm instructions for padlocks to be put on all the spinnakers, because he didn't want to be called up for a sail change. As it was he was up most of the night. The dying wind played elaborate games of hide and seek, coming from the south, then the west, increasing to a fresh breeze, then falling to a whisper.

The next day we sighted Cape Reinga on the north-west tip of New Zealand, and sailed slowly towards it in a gentle south-west breeze. The land was a beautiful sight, so green and pleasant and, because it was New Zealand, warm and inviting too. We knew that a great welcome awaited us on our arrival in Auckland. We also knew that Auckland was 160 miles away down the east coast of this, the North Island. Hardly daring to hope, we kept the breeze all that night and rounded the North Cape. Altering course down the eastern seaboard, our excitement rose with every mile.

Then the wind died.

A tiny breeze appeared now and then but to all intents and purposes we were becalmed. I kept reminding myself that it could have been a great deal worse – we could have been becalmed days ago. Oddly enough it was Robin, so controlled and reserved, who stamped around muttering about the bloody wind and how ridiculous it was for this to happen now. The rest of us took the opportunity to clear out lockers, sort out shore clothes and generally tidy up.

As we sat idly two miles off the coast, staring at the beautiful land, an extraordinary thing happened. A seaplane flew over, circled, and flew off again, followed by a larger plane which also circled and flew off again. Then the seaplane returned and dropped a yellow flare to shoreward of us. 'They're saying hello!' someone said. It seemed a strange way to say hello, but seeing nothing else in sight we assumed they were trying to communicate with us. We turned on the radio but heard nothing so, seeing the seaplane returning yet again, we let off a white flare to say hello in return. It seemed a friendly sort of thing to do. Imagine our surprise when, a week after our arrival in Auckland, someone told us it had been an emergency and that the planes were trying to attract our attention to a fishing boat which had been drifting for three days without an engine. However, we did not feel too guilty about our lack of response. It was flat calm and the fishing boat cannot have been in terrible danger. Also, a powerful motor vessel would have been better equipped to tow the boat back to port. Finally, we hadn't seen a sign of any other boat so, even if we had realised our help was needed, we wouldn't have known which direction to look in. It was a pity neither of the planes spoke to us on the radio for all the confusion could then have been avoided.

The wind whirled round in faint, gasping circles all afternoon and we managed to trickle along at a quarter or half a knot. Not a great speed, but not unpleasant when you have beautiful, green, rolling hills to look at, and many coves and inlets to examine through the binoculars.

Steeling ourselves for a long windless night we were unprepared for a sudden surprise. A faint but firm breeze sprang up. In no time we were roaring along close-hauled in a brisk, fresh land breeze. We could hardly believe our luck as we hammered along for hour after hour, past island after island until we saw the unmistakable glow of the lights of a big city. Excitedly, we made contact with the host yacht club on the VHF radio and put through a call to Eve's mother, Diana, who had flown out to meet us. It was the most thrilling finish of the race because it was so unexpectedly fast.

As dawn broke and the islets and volcanic hills surrounding Auckland harbour grew into soft, distinguishable shapes, Jacques and I grinned at each other. It was a great milestone – halfway round the world and down under. Of all the stops, this was the one we were most looking forward to. Here we would spend Christmas and, with well over four weeks until the scheduled restart date, here we would also take a well earned holiday. After 13,000 miles sailing round the world we could think of nothing better than a long, restful time away from it all and away from the sea!

CHAPTER 8

Christmas in Auckland

It was just half past six in the morning as we started to tack down the channel between the many islands off Auckland Harbour. A small fishing boat hove into view and came over to give us a wave and a cheer, a warm gesture indeed. As we identified the finishing line some mile or so away a large motor boat swept around the headland and made straight for us. It was covered in waving, cheering people. Not only was Eve's mother, Diana, there, but Peter Blake from *Condor*, Bob Saunders of the BBC, and many others whom we later discovered to be representatives of the host yacht club. Knowing that all these people must have got up at half past five in the morning, we were overwhelmed to see them. To express our gratitude we put on a show of racing techniques by sitting out along the side of the boat in the fashion of the fastest racing machines at Cowes. Sitting in a row was also quite handy for passing the champagne back and forth. When we crossed the line and handed the sails, we then performed a Maori war dance we had been rehearsing for the last two days – we always liked to put on some kind of show for those who were kind enough to come out and meet us. The dance consisted of roaring, jumping, stamping and making aggressive gestures, and was performed to a loud chant. Everyone forgot the words and most people the steps, but what we lacked in rehearsal time we made up for in enthusiasm. We were particularly fond of the end of the dance where we emulated the Maori warriors and tried to frighten our enemies by leaping into the air, opening our eyes till they stood out like ping-pong balls, and sticking out our tongues. The audience gave us a rapturous round of applause – mainly, I suspect, because they were so astonished.

We finished at six minutes past seven, five weeks and one day after leaving Cape Town. We became sixth boat to finish and – although we had to wait two days to be sure – seventh on handicap for the leg. What was more, our position for the two legs so far was seventh, two places up on our ninth at Cape Town. The small boats had done very well on this second leg and had taken the first two places. Even if we had gone further south and had the advantage of the stronger winds, it was doubtful we could have finished better than fifth. Seventh? Well, it was better than ninth and as long as our position was improving we were happy!

'Well done, Missus,' said Jacques, giving me a big hug. And it was not the only hug I got at the finish – Tony and Sam both gave me lovely bear-like embraces! Indeed everyone was over the moon. We were halfway round the world and, somehow or another, still in one piece. We had a lot to celebrate.

OPPOSITE
A fine breeze for the finish at Auckland (*photo: New Zealand Herald*).

The next boat to arrive was *33 Export,* just eight and a half hours later. We had not managed to shake her off ever since sighting her in the early stages of the leg. Her time was sufficiently fast to give her a well deserved first place for the leg. It was a popular win – *33* was a slim, light boat which had been sailed with great flair and determination by her crew, and at some cost in personal comfort. A look around the boat's interior revealed the most appalling conditions – cramped space, little headroom and several days' unwashed dishes.

A large meal and a hot bath was everyone's first thought on arriving in port. After tying up at a wharf right in the centre of town, we dealt with the local formalities as quickly as possible. All our remaining fruit and vegetables were handed over to the Agriculture Department for destruction to prevent plant disease entering the country. We had been so anxious to waste no time getting ashore that we collected the fruit and veg the day before. The Customs Officer tried to gather everyone's signatures on his forms but, seeing how difficult it would be now that the crew were chatting and laughing with the crowds on the next-door boat, he and I came to an arrangement and I signed for everybody.

The Royal New Zealand Yacht Squadron, our hosts, had arranged for two families to look after each yacht. *ADC*'s families arrived bearing baskets of exotic fruit and fresh bread, butter, bacon and eggs for breakfast. The Paykels and the McKenzies were to look after us very well during our stay. Their most noble gesture was to offer to do our laundry, which consisted of twelve large and unsavoury bags of clothing accumulated over five weeks of hard sailing. There is something rather embarrassing about handing over such obvious evidence of a squalid life to people you have only just met. However, a moment's consideration of the alternatives – launderettes and so on – and we didn't hold back for long.

The local press arrived and I heard Bumble say to one reporter, 'I thought I'd be terrified but I was only frightened,' which was a pretty fair summary of how we had all felt about the second leg. Another reporter asked her what it was like to sail the world with nine men. 'Oh, it's *lovely!*' replied Bumble, eyes dancing. 'I'm absolutely beastly to them and all they do is hug me!'

Once our official welcome was over we all made a rush for hotel rooms. Only those of us who were completely broke stayed on the boat that first night. After a long hot bath and an enormous New Zealand breakfast Jacques and I went down to the hotel lobby and burst out laughing as we saw Tony and Beat checking in. Beat, unaware that he was now back in civilisation, was standing at the desk in sea boots, Puffa jacket – and baggy, woolly longjohns.

It had become a tradition that we all ate together the first night in port, so at eight that evening we left for a restaurant in three taxis. With us in our taxi, driven by a smiling Maori with an enormous frizzy hairdo, was Robert. He was not his normal outgoing self. Eventually, looking a bit sheepish and shaken, he told us why. That afternoon he and Robin had gone into town in search of a little relaxation. Ensconced in a dark and friendly bar, they had soon found themselves chatting to a warm and vivacious blonde. Never slow on the uptake, Robert had soon established friendly relations with this glamorous piece and was looking forward to spending a few hours in her company. It was a good half an hour later that the barman passed him a note.

At this point in the tale Robert's voice faltered and he giggled nervously. But after a few promptings he eventually spat it out. The note had read, 'That lady you're with is a fella.'

'I should have realised,' groaned Robert, 'when she said her boyfriend was a sailor.'

This was a mortal blow to such an enthusiastic heterosexual as Robert and he was still in a state of shock. His composure was not improved when the taxi driver joined in the general laughter.

'Don't laugh, mate,' said Robert to the back of the taxi driver's head. 'It could have happened to you!' This made the taxi driver laugh even more for, on turning round, it was revealed to be a woman. Twice in one day was too much for Robert and he took to drink, recovering only the next day when he made successful contact with a guaranteed genuine New Zealand woman.

We decided to get most of the work done on the boat as soon as possible, leaving ourselves free to take a holiday before Christmas. Thanks to the efficiency of the local firms and the excellent organisation of the yacht club, everything was soon in hand. The local sparmaker took our spinnaker pole away to be straightened and sleeved. Hoods started to make a new Number Two genoa to replace the one lost on our first broach, and to carry out the major sail repairs. The only difficulty was to get the boat out of the water quickly so that we could examine her for the problem suffered by *King's Legend* and *Disque d'Or*. This took time because of the shortage of boatyards capable of lifting big boats, but we eventually found a small yard with an old-fashioned greased slipway which could take us in a week's time.

Jacques and Tony wonder how to tackle two of the many repairs (*photo [left]*: Beat Güttinger).

General Motors kindly lent us two cars, which enabled us to drive to a yard many miles out of town where *King's Legend* and *Disque d'Or* were hauled out of the water. The repair work on their skegs had already started, but we could still see where the problem had occurred. According to the yachts' builders, who had flown out from Finland to supervise the repairs, the damage had been caused by worn rudder stock bearings which had caused the rudder to move on a lateral plane. Whatever the cause, the damage to *Disque d'Or* was obviously serious. One could make her skeg waggle by pulling on it with one hand. Whole areas of her hull had delaminated and could be seen to move in and out with the movement of the skeg. Although we were not experts, we thought the repairs being carried out were far from adequate.

We were naturally rather worried in case *ADC* should have the same problem and could barely conceal our impatience during the week before she was lifted out. But once she was pulled up the slipway we breathed again. A close examination revealed that her skeg was as firm as a rock and there was very little lateral movement in the rudder stock. To be on the safe side, we asked the builders to glass in more supports around the stock just inside the hull. That done, we had every expectation of completing the race without the same problem as the other two Swans.

With most of the major jobs under way we could appreciate life on land to the full. Diana Bonham had the brilliant idea of taking Eve, Bumble and me off to a health and beauty parlour where we enjoyed a sauna bath, a massage and a facial. We even had a manicure, although there was not much left of our nails after so much rough handling of sails and ropes. Bumble emerged with lovely black eyelashes which she fluttered at everyone, asking, as she put her face two inches from people's noses, if they noticed anything astoundingly different about her appearance. Apart from Bumble's eyelashes, it would be difficult for anyone to spot any change in our looks, but it did not matter – the afternoon's treatment had left us feeling like a million dollars.

We found the food in Auckland to be very good indeed and enjoyed some memorable meals. We all put on weight, but it was Eve and Diana who positively grew before our eyes. They were staying with one of the Samoan royal families, their blood brothers and sisters by adoption from many years before when the family had formed a Polynesian dance group, come to England, and found themselves stranded without money by an unscrupulous manager. The Bonhams had taken the whole family in and looked after them and, in appreciation, the Samoans had invoked an old island custom by making them blood brothers and sisters. Most of the family now lived in New Zealand and were determined to treat Eve and Diana to the best of their traditional hospitality – which meant gargantuan meals. Eve and Diana had a wonderful and very fattening time.

The New Zealanders were extremely warm and hospitable towards us. They were tremendously interested in the race, not only because it was the first time the event had stopped there (the first race had gone to Sydney), but because they were sailing-mad anyway. New Zealand must be one of the best, if not the greatest, cruising grounds in the world, rich in beautiful bays, islands and harbours. With only three million people in an area the size of Britain, it is a

144

country where the coastline is unspoilt by mass developments or industrial
ugliness. Most Aucklanders possess boats and are avid sailors. Many were
anxious to come and see the fleet, meet the crews and to offer us hospitality.
Unless we were careful, we were not going to have any rest at all.

One of the most memorable parties was held at the Royal Akarana Yacht
Club on a Saturday night. Since it was a Roman party we went suitably attired

in togas and laurel wreaths. Any idea about the New Zealanders being quiet and reserved was quickly dispelled by the wildness of the party, which culminated in a series of chariot races up and down the car park. This impression was reinforced the following day when we arrived at the beach to have an inter-yacht race in Laser dinghies. There we saw a man in a full suit of armour, looking for his seaplane. He was soon joined by a man in full naval mess kit of circa 1800, telling him the seaplane had gone hours ago. This was the annual breakfast gathering of a men's club, whose members enjoyed dressing up for the occasion.

The Laser race itself was a great success. *GB II* cheated by pulling a local champion into their team. *Condor* also cheated – so we maintained – because they had three New Zealanders in their crew, all with 'local knowledge'. (They won of course – or was it *GB II?* It didn't seem to matter.) Cheating or not, it was a marvellous day during which the crews exhibited their skills – usually far in excess of their skippers'. Bumble, not discouraged by the fact she had never sailed a dinghy before, entered a race and caused bedlam at the start by capsizing twice on the line.

After two weeks' work on *ADC* we put her back in the water and took our holiday. Some of the crew went to the South Island, some to the top of the North; some borrowed cars, some hitch-hiked, some walked, some flew. Whatever the mode of travel, we were all keen to see as much of the beautiful country as we could. Jacques and I went to Rotorua first, with Bob Saunders and the BBC camera crew who wanted to film us seeing the local sights. Rotorua boasts many hot springs and other volcanic phenomena and we inspected bubbling mud pools, high geysers – which never went off while we were there, though we waited for hours – and thermal springs. Other strange sights included a herd of performing sheep, really a group of bewildered sheep forced from platform to platform to amuse the tourists, and a trout farm where the fish lived in idyllic surroundings, jumping into the air to feed off spoons of food we held just above the water. We also visited some old Maori villages built amid the hot springs and enveloped in the strong smell of sulphur. It was most impressive to see the way the hot spring water was channelled down aqueducts until it reached the right temperature for washing clothes. Similarly, the hotels and modern houses used the spring water for heating their rooms and their fresh water. However, we discovered that the spring water was not ideal for bathing in – after a visit to the local Polynesian baths I found the sulphur caused two layers of my best skin to peel a few days later.

One evening we went for a meal to find ourselves sitting next to Admiral Steiner, the RNSA race organiser who had come out from the UK to supervise our stay in New Zealand. We joked about coming out to Rotorua to get away from each other and decided we would obviously have to go further afield for peace and quiet. The next day we went to a beautiful lake deep in the hills which could be reached only by a long, narrow track. Apart from the inhabitants of a small fishing lodge which was the only building on the lake, there was no-one there – until we saw two people arrive and identified one as a crew member of *33 Export*. This was ridiculous, Jacques and I agreed, and the next day we said goodbye to the BBC and left for more isolated places.

We drove down to Lake Taupo, and on to Ruapehu, the great volcanic mountain which has become a popular ski resort. Being mid-summer, the place was deserted and we were able to walk among the moorland hills without seeing another soul. Having enjoyed uninterrupted sunshine in Auckland, it now decided to rain and drizzle ceaselessly so we left and headed east again for Lake Taupo, to see if we might catch some friends who had a holiday lodge there. As we followed the track to the lodge a passing car screeched to a halt and we were greeted by John and Marie-Christine Ridgway, also on a get-away-from-it-all-holiday!

From Taupo we went east, meeting most of the country's eighty million sheep on the way. We then worked our way back towards Rotorua and discovered that the east coast attracts twice as much rain as anywhere else. But we did not mind the weather for we were soon bewitched by the wild, beautiful and rich hill forest of the Urewera National Park, so isolated that it could only be reached by unmade roads. Nestling in the peaks of the mountain range was a great lake, cold, still and untouched, fed by massive and spectacular waterfalls.

With Christmas fast approaching, we finally had to make our way back towards Auckland. We stayed one more night in Rotorua, choosing a motel where each room boasted a private, spring-fed, heated plunge pool of its own, and then headed back to the city.

Our holiday had been short and we had seen only a small part of that beautiful and spacious country, but it had been a wonderful ten days nonetheless. In three years Jacques and I had never had a real holiday and since our marriage we had enjoyed precious little time on our own. Those ten days were the honeymoon we hadn't had time for the previous July.

In Auckland we soon became engulfed by preparations and repair jobs again. With the restart fixed for Boxing Day, it was necessary to have everything ready and all the food loaded by Christmas Eve. But once all the work was done, we had our own Christmas dinner party complete with crackers, Christmas pudding, funny hats and presents. It was the nearest we could get to having a traditional Christmas, although the hot mid-summer weather seemed a little incongruous to us Europeans. On Christmas Day itself, Whitbread had arranged a day's outing around the nearby islands on a pleasure steamer. They laid on an enormous Christmas lunch, with cold meats, salads, mince pies and, of course, Christmas pudding, which we were encouraged to dance off to the music of a live jazz band.

By the restart day, we were groaning with food, but very happy. It had been a restful, enjoyable and interesting four weeks in a warm and hospitable country and, in many ways, we were sorry to leave. However, the restart would also mark the beginning of our long journey home and, having been away four months, we were beginning to look forward to our return. From another point of view, it was high time we left. Nick had collected his usual ration of parking tickets, while Jacques and I found that the car we had been using had got dented when left parked in the middle of town. Last but not least, we were fast running out of money.

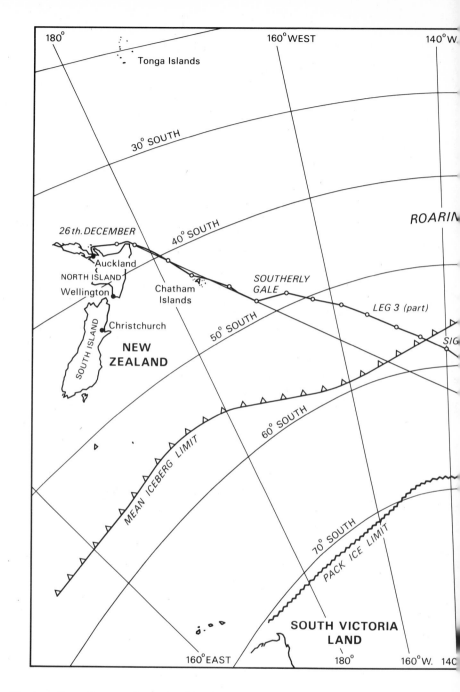

The handicap distance from Auckland to Rio de Janeiro was 7,400 miles. The great turning point on the leg would be the famous Cape Horn. Here, at 58° south, the wind and seas are funnelled between South America with its high Andes, and Antarctica reaching up from the south, creating one of the stormiest areas in the world. The great circle or direct route from New

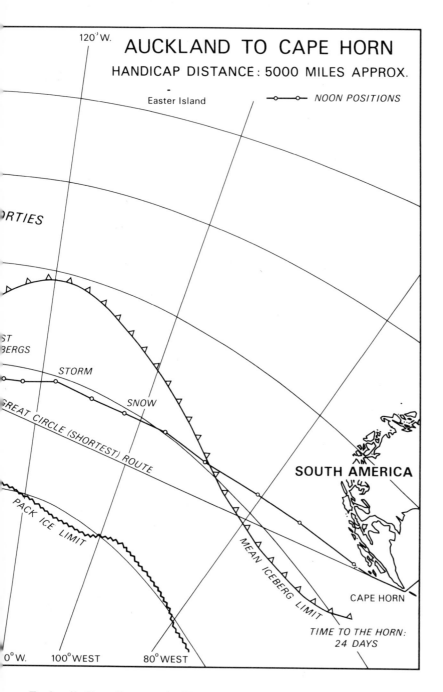

AUCKLAND TO CAPE HORN
HANDICAP DISTANCE: 5000 MILES APPROX.

120° W.

Easter Island

●—○—○— NOON POSITIONS

RTIES

ST
BERGS

STORM

SNOW

GREAT CIRCLE (SHORTEST) ROUTE

PACK ICE LIMIT

SOUTH AMERICA

MEAN ICEBERG LIMIT

CAPE HORN

TIME TO THE HORN:
24 DAYS

0° W.   100° WEST   80° WEST

Zealand's East Cape to the Horn went down as far as 63° south. As on the second leg we were faced with the question of how far south we should go. The Southern Ocean had been very kind to us on the way to Auckland – would it be as kind again? Also, we wondered at which point we would run into easterlies rather than the westerlies we needed. Before, *Debenhams* had gone as far as 58°

without running into headwinds, but whether the same would be true of the coming leg was difficult to tell.

Having stayed too far north on the way to Auckland, we decided to take the bull by the horns and head down to 60° south. If we ran into adverse weather we would turn north again. At least, that was the theory.

We would meet icebergs on this southerly route but with the short summer nights, the visibility should be good enough to avoid them.

We were to see an addition to the fleet on the third leg. The famous *Pen Duick VI*, skippered by the legendary Eric Tabarly, was to join us for the second half of the race. Eric and his boat had won the Transatlantic Singlehanded Race and several other important events after a disastrous first outing on the first Whitbread Race. Then, *Pen Duick* had lost her mast not once but twice and, having been hot favourite to win, had retired from the event. There was one minor problem surrounding *Pen Duick's* entry which none of us paid much attention to, unaware of the furore the whole matter was to cause a short while later; *Pen Duick* was late in sending a valid rating certificate to the organisers, a vital pre-requisite to being allowed to race. Without it, the boat's handicap could not be calculated, nor her time allowance announced. When the certificate was finally produced, *Condor* lodged a protest over a technical

A mile after the start at Auckland, we round the first mark. Next mark, the Horn (*photo: New Zealand Herald*).

matter involving so-called exotic materials. *Condor* had been penalised for having a carbon fibre mast on the first leg (the mast that had broken), while *Pen Duick* had no penalty for her spent uranium keel, a truly exotic material. The organisers went into a huddle to try to sort the matter out but, by the starting date nothing had been settled and the matter was referred to an international yachting body sitting in London. The storm was to break when the fleet was at sea and in a small way even *ADC* was to be dragged into the row.

On Boxing Day there was a large crowd at the quayside to see us off. Eve's Samoan family were there to give us lucky beads and garlands of flowers. People showered us with cakes, mince pies and fruit. To show our appreciation, we danced our Maori war dance again which, with no rehearsal at all, was even more shambolic, and certainly wouldn't have frightened our enemies. Waving and shouting, we said goodbye to the many friends we had made and, with much sadness, pulled away from the quay.

It was a glorious summer day for the start, with sunshine, blue skies and a fresh easterly wind. Being a holiday, the spectators had come out in force and it was estimated that 2,000 craft were there to see us off. We made a rip-roaring start, all sixteen boats reaching fast for a harbour buoy we had to leave to starboard. There were so many spectators about that we could not see the mark for boats and nearly overshot it. There was chaos and confusion as we all raised spinnakers and bore away for the mark. As we rounded it we were happy to see we were ahead of *Flyer* and *King's Legend* – if only for the moment.

The spectator craft followed us for an hour or so, the enormous fleet hurrying to keep up with us as we roared along at a steady ten knots. Then, as they dropped behind, we were on our own, looking back at the sparkling blue waters and fertile green islands of lovely New Zealand, where we had passed such a happy, landbound four weeks.

151

CHAPTER 9

Heading South Again

'Ughhh. I'm beginning to think all that Christmas pudding was a mistake,' groaned Bumble as we hit a short, choppy head sea between Great Barrier Island and the mainland. And Bumble was not the only one. Robin was already draped over the rail, white as a sheet, while the rest of us were wobbling about, looking pale and nervous. It was almost a relief when the wind dropped away and, by the next morning, we found ourselves nearly becalmed in the Bay of Plenty. After four weeks ashore we needed time to regain our sea legs, not to mention our stomachs.

For the whole of that day we slopped around in the bay, staring at White Island, a lively and smoking volcano. Only in the late afternoon did we pick up a breeze and head off towards East Cape which we rounded next morning in company with the rest of the fleet. In a gentle easterly we reached off towards the Chatham Islands on our great circle course for the Horn.

We soon had our first surprise. A supposedly full gas bottle which should have lasted ten days ran out. Robert, who was in charge of this department, shook his head in disbelief. He checked the connections and the cooker for leaks, but could find none. In all probability, the bottle had been overlooked when our six bottles were being refilled. But to be on the safe side we decided to ration the gas until we discovered how long the next bottle was going to last.

A call on the radio from *Condor* alerted us to the next problem. Like us, they had bought some fruit juice in plastic bottles and reported that their plastic containers were beginning to swell and leak in an alarming fashion. A quick search through the lockers revealed that we had the same problem – the fruit juice was fizzing and bubbling and expanding until it was bursting the bottles. When the word 'fermenting' was first mentioned, there was some stirring of interest among the crew. But after one sip we decided that the juice would never make good wine and that it would have to be jettisoned forthwith.

As always, settling back into a life afloat involved making minor adjustments. Resolving the matter of who was sleeping where was a subject of much discussion and one day Robin, with all his worldly belongings – a sleeping bag, a pillow and a copy of *Playboy* – changed bunks three times in the space of five minutes. Tony's nose started peeling again. My face burnt in the glare of the water-reflected sun. And Nick developed a heavy cold – for which I prescribed vitamin C!

Fred tried to run the engine, only to find he could not see the temperature gauge or rev counter. These were situated in a panel with a transparent door just near the steering wheel, very convenient for the smokers. This small

FACING PAGE
Above left: A severe gale on the nose for New Year (*photo:* Beat Güttinger).

Above right: Surfing under storm spinnaker.

Below: Seventy knots of wind at 60° south.

OVERLEAF
Riding big seas during a storm.

compartment was full of tobacco pouches, matches, cigarettes and tubes of sweets. 'Would you mind removing the confectionery shop?' Fred asked plaintively. 'Otherwise I won't be able to tell you when the engine's about to blow up.' Jacques and Beat removed their belongings, only to slip them back into the same spot five minutes later, for there was no other place which was both handy and watertight. They did, however, arrange their smoking equipment a little more tidily.

Sam pointed at Jacques, 'I saw you, Sooty!' Jacques was Sooty because he knocked his pipe out on the side deck and, according to Sam, deposited a mass of black ash on the side of *his* clean boat.

'British git,' replied Jacques, his soft French accent adding new dimensions to the words.

On the third day we threw a pot plant and some cut flowers over the side, all collected during our stay in Auckland. I also lost a hat in the same direction, although not intentionally. I managed to do this regularly every few thousand miles, so it was nothing unusual.

It was a long reach to the Chatham Islands. There was little sail-changing to be done and no exhausting spinnaker work, so it was a relaxing time. I took the opportunity to do some navigation to keep my hand in – but disgraced myself by not checking the error on the chronometer and putting us ten miles west of our position. It was not surprising that we passed a little closer to the Chatham Islands than we anticipated.

Just to the east of the islands lay the Date Line where we would put our clocks back twenty-four hours and have a second day with the same date, a very confusing idea until one remembered that we had got ahead of Greenwich Mean Time by twelve hours and were now adjusting our clocks to be twelve hours behind it. Thus, as we sailed on eastward and continued to put our clocks forward, we would slowly catch up with GMT again until we arrived back in England using the same time and date as everyone else.

We were due to cross the Date Line on the evening of the 30th December, but rather than have two 30th Decembers, which would be rather uninteresting, we postponed our date change until the next day which was, we had noticed, New Year's Eve. In this way we could have two celebrations. If we included the British New Year we could have three, and even five counting the French and Swiss. We soon discovered that most of the other yachts had the same idea and we arranged a radio schedule for midnight, local time, New Year's Eve Number One, to exchange toasts and good wishes. Only *Adventure* was planning a party the following night, a decision they must have regretted.

We had some inkling that bad weather was on the way from the news on the New Zealand radio. Their bulletins contained reports that the classic sailing event, the Sydney–Hobart Race, had been hit by a bad storm, forcing a third of the fleet to retire and even a few to sink. Bad weather should never be believed until it arrives, but we couldn't help noticing that the barometer was dropping downwards in something of a hurry. Our latitude was 46° south, well into the Roaring Forties again. Unless the storm had blown out, it was reasonable to assume that it was speeding across the Tasman Sea straight for

FACING PAGE
Beautiful but cold, a week from the Horn.

153

us. On the morning of New Year's Eve we picked up another news bulletin, reporting strong winds and driving rain across the South Island. It appeared that the bad weather was well on its way.

Looking at the sea and the sky, it was difficult to believe. We continued to close-reach in pleasant conditions, the wind remaining steady at Force 4. Our only concern was the rigging. Although we had retuned it in Auckland, the main mast was still falling off badly at the head and no amount of tightening of the shrouds seemed to bring it up. The problem lay in the intermediates which were the only shrouds we could not adjust at deck level. While the conditions were still moderate Tony ('we know you love it up there') Bertram went up to see if he could loosen them off. It was a terrible job, requiring the use of two hands and some heavy tools. In the end the bottlescrews proved to be too tight and Tony had to return to the deck, defeated, tired and a little shaky. It is said the modern metal mast can take a lot of punishment and, watching it bend sideways in a way it was never designed to bend, we hoped it was true.

Our New Year's Eve celebration was congenial but subdued. The advent of another year turned people's thoughts to the future and we talked about what we would do on our return. Robert and Robin thought they would return to their jobs. Nick wanted to have a serious go at his FRCS. Sam thought he might like to become a sailmaker – even though he reckoned he'd sewn enough sails to last him a lifetime. Far from turning us into a group of adventurers who dreamed of sailing on for ever, it seemed that a trip round the world had given everyone the ambition to stay firmly on dry land. Eve made no bones

It starts to blow up; the deck crew move forward for a sail change.

about the matter. 'I wasn't made for this life,' she said wearily, 'and I'm afraid it brings out the worst in me. *If* and *when* I go to sea again, it'll only be for the odd weekend!'

Only Tony and Beat talked excitedly about the sailing they would be doing the coming summer. They both hoped to crew on hot boats in round-the-buoys events and Beat was planning to enter the Round Britain Race in July. It was a love of racing that gave them their love of sailing and, as long as there was an exciting event in the offing, they wanted to be there taking part in it.

Jacques and I wanted to do some sailing too – but very gently and in no hurry. We were looking forward to getting our own *Gulliver G* back in the water and refitted for cruising. Then there was the house to decorate, all the photographs of the race for Jacques to develop and catalogue, a book to be written . . . the six months after the race would be very busy.

When we resumed our celebration half an hour before midnight, we were all half asleep and rather quiet. But once we got on the radio and listened to the noise and hullabaloo on the other yachts we soon regained our party spirits. Many toasts were drunk in many languages that evening and by midnight there were few people within 200 miles who were entirely sober.

The next day it began to blow from the south – just off the starboard bow. In one way we were quite pleased about this, for we reckoned to do well against the lighter boats in heavy weather. We were lying in a good position – as on the second leg, we had managed to do well in the first few days – and we expected to consolidate our position in a hard windward blow. *Disque d'Or* was a little to the north and behind, and that was where we wanted her to stay. By the second New Year's Eve night, it was blowing Force 7 from the south and the barometer was still low. All thoughts of a second celebration vanished as we battened down the hatches for a wet, windward slog. We had not had a hard windward blow since the first leg and we had almost forgotten what it was like. Now we began to remember with burning clarity. Someone wrote in the deck log, 'Pretty shitty, eh, Folks?' and that about summed it up. As a reply I wrote 'Think . . . it could be dead calm or blowing 125 knots. You lot just don't know when you're well off!' This impressed no-one. As the wind steadily increased through the night to Force 9, the boat became wetter and more uncomfortable, until it was difficult to sleep for the noise and hullabaloo. We shortened sail down to treble-reefed main and small jib topsail, but the boat was still going too fast. She was jumping off waves and landing with such a crash that those in the forward cabins were having a hard time staying in their bunks. After one spectacular crash, Sam was heard to say, 'Another mile gone. Sounds like we're backing over them now.' Every time the bows shuddered into a wave we feared that something would break and we decided we would have to shorten sail again, putting up the previously unused storm jib. This was one of the few sails we had kept from the original wardrobe. It looked good and strong and brand-new and we put it up with confidence.

Half an hour later, it ripped. My views on the sail loft that had made it were not very charitable. Storm jibs just do not rip – they should be built like fortresses. Yet this had proved to be as flimsy as a piece of silk.

We were now in a spot. There were no other sails we could put up. We were carrying a staysail and a reefed main, but our speed had fallen drastically. We put the staysail onto the main forestay and settled down to repairing the storm jib. Sam told me it would be no easy matter. Each layer of the sail cloth would have to be peeled back, fitted into place and resewn. It would take hours. There was nothing we could do but sit back and wait.

For the next eight hours we sat it out, our speed reduced to five or six knots, and the conditions getting worse as the seas built up. Everyone began to feel a little ill and even Jacques could not face his pipe. Eve sweated away at the sewing machine, handing over to Sam or Bumble when sickness overwhelmed her and she had to shoot up on deck. More comments appeared in the deck log; 'I think it might clear up and get wet', 'Still dry enough for a fag!' and 'I feel sorry for the next watch.' A tin of milk powder flew across the galley and exploded in a white sticky mess everywhere, finding its way behind the cooker, and into the lockers until it glued up the hinges.

Those of us who had been up on the foredeck were soaked and, on going below, found our bunks were little better. A tiny deck leak dripped straight on to the bunk where Jacques and I tried to grab the odd hour's sleep, wetting the pillows and the mattress. We rigged up an elaborate plastic sheet arrangement to deflect the drips, and it proved to be moderately successful – the moisture slid down the bulkhead and soaked the mattress from underneath instead of on top.

The wind showed no signs of moderating. On Chat Hour we heard that *Disque d'Or*'s leak had started again, which was not entirely surprising in view of the cursory repairs carried out in Auckland. *Condor* were worried about their mast which was too slim and flimsy for the boat. It was whipping back and forth so violently that they were frightened of losing it and had been forced to slow down. *GB II*'s mainsail track had been pulled out of the mast and they were unable to raise much mainsail. We did not hear from two of the boats at all, the beginning of a widespread attack of radio failures that would break out during the leg. Not for the last time I blessed our Marconi transmitter which was standing up to the punishment so well.

When steering we were forced to wear goggles and face masks to protect ourselves from the spray which flew across the deck like thousands of sharp hailstones. To prevent the whole deck crew from becoming wet and cold, only two would stay on deck, while the other two went below to dry out for a while. The sky was deep grey and the seas were high, with foaming white crests. It was exhilarating to steer, letting the boat climb the waves then flicking her nose up into a crest, to prevent her from being knocked sideways. Up and over, riding the great waves in the powerful machine, feeling the strength of the wind against the sails – I loved it, just as I have always loved bad weather. I was only sorry we couldn't go faster still.

Whenever I was about to go on deck in this kind of weather Jacques would give me a critical look to make sure I was wearing a safety harness. I found harnesses a blessed nuisance and hated wearing the things but, quite rightly, Jacques would often insist. It was not a matter of setting a good example – the others were extremely diligent about wearing theirs – but of fear. Jacques and I had a deep and horrifying terror of losing each other at sea. Falling overboard

Nick takes over the helm and the goggles (*photo:* Fred Dovaston).

is not a very nice way to go and the possibility of it happening made our blood run cold. It was bad enough for one of us to imagine losing the other, but the manner in which it would happen, the desperate feeling of helplessness as we would try to turn the boat around and search in the large, grey seas was extremely painful to contemplate. It was over the wearing of harnesses that Jacques and I had our only disagreements. I always feel as safe as houses on the deck of a boat and, while I could concede that a harness was necessary in really bad weather, it was difficult to agree as to where good weather ended and bad began!

It was difficult to sleep while the gale was blowing and when I went below for a rest I read Chris Bonington's account of his successful Everest expedition. It impressed me very much, not only because it was a good story well told, but because of the many and various difficulties the expedition had encountered – in organisation, in the climbing itself and in the leadership of such a mixed group of strong and varied personalities. It was interesting to read how Chris Bonington had solved all these complex problems and I was particularly fascinated by his solutions to the difficulties of leadership. The rest of the crew read the book over the next few weeks and were all equally impressed. The next time someone went up the mast, the first spreaders were referred to as Camp One and the deck as Base Camp.

The weather had gone from what Tony described as 'very average' to 'below average'. Now the barometer was falling further and I kept calling up from the chart table to ask if there was a visible change in the conditions. 'A marginal change,' Tony replied, 'but I'm not sure in which direction.'

I wrote in the deck log, 'The barometer's falling again – you ain't seen nothing yet!'

But I was wrong. A few hours later the barometer levelled off and at long last the wind began to moderate. The reply in the log – it was Sam's writing, of course – read, 'The barometer's fallen and we ain't seen nothing!'

Later he added the observation that it was 'an impudent little morning', and indeed it was. In the usual way of the sea we had only just put up the repaired storm jib when the wind moderated sufficiently to raise the Number Two topsail. However, it stayed at a lively Force 7 for a long time and water and spray continued to cover the decks. Below, the cabins were still running with condensation and damp and, to add to the feeling of discomfort, we slept in our wet clothes to avoid getting yet another set of dry clothes wet when we next went on deck. It was easier to sleep in wet clothes and dry them out a little in the process than to take wet clothes off and attempt to put them on again when going on deck. There are few things more unpleasant than donning wet clothes when they are cold and clammy.

Finally, the wind moderated to Force 4 and veered to the west and then to the north. With a sigh of relief we opened the hatches and aired our clothes. A watery sun came through the cloud and, although we were now at 54° south, it was warm enough to dry the boat out and take the worst of the moisture from our clothes. There is something wonderful about the aftermath of a gale, a feeling of contentment and relief that makes the simplest things particularly pleasurable. The tiny shafts of sunlight and the splashes of colour on the waves were a beautiful sight.

The next day we had a chance to try a new idea that we had heard about in Auckland. When chatting with the skipper of *Neptune*, he had told us how they had found a way to release their spinnaker from the guy and therefore the end of the pole by remote control. They did not need to ease the pole forward, nor let the guy fly through the pole end, the two conventional methods of going about the problem. They also boasted that their method was so efficient, they could leave a spinnaker up until the last hair-raising pre-broach moment and lower it instantly. At first we were a little sceptical about this magical method, but when it was described to us we began to see that it might work.

That day, when we hoisted the heavy spinnaker in a fresh westerly, we tried it, rigging up the necessary extra guy and looping a small piece of cord through the trigger of the snap shackle in the way we had been told. To our amazement and then our delight it worked. By tightening up one guy and easing off the other, Bang! The spinnaker suddenly flew away from the end of the pole and could be safely gathered in under the main boom. It was so quick and easy we were taken aback. And, like all clever ideas, it was so very simple.

From then on, we rigged the pole to quick-release whenever we had a heavy spinnaker up – that is, when there was a stiff breeze and possibility of squalls and therefore broaches. At every opportunity we would try the system out and for the most part it worked extremely well. We were caught out a couple of times, especially in those early days before we understood the limitations of the system. On one occasion we tried to release the spinnaker when the pole was well forward, something it just would not do. We managed to fight off a broach while we lowered it in the conventional way, but it was a near thing.

As we ventured further south it became dank, foggy and cold. Though the nights were becoming even shorter, the few hours of darkness froze our hands and numbed our feet. A few more days of southerly sailing and there would be no night at all – just as well because we were fast approaching iceberg country.

It was difficult to get a good idea of our position because *Disque d'Or* had now lapsed into radio silence, almost certainly due to a faulty transmitter. We did not hear from *King's Legend* either. Much later in Rio, they admitted that the radio had been subjected to a very unfortunate accident. When the boat had given a heavy roll, the contents of the aft loo had flown across the boat and soaked the radio, not guaranteed to bring out the best in even the most robust sets. *B & B Italia* was also off the air, while some of the other boats were having trouble in making themselves heard.

Pen Duick, the newcomer to the fleet, was getting in contact every few days, not bad considering that Eric Tabarly was known to dislike radios and other gadgets. *Pen Duick* was doing very well, ahead of *Condor* and vying with *GB II* for the lead. It was on 6th January, four days after the gale, that the thunderbolt struck and we got caught in the middle of the ensuing furore. At Chat Hour it was necessary to relay messages up and down the fleet because we were already well spread out. From behind, *Adventure* made contact with us and, unheard by nearly all the other boats, relayed a devastating telegram from the race organisers – *Pen Duick* was disqualified. There was no mention of exotic penalties or extra time penalties or any of the normal measures one

Dank, misty, and cold as we venture south.

would expect for minor rule infringements – it was a bald, final, disqualification. The telegram was, of course, addressed to *Pen Duick* and it was now our job to pass the message on to her – a moment we did not enjoy.

To understand the outcry that swept the fleet and the whole of France, it is necessary to appreciate that Eric Tabarly is a national hero in his native land, having been awarded the Légion d'Honneur and other such accolades. The reaction of the other boats was first bewilderment and then indignation. The French boats said some angry words about unfair decisions, biased committees and some even threatened to withdraw from the race. However, this was nothing compared to the outcry in France. Strong, emotional and sometimes scandalous accusations were bandied about – *Pen Duick* had been disqualified because she was winning; the British boats were so jealous that they had brought about the disqualification; Eric was being victimised, and so on. One paper even reported that the British yacht *ADC Accutrac* had been chosen to deliver the message as the committee had not dared deliver it direct.

All this was nonsense, of course. We eventually discovered that the committee had been forced to disqualify *Pen Duick* after the international body had decided she should never have had a rating certificate in the first place, and certainly could not have one now. As to the telegram, we had merely relayed it as a favour, as did all the boats when requested to by a shore station.

Pen Duick continued to race nevertheless, and the rest of us considered her to be another competitor just as before. The discussions could wait until Rio.

As it became progressively colder, we put on more clothing – long silk underwear, woolly longjohns, polar suits, sweaters and Puffa jackets. On our heads we wore balaclavas and on our feet a pair of thick socks and then boots. Even so, I always had cold feet and, on turning in, would make Jacques scream by placing them against his relatively warm feet, until I could get to sleep. John had cold feet problems too and would dance up and down the deck for hours, trying to persuade some circulation into them. We decided his blood had got thin from spending all his time in the West Indian sun.

However, the cold was not unpleasant and we were able to stay on deck for long periods of time without freezing up. Steering always made us warm, particularly when we had a spinnaker up, although this was less often than we expected. The wind pattern was giving us less running and more reaching and windward work than on the previous leg. However, this provided plenty of variety and activity, so we did not complain. At the handover of the watch one day someone came on deck and asked, 'What's been happening?'

'Got half an hour to spare and I'll tell you, old mate,' came the reply. Sometimes the wind shifted so quickly the watch would finish a sail change only to start another.

There were odd, quiet moments when we would recount our Most Embarrassing Experience Ever, or some other such riveting subject. Fred, having run out of stories, would recount seafaring yarns or tales of Glaston Dock, where he used to live. Sometimes one story would become so involved that Fred could spin it out to last a whole watch, picking up the threads of the tale between sail changes.

160

A twinkle in his eye, John would still tell us how things were done on his own *Tangaroa*. We had no idea of real sailing, he said, until we tried a boat with carpets, soft covers, hot showers and a barbecue over the stern.

Despite the many subjects available, conversation at the saloon table always seemed to get down to basics. One day Jacques announced that our talk was getting far too lavatorial and that he couldn't stand it any more, particularly at meal times. Everyone murmured assent – then started talking about their stomach ailments, spots and other horrors. In an attempt to be reasonable Jacques threatened to throw bread, catapult custard and eventually to eat elsewhere. When this failed, he resorted to new tactics and started to sing loud French songs whenever the conversation turned to basics.

For a week after the southerly gale we plodded south-east, going further into the depths of the Southern Ocean. Out of the Forties and into the Fifties, entering the most isolated stretch of ocean in the world. There were no islands here, nor ships, only the cold, icy sea encompassing the frozen Antarctic continent 1,000 miles away. The occasional albatross circled the boat and swooped across our wake. Sometimes we saw smaller seabirds, but often there would be nothing.

At the fifty-eighth latitude, the fog, mist and cold reminded me of the Grand Banks of Newfoundland in the North Atlantic, another area of icebergs and cold waters. After two weeks at sea we had not yet spotted icebergs, but the water temperature was dropping rapidly and had now reached 3°C. The air was taking on a chill that made our breath steam and our noses turn red. Someone (Sam) wrote in the log, 'Do you know any brass welders?'

The mist and cloud made navigation difficult and without any sun we could only estimate our position. This did not matter for the odd day or so but after a while we became anxious for a definite fix, not so much to determine our position in the ocean, but to find out what kind of runs we were achieving.

On Chat Hour, *GB II* reported seeing three icebergs and gave us their positions, while *Condor* reported having passed two more. I replied to Rob James on *GB II,* giving him our position and saying that, although we were well south, we had seen nothing. At the very moment I spoke there was a shriek from the deck and a clamouring of noise and excitement. Someone put his nose down the hatch and yelled 'Icebergs!'

'Hello, Rob,' I said over the radio. 'About what I just said. I'll just change that. We've got them here, too.' With which I leapt up on deck to have a look. They were magnificent. Tall, angular and brilliant white. There were two of them about two miles apart, both large and both solid. Fortunately we were going to pass clear of them without having to alter course. The only danger would be to leeward of the bergs, where we might run into bergy bits and growlers. We kept a sharp look out but the only growlers we saw were very close to the main bergs.

As we drew abreast of these white mountains, Robert and John, who had disappeared down below a few minutes earlier, suddenly shot on deck wearing nothing but towels around their waists. 'We're tough and hearty!' they cried and pretended to wind hard on a winch. 'We don't mind the cold!' By this time their teeth were chattering and they rushed up and down the deck to get warm.

We sight our first
icebergs – Robert
and John show us
how tough and
hearty they are.

For five minutes these two hearty Antarctic explorers kindly posed for photographs then, their heartiness evaporated, shot below as rapidly as they had come up.

For a week after that, we saw two or three icebergs every day, all of them magnificent. One was shaped like a giant ice-cream wedge with ripples of ice down the sides. Another had a tall, thin finger at one end which slowly broke away from the main berg as we watched. For one moment it balanced precariously in the air, then it fell in a mass of spray and turned turtle, its round, smooth, underwater section showing watery white above the surface. To the side of it a scattering of bergy bits appeared and we guessed the long finger had broken up.

At nearly 60° south in mid-summer, the nights were almost non-existent. A faint greyness came over the sky during the long dusk and dawn, while the three-hour night was never darker than an English twilight. Often the sky was clear to the south and we would see a rich, blood-red sunset move across the southern sky from the south-west to the south-east, to become a yellow-gold sunrise a few hours later. The icebergs could be seen clear and cold on the east horizon even at midnight, so we had no fears about collision. Only fog could create a hazard and, while it did become misty from time to time, the visibility never deteriorated to less than a mile.

The long days without darkness also made steering much easier. Having decided the course we wanted, we would point the boat as close to the course as possible – when downwind we might only be able to make a course 20° either side of the ideal, because it was never possible to sail dead downwind. We would then trim the sails to that course, and settle down to steer by the wind direction indicator, keeping the wind at the right angle to ensure we were getting the most speed out of the sails. An occasional glance at the compass would reveal if the wind had changed. Daylight always helped steering tremendously because the helmsman could also see the horizon. Watching the horizon would tell the helmsman which way the boat was tilting and therefore the way she was about to veer. He could then correct the veer before it happened.

As we went south there was only one major problem – lack of wind. Sometimes it blew a fresh breeze of Force 5 or so, but all too often it fell to Force 2 or 3. Although we had received no news from some of the other boats because of their radio problems, we did know that most of those up at 55° south were getting plenty of wind. They had a greater distance to cover at that latitude, but their extra speed seemed to outweigh it, and they were catching us up. *Condor* was on roughly the same latitude as us, about 60° south, but she was now losing out badly to *Pen Duick*, who had stayed in the mid-Fifties. It seemed we had taken the less windy route again! However, we still had a long way to go to the Horn and anything could happen. As before, it would not be worth changing tactics at this stage so we would just have to sit it out – and hope.

It was about this time that Robin discovered the barometer. He suddenly realised that if it went up or down rapidly, the wind was probably going to blow, but if it stayed more or less level, then the wind was probably going to drop. He became fascinated by the instrument and would look at it every time he passed the chart table. Whenever it showed a sign of change he would come and tell us. I'm afraid we all laughed at him and from then on Robin would look at the barometer secretively and keep his comments to himself. On top of this Robin was still ribbed about his appetite, his surreptitious second helpings and midnight feasts. But he always took funny comments in good heart. Inevitably, some people suffered more ribbing than others but it was always friendly and, since the favourite victim changed fairly regularly, it was spread over the whole crew.

After sixteen days at sea, we found ourselves pushed down to more than 61° south – and decided that was quite far enough. There was no sign of any more wind and the temperature was dropping even further. We drew a course due east until such time as we must head north-east for the Horn, still 1,800 miles away. We were not surprised to find that we were the most southerly of the yachts. Even *Debenhams* was further north than we were – one sortie into the pack ice had obviously been enough for her.

While the winds were moderate – in the Southern Ocean, anything under Force 6 – we did repairs and chores. Never had the boat looked so clean and well scrubbed below. Beat went up to Camp Four, the mast lights, to try to replace a bulb, but the light fitting had corroded onto the aluminium mast and he could not gain access. I sweated away at the radio, trying to make contact with Wellington. Over and over again I would transmit our call sign, Two Oscar Victor November, until I almost spoke it in my sleep. I would try to make contact at any time of the day and night, but often without success. Even when I got through and Wellington tuned me in and found a line to London,

The standby and off-watch crew relax below (*photo:* Beat Güttinger).

the quality of the transmission would sometimes deteriorate so rapidly that we would have to abandon the call. Capital Radio were now used to taping whatever they could get, and broadcasting only those fragments that were more or less audible. We could not see if the Southern Lights were particularly active for it was always overcast, but since we were now in an area of 40° variation and fairly near the Magnetic Pole, it seemed probable that magnetic activity was the culprit.

The heater also kept us busy. It continued to smoke and spread fumes through the boat although Fred had thoroughly overhauled it in Auckland. At first Fred could not believe it was not exhaust fumes being sucked back into the cabins from the flue and tried closing all the hatches. He was finally convinced the problem was in the system itself when everyone rushed up from below choking and enveloped in smoke.

Just for old times' sake, the starcut ripped again. This time it was the fault of the helmsman who let the boat come up broadside to the wind just as we had the pole forward and the sheet hard in, ready to lower it. Soon the sewing machine was going full speed again, Sam's head lowered over the rapidly moving needle in close concentration. I asked him if the sail had any strength left in it at all.

'Oh yes,' replied Sam, 'It'll be fine as long as you put it up in its bag.'

On the seventeenth day the wind swung round to the south-east and it became bitterly cold. It started to sleet, then hail, and being almost close-

164

hauled we had to wear face masks to protect our faces from the sharp, dagger-like hailstones as they hit us like bullets. Even when facing away from the wind it was wise to wear a mask to prevent one's face from freezing, so icy was the wind. At midnight the mainsail ripped across the top, a result of chafe, and we had to take the sail off for repair. It was impossible to touch metal for more than a minute without losing all feeling in one's hands and then suffering terrible pain, so it was a long, slow job to remove the sail from the mast track and the boom. Although we wore gloves as much as possible, these got soaking wet very quickly and anyway had to be removed to handle the gear effectively.

While the old mainsail was being repaired we put the new main up, an equally laborious and difficult job. Fred, as diligent about the filming as ever, appeared in the middle of the performance with camera and lights, followed by Bumble who was to operate the sound. Together they stumbled about the deck, linked by an umbilical cord of cable, recording the whole scene. By the time they returned below they and most of the equipment were soaked. But Fred reckoned he'd got some good shots, making it all worthwhile.

Throughout the night the deck crew took it in turns to go below and thaw themselves out and, come the change of watch, they turned in with relief, anxious for sleep and warmth. Hot-bunking had tremendous advantages if the crew were quick to jump into their sleeping bags – having been vacated a few minutes earlier, they were still warm. There were fewer complaints about other people's bedding, clothing and nasty personal habits, too. Everyone wore so many clothes both on deck and asleep that unwashed bodies were well camouflaged. Only when Nick announced he was going to hot-bunk with X, known as 'the greatest wind machine after the jet engine', did Robert say, 'You'll be needing a mask and flippers, mate.'

By the next morning the wind was up to fifty knots, Force 10, from the south.

'What's the barometer doing?' I asked Robin.

'Still falling,' he replied, staring at the instrument. 'More wind?'

Indeed the wind was not likely to moderate yet. Already the boat was taking a lot of punishment, the heavy beam seas rearing up and hitting her hard on the side so that she rolled and yawed in a mass of spray. As we worked to reduce the sail area, water would shoot over the deck, sweeping us off our feet. After a large wave had hit, we would automatically look around the deck to make sure everyone else was still there. The water was so cold that our hands froze as they touched the ropes, the winches or the sails and each dribble that seeped down our necks and into our clothing felt like ice.

At midday the barometer started to climb rapidly. If the pattern ran to form the wind would, if anything, blow even harder. Since it was already blowing Force 10, I wondered what was on its way. I watched the large, grey seas with their white, torn crests and listened to the wind howling in the rigging, and thought here at last was the real Southern Ocean. This was what we had come to find and sail through; this beautiful, powerful, magnificent ocean. As I watched I felt no fear, only simple admiration.

CHAPTER 10

Storms, Squalls and Cape Horn

The wind shrieked and roared in the rigging like an angry demon. The grey sea was now almost white as the wind tore the wave crests into spume that flew down the slopes of the waves in long, ragged streaks. It was blowing up to seventy knots, Force 12. Fortunately, the wind was slowly veering to the west of south so that we were able to take the seas aft of the beam and lay our course. At 0900 we fought to lower the mainsail, fearful that it might rip despite being reefed well down. We then raised the storm trisail. The operation took an hour, so slowly did we have to work and so cold were our fingers.

From the grey south-western horizon heavy, tawny yellow clouds appeared from time to time. These clouds, their wispy fingers reaching down to the sea, would overtake and envelop us in a flurry of driving snow, reducing the visibility to under a mile. As we rushed on into the yellow murk we were unable to see much except for the white, corrugated wave slopes before us. One cloud, darker than the rest, enveloped us for many minutes until we saw, silhouetted against a tiny arc of light that glowed white and gold on the black northern horizon, a massive iceberg. First black against the brilliant arc, then lit dull silver white by a shaft of watery sun, the berg stood solid and impenetrable against the onslaught of the sea. Waves broke against the massive white walls, sending sheets of silver spray hundreds of feet into the air, almost over the ice mountain itself.

The seas slowly built up. They were still long and well spaced, but now higher, with sharper crests. We turned *ADC* slightly north to take the seas on the quarter and prevent a violent corkscrewing motion. By 1400 the wind had veered further to the west-south-west and we were able to lay a course due east again. For a while the change in the wind quietened the sea so that our downwind run was a little less wild. We boomed out a jib and surfed down the long, white waves, the snow and wind strong and cold against our backs.

In the afternoon we huddled round the radio, keen to hear how the other boats were faring in this wind. To our amazement we found that neither the boats ahead of us nor the boats behind had a wind anywhere near storm force. Ahead, *Condor* had head winds – possibly the same south-easterly we had encountered at the beginning of the blow – and behind *Adventure* reported only fifteen to twenty knots of wind from the south-west. Extraordinary though it was, the storm seemed to be a local affair, probably born further south and only now sweeping northwards. Again, there was no news from the boats we suspected of having radio troubles, and we transmitted to them 'blind', asking them to call us on their emergency transmitters. We heard nothing but, although two of the yachts concerned – *King's Legend* and *Disque d'Or* – were the ones who had leak problems, we felt there was nothing to worry about. Both were good, strong boats and both had suffered radio problems before.

The wild corkscrewing motion soon affected Eve and Robin, and the two of them were laid low with seasickness again. Eve's queasy stomach was not helped by having to spend hours bending over the sewing machine trying to repair the old mainsail we had ripped some days previously. Down below, it was as damp as before. Optimistically, everyone hung clothes up over their bunks to dry but it was little use. The clothes were salty and moist and would remain so as long as it was wet and cold. Having damp skin all the time, there was a bad epidemic of spotty botty and cold sores. Some of us had developed bad chilblains. John lost the feeling in the end of his toes while I gradually developed numb fingertips – cold injuries which were to take many weeks to mend. On deck we would hit, rub and pound the feeling into our fingers and toes but they would become ice-cold all the same, then hurt until we gasped with pain.

At the height of the storm two cups of freshly made coffee leapt off the stove when the gimbals were unable to keep up with the boat's motion. At the same time the loos became almost unusable because the water inlets were so often out of the water. In the cockpit, conditions were 'below average' as Tony described them. Water shot up our sleeves and down our necks as large waves broke against our quarter. All was dampness and cold.

Yet the sailing was exhilarating and, despite the constant wetting we were receiving, we were enjoying ourselves. Steering was a matter of lining the boat up to take a crest as kindly as possible, then letting her roar off down the long slope of the wave. Helming was demanding but not difficult. However it would become harder if the wind stayed at seventy knots for much longer. The seas were building up again and the crests curving more steeply. It was best for the helmsman if he didn't look behind – now and then it seemed the boat would never lift to the large waves. Yet, as long as the helmsman lined her up properly, she always did.

For eighteen hours the storm blew and *ADC* rushed eastward in a flurry of snow, wind and white seas. Then, almost imperceptibly, the wind began to ease. After another three hours it was falling fast. This was the most dangerous time of all – with the wind down to Force 5 and a large, floppy sea running, we could easily be capsized or pooped. It was imperative to pile on as much sail as possible to maintain our speed and stay with the waves. We put up a large jib, then a small spinnaker, although it was difficult to control the boat in the twisting seas. A couple of peaked waves broke against the quarter and drenched the helmsman but, by three the next morning, the worst was over and we could afford to relax.

Even then our difficulties were not quite over. The wind swung round to the south again and brought freezing temperatures straight from the Antarctic. Never before had we been so cold. The wind cut through small gaps in our clothing and froze our wrists and necks, while our noses felt like blocks of ice. If this was summer in the Southern Ocean, we wondered what winter must be

Sixty knots plus
and we run fast
before the waves.

like! Admittedly we were further south than sailing vessels normally used to go. The clippers would stay up in the Forties or, if the weather was good and it was mid-summer, they might venture down to the mid-Fifties. The singlehanded adventurers and the yachts in the previous Whitbread Race had all stayed further north – and perhaps they had good reason. Nevertheless, the southern route was shorter and, with a long way still to go to the Horn, it might prove the faster.

In addition to the cold-injured hands and feet, salt sores and chapped lips we suffered, we now had cuts and abrasions that would not heal. On hands even the smallest cut would stay open, to be knocked time and time again on winches or sharp fittings until it seemed they would never close. Hands swelled until the skin cracked and hardened. Knuckles were red and sore.

While it was so cold only two of us remained on deck at one time, one steering, the other ready to summon the others from below should it be necessary. At breakfast-time one day John and I were on deck, waiting for the first two members of the next watch to appear from the companion-way. We were very cold and looking forward to getting below for a mug of hot tea. When there was no sign of life at five to eight, we hatched a plot. Putting the wheel-lock on, we left the helm and balanced the boat with the sails so that she sailed in a straight line by herself. At eight o'clock precisely, we opened the hatch and went below – leaving no-one on deck. At the bottom of the companion-way we met Tony and Beat, struggling into layers of oilskins, neck towels, and gloves.

'Morning,' we said nonchalantly.

'Morning,' they replied.

'Very cold. Wind about fifteen knots from the south. Full main, mizzen and Number Two genoa,' I told Tony.

'Take your time,' added John. 'Nothing's happening up there.'

'Who's on deck?' Beat asked.

'A very good question,' we replied, bursting into giggles. Tony laughed nervously, then went pale. Pulling on his last glove, he shot up the companion-way, looked around and shouted over his shoulder, 'Jesus! There's nobody!'

Beat bolted up the companion-way behind him and the two of them rushed to the wheel to check that all was well. John and I had been keeping an eye on the boat speed read-out at the chart table and, seeing it had stayed constant, knew the boat was still on course.

A few minutes later, Tony put his head down the companion-way. 'Blimey,' he laughed. 'You really conned us there. And with all these growlers around!'

'Come on,' I replied, 'growlers indeed! One tiny iceberg miles away and you give us growlers. Good try, Tony!'

'You mean, you didn't know?' One look at Tony's face, which could never stay straight if he was joking, and we knew there were growlers. Going up on deck again I saw small white pieces of ice floating about the boat. 'Ooops, deary,' I murmured. The laugh was definitely on us!

That relatively quiet day also revealed a problem. The engine, which had refused to start during the storm, was not responding to Fred's expert care. At first he thought the problem was air in the fuel system, but now the starter

170

motor was refusing to turn over. Fred removed the starter and took it apart, to discover it had burnt out. Painstakingly Fred unwound the thick copper wire of the outer coil and reinsulated it. The next day he had the motor assembled, ready for another try. It gave half a turn and then burnt out again. This time the inner coil was black and charred. Jacques suggested that the engine itself might be seized, causing the starter to burn out, but Fred thought it was just a question of reinsulating the starter properly. So began a saga which lasted for the whole of the next week, all the way to the Horn. For three days we ran a kind of factory, one person cutting the wire, another insulating it, another soldering the end connections, and me weaving the wire back into its intricate pattern. It was a mammoth job, but a very absorbing one. After three days we tried again. It burnt out.

Next, Fred rewired the thing with ready-insulated, but rather thin wire. It burnt out. Finally, Fred took a look at the engine and discovered one cylinder full of water and the whole thing seized. Either water had got past the water trap in the exhaust during the storm, or the exhaust-cooling water was leaking into the engine. Whatever it was, we decided not to attempt to start the engine until Rio. Fred filled the cylinders up with oil to stop them corroding, and we were back to the energy-conservation routine. At least the outside temperature was keeping the freezer cold and there was a good chance of the meat lasting ten days or so.

It snowed several times a day and the deck was often covered in a thick carpet of white. Snowball fights were very popular with everyone. One morning John came up the companion-way with a thermometer to take the air temperature for his weather report. 'Do you want a weather report?' asked Tony.

Icy winds and snow at 60° south.

171

'Er, yes, please,' said John uncertainly.

'Here you are, then.' And Tony thrust a large snowball down John's neck.

I too got taken in by the snow. Coming up on deck soon after we had raised the heavy spinnaker one day, I suddenly yelled, 'Let's get it down!' I could see daylight between the panels – the sail was coming apart in at least four different places! Only after everyone looked and laughed did I realise that I was seeing snow sitting in layers above the seams, and not daylight at all.

When the wind blew from the west again the temperature rose a little but the weather brought a series of vicious squalls. Now 900 miles from the Horn, it seemed as if we were already under its influence. As a squall hit the wind would leap from ten to forty knots over the deck and we would be enveloped in snow or hail. We ripped the starcut again. We were on the point of broaching a dozen times a day. Nevertheless we hung on to the spinnaker in the worst of the gusts, hoping we could control the boat until the squall had passed. The alternative was to lower the spinnaker every time a squall hit, which would lose us a lot of time and mean lowering and repacking the spinnaker at least once an hour. The boats to the north, *Tielsa, Disque d'Or, 33 Export* and *Gauloises,* were all rushing for the Horn. We might just hold them if we pushed really hard. Now that we were nearing the end of the fast downwind stage and only four days from leaving the Southern Ocean, we were in no mood to hold back. It was all or nothing. We had the confidence to hold the spinnakers in the gusts and when we broached we would shrug if off and get back on course as soon as possible. Bumble, carried away by the excitement, cried her usual 'More sail, more sail!' She was a girl after my own heart. I often horrified the others by wanting to put up more sail. I had a great ally in John who was also keen to press hard. Tony and Beat were a little more moderate but, once the maximum sail was up, they would steer with a look of wild excitement on their faces. Controlling the boat during each squall became a personal challenge for the helmsman and the closer to the limit we sailed, the more we enjoyed the wild ride. Nick and Robert were also enthusiastic helmsmen, while Jacques was the careful one who quite rightly tempered our enthusiasm with common sense and pleas for moderation.

Now and then we got caught out. In one powerful gust of fifty knots we broached and didn't come out of it. Neither could we get the quick release to work because the pole had strained so far forward. Tony rushed to the bow and stood ready on the pulpit to release the sail in the normal way, but it would be no easy matter to let the pole forward. The guy, under the most fantastic pressure, had to be eased out on the winch. I had developed my patent system for doing this, guaranteed not to remove your fingers, but still a bit hairy. I would take the tail of the guy off the cleat, make it up again a few inches further down the tail, and then stand clear. With a loud crack like a rifle shot, the guy would shoot out by the amount I had eased off the tail, and this notwithstanding the five full turns on the winch barrel. Once the guy was far enough forward Tony reached up and released the sail. In such a wind it took five people to pull the spinnaker in under the main.

Of course, as soon as the sail was safely down the wind dropped – so we repacked the spinnaker and put it up again.

This hard, fast sailing was the most exhilarating we had yet encountered. Gone were our old fears of broaching to leeward, for we never repeated the disastrous occurrence of the second leg. Gone, too, were most of our worries about broaching to windward. We had the spinnaker trimming and handling down to such a fine art that most broaches were minor affairs, soon controlled and causing no damage. With so many miles behind us and so few to go to the Horn, we had lost much of our awe of this isolated ocean. We were reckless, maybe, but those days were incomparable for a feeling of excitement and achievement.

One wild night Tony came off watch and, grinning quietly, said, 'Call me when you need the bolt cutters.' The possibility of losing the mast and having to cut it away was hopefully remote – but off watch both Jacques and I kept our boots standing in our oilskin trousers beside the bunk, ready to receive feet and rush on deck at a moment's notice. With the mast and rigging under such strain, anything could happen.

The wear and tear on the gear was terrible. Every other day the guys had to be shortened and rebound where they passed through the poles. Shackles broke under the sheer load of the spinnakers. The wheel and rudder started to develop some play in their bearings. The mainsail was chafing against the shrouds again. In a race against time we repaired what we could and patched up the rest. Every time we broached, the main boom buried itself in the water and the vangs, which held the boom down, broke. On the previous leg,

For some, helming was both exciting and enjoyable – but it was best not to look behind.

173

The remorseless wear and tear necessitated constant repair work.

broaching had proved very expensive in the rope and blocks that made up the vangs, but now we had tied small strops between the block and the toerail. When we broached these would break and not the vang. If they had not broken and the vangs had held, the mainsail would have been ripped to pieces as it was dragged through the water.

'Iceberg two points off the starboard bow!' cried Robin one day.

'Yer what?' asked Nick. 'What's two points, Robin?'

'Er. . . well, just off the bow, you know.'

'Okay,' laughed Nick. 'Two points off the bow it is.'

From then on, the crew took delight in asking Robin how many points off the bow an iceberg, an albatross or a cloud might be. However, as we inched northwards towards 58° south, the icebergs became less and less frequent. It was just as well for we had enough to worry about – the wind became more and more violent, squalling from ten to forty-five knots and changing direction by 50° in front of a cloud, and then swinging back after it had passed. It was crazy sailing as we put spinnakers up, took them down, gybed them and then broached with them. 'Wow!' read the log.

Family life below had reached its usual stage after nearly four weeks at sea. The routine of eating, sleeping and watch-keeping was so embedded in our subconscious that we followed it automatically. At the same time some of us became a little ratty. Sam reacted like an old woman when Eve suggested that, for once during their standby, he might like to take the uncomfortable berth in the saloon and give up the bunk in which he managed to stay all through the trip. Sullenly, Sam agreed and stomped off with all his bedding – his two sheepskins, his sleeping bags, his pillow and his rug, tutting and blowing through his mouth as he carefully rearranged it all in the saloon. Eve too was showing signs of strain, rising to every bait anyone put in her path. Nick was an expert at getting a rise out of Eve and they would badger each other continuously. Worried that it might develop into a bad situation, I suggested one of them might like to change watch. However, they were horrified at the idea. Both swore they adored each other and their little contretemps – neither wanted to change watch. What a suggestion!

Everyone had fallen into their old habits. Robert was lively, funny – and always late on watch. Jacques was as worried as ever about being overcanvassed and pushing the boat too hard. I nagged everyone about packing sails and putting them away. And Bumble shrieked with disbelief when she found dirty pans in the galley every single morning. This was the result of a system that didn't work. Leftovers were left in the pans on the stove for people to pick at during the long, cold night watches. Whoever finished the contents of a pan had then to wash it up. Being extremely crafty, the secret eaters would consume everything except one small mouthful, leaving the washing-up for someone else. Of course the last mouthful became eminently resistible to everyone and, lo and behold, all the pans would be there, dirty and unwashed, in the morning. After so many months together, the twelve of us knew each other as well as any member of our own families. We knew each other's foibles and weaknesses, each pet irritation and dislike. And, as in most families, we tolerated them with good grace.

Six hundred miles from the Horn, there were two great questions. Would we beat *Tielsa* and the other boats to the great headland? And would we arrive in time for Sam's birthday? Sam had no doubt about it, the 18th January it would be and he would like cake, champagne and a special five-course supper please.

By the 17th January it looked as though we would indeed make it by the next day and, more important, in daylight – it would be disappointing to pass the Horn during the ever-increasing hours of darkness. The overcast, squally weather had prevented John from getting any sun or star sights for several days and we had been running on dead reckoning, just when we most needed an accurate position. Fortunately, as if in answer to our prayers, several breaks started to appear in the clouds late in the morning and John, Jacques and I managed to get several sun sights over the space of three hours. When we had plotted a position we were hardly surprised to find that we were going to have island trouble again. The Diego Ramirez Islands, sixty miles south-west of the Horn, were dead ahead. Although the islands were small and closely grouped we knew that, if our past experience was anything to go by, we would find them straight across our path.

The weather remained as squally and wild as ever. The temperature had risen, however, and the snow was slowly turning to sleet, hail and even rain. We carried spinnakers as much as possible to maintain a high speed and reach the Horn in daylight the next day. No sooner had we raised one spinnaker than we had to gybe it or put up another. Inside our oilskins we sweated and glowed with heat as we winched and hauled on the lines. Spinnakers disappeared down the hatch for repacking, came up again carefully stopped in elastic bands and were put up again. Now that the sun was breaking through, the beautiful, rolling seas were illuminated blue-grey, turning dark gunmetal grey streaked with white as each squall came over. It was not difficult to see the squalls coming. Behind, the blue sky would darken as a heavy, black cloud came skimming over the sea towards us. Underneath there would be a grey blurr of rain or snow reaching down to a mass of white as the waves were churned up by the gale -force winds beneath. When in doubt about lowering the spinnaker, we hung on to it, and often found ourselves surfing along out of control in forty-five knots of true wind, Force 9.

At eleven the next morning we sighted the Diego Ramirez Islands. They were dead ahead. To avoid them, a gybe or a long detour would have to be necessary, so we decided to go straight through the middle of the islands, using a well-charted channel. Eve came up on deck as we approached the mile-wide gap between the islands but, looking to starboard, did not realise she was seeing only half the islands. 'Which gap are we going through?' she asked, eyeing the mass of small jagged rocks and islets with horror.

'Oh, that one there,' I said, pointing at a minute and highly dangerous gap.

Eve's mouth dropped open and she stared at me in disbelief. Only when she looked round and saw the other half of the island group safe to port did she realise we were going to survive the next half hour. Putting a hand to her heart, she sighed, rolled her eyes and told us we were rotten skunks. Tony also came up a few minutes later, unaware that we were anywhere near land, and received a severe shock when he saw the towering, moss-green cliffs just a few hundred yards away.

As we left the islands behind, some real Cape Horn weather came up. The wind increased to a steady gale and the sky became overcast with low, grey clouds. The colour of the sea changed dramatically from grey-blue to a translucent pale green. Most noticeable of all, however, were the seas themselves. They became shorter and steeper, their slopes angled so that they reared up behind the boat like ice-green walls. We could sense we were nearing the Horn.

As the visibility diminished I asked the helmsman to alter course slightly northward, so that we could be sure of seeing the Horn. The wind had become too much for the storm spinnaker and we took it down, putting a boomed-out jib in its place. Without the distractions of the spinnaker, we spent our time peering out to port, looking for signs of land. As we marked the miles off on the chart and realised we must soon be there, Bumble appeared in the hatch with Sam's birthday cake, followed by Robert with two bottles of champagne.

The first thing I saw was the vague suggestion of land abeam then, as Jacques and I stood on the foredeck staring ahead, we saw a shadowy, grey outline of a giant cliff some five miles away. The clouds swept in again and it was lost but, a few minutes later, we saw the giant cliff again, the unmistakeable craggy shape of Cape Horn. Jacques and I hugged each other, too overcome to speak, then stood and stared again. When one place has been the subject of so many legends and myths it is difficult to believe you are looking at it with your own eyes. The rest of the crew came to stare too, then

176

Robert opened the champagne and the silence was broken by Sam.

Cape Horn at last.

'I told you we'd get 'ere on me birthday! Now where's this 'ere cake. If you lot think you're gettin' any, you're in for a big surprise.' There was an ugly scramble for the cake, a cry of, 'Now, children, this'll only end in tears!' and our celebration began. Everyone posed for photographs and, when the light improved for a few minutes, we took some close-ups of Cape Horn. Wondering how close to the cliffs we could safely pass I ambled down to the chart table, and quickly shot back on deck to ask for a very hasty gybe – we had gone in so close that we were in danger of running into some submerged rocks that ran half a mile out from land. It would have been no joke to have been shipwrecked on Cape Horn – although it would certainly have been historic.

As we sped away from the Horn, the weather closed in again and we had our last sight of the jagged crag in its lonely position at the tip of the world.

On Chat Hour that night we heard that *Tielsa, Disque d'Or* and *Neptune* had slipped round ahead of us but it did not detract from our feeling of achievement. Behind us were several of our old adversaries, *King's Legend, Gauloises* and *33 Export,* so there was every reason to be pleased. *King's Legend* and *33 Export* rounded together, racing neck and neck and so close that they almost collided when one of them broached. *Gauloises* was only a

FACING PAGE
Above: A fast reach north of the Falklands.

Below: Rio at last, in time for the Carnival.

177

Sam's birthday presents: the Horn and a chocolate cake.

few hours behind us and lived up to her nickname of the Blue Submarine by nose-diving into one of the steep Cape Horn waves, doing a violent leeward broach, and bending both her spinnaker pole and her main mast. It did not, of course, prevent her from continuing to race flat out. She was leading the leg on handicap and was not about to give up the prize.

Pen Duick had been the first round the Horn by a long way, followed by *Condor, GB II* and *Flyer*. Unless something went seriously wrong on the last leg, *Flyer* would live up to her name and take the Whitbread trophy for the race. It was sad for *Gauloises* who, had it not been for the loss of her rudder on the second leg, would have had a good chance of taking the prize from her. However, there was still a long way to go and anything could happen. For us on *ADC* the race was still far from over. We had a good chance of picking up another two places, to fifth position, if we could overtake *Neptune* and hold off *Adventure* on the next section of this third leg. Although we had rounded the Horn and completed the most hazardous part of the trip, there were still 2,300 miles to go to Rio.

Our run to the Horn had been squally, but the night that we flew up from the Horn to the Le Maire Straits was even wilder and windier. The wind came screeching down off the hills like a wild cat, clawing the water and howling in

178

the rigging. Poor Beat, who was watch-leader while Tony was on standby, thought the squalls had subsided and put up a spinnaker. No sooner was it up than the wind increased to forty knots over the deck. Luckily Fred was at the wheel and, tiger that he was, managed to hold the boat steady for a long time, mainly because the seas were relatively small in the lee of the land. Then a powerful gust hit the boat and, despite everything, over she went. Fred fought to bring the boat back under control but, even when she was upright again, had to admit that he might not be able to keep her there. Only too pleased to get the wild beast of a spinnaker down again, we all rushed to the winches and fought it to the deck.

Our passage through the Le Maire Straits and north towards the Falklands was marked by lighter winds and a couple of serious navigational errors. The navigational errors consisted of a delayed gybe, which put us uncomfortably close to Tierra del Fuego, and a misreading of the currents (north of the Straits we found it strong westerly not easterly as we had supposed). The last error resulted in us being becalmed while *33 Export,* further to the east, held the wind and caught us up. Also, we nearly missed our rendezvous with HMS *Endurance,* the naval Antarctic survey ship who was trying to intercept us to say hello. Fortunately she found us, despite our being miles further west than

Rendezvous with HMS *Endurance* (*photo:* Slim MacDonnell).

we had reported, and we were able to exchange greetings and a few cheers. In expectation of having their photograph taken, the crew had pressed their oilskins and combed their beards . . . so they said, but no-one would have known the difference.

After *Endurance* had left us to steam south, I pondered the problem of the navigation and concluded that John should be given more time to concentrate on it, at the expense of running a watch. However this would be a problem, since I knew that John enjoyed both jobs. In the end, the matter resolved itself with a very bad broach just north of the Falklands.

It had been a blustery day. Once again, we had encountered island trouble and found ourselves heading straight for the Jason group that straggled out to the north-west of the Falklands. Rather than weave around the islands and lose time we went straight through. After a couple of gybes we were clear and Tony and I decided to raise a spinnaker again. The wind was a bit fresh, but nothing we couldn't handle. The trimming of the spinnaker was delicate but, after the usual trial and error, we got the boat finely balanced and going like a train. Then John's watch took over. Hardly had I gone below for a moment than I heard the spinnaker being retrimmed. Even after such a long time, John still felt his way of trimming a spinnaker was superior. Within five minutes the boat had taken a terrible roll to windward, then leeward, then broached. It was no minor broach either. It was so severe that the storm spinnaker got wrapped around the spreaders and tore into three sections, the first time such a thing had happened.

It was not the first time that I had felt John's judgment to be at fault and, although I disliked having to do it, I asked John to stand down as watch-leader. John was very understanding about it and, although he remained convinced that his method was the right one, he understood that severe broaches which damaged the gear had to be avoided. In good heart and cheerful as ever, John settled down to concentrate on the tactics and navigation while Jacques and Beat took over his watch.

The other matter that concerned me was communications. All the way to the Horn I had kept radio contact with Wellington in New Zealand. Once in the Atlantic I had hoped to make contact with a South American station or even Portishead but after many hours at the transmitter I was forced to try Wellington again. I don't know who was more surprised when I got through, them or me, but the quality of the contact was poor and, after saying hello, we had to abandon the call. Jacques tried an Argentinian station, speaking in his best Spanish, which was very slow and hesitant. They told him there was no-one who spoke English at the station – although it is the international radio language – and they could not anyway get a call through to England. It was our first indication that the standard of South American communications was very poor, normally not a matter that would have bothered us, but one which was to have serious repercussions for a badly injured crew member some days later.

While I tried to make radio contact with Cape Town or Portishead at all hours of the day and night, the sailmaking team of Eve, Sam and Bumble worked hard to repair the storm spinnaker. Fred, too, was busy oiling and

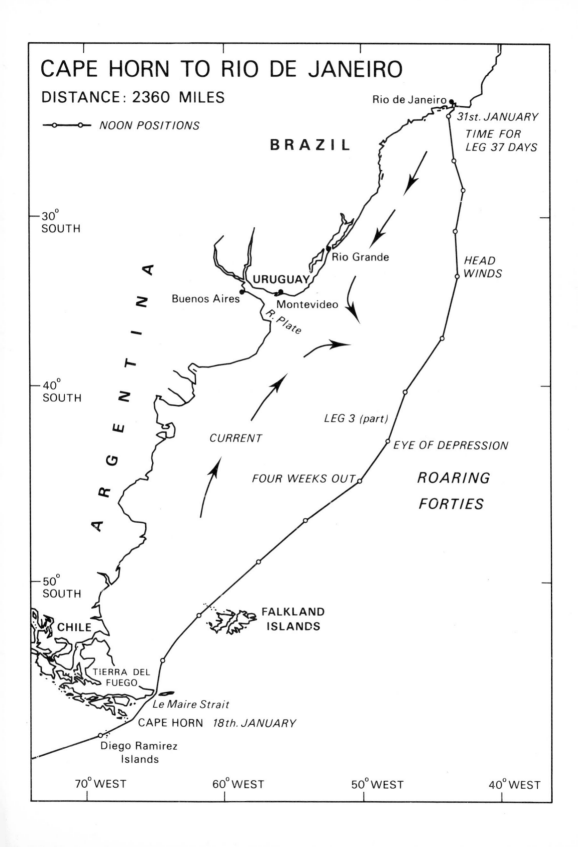

CAPE HORN TO RIO DE JANEIRO

DISTANCE: 2360 MILES

○—○—○ *NOON POSITIONS*

B R A Z I L

Rio de Janeiro ●

31st. JANUARY
TIME FOR
LEG 37 DAYS

—30°
SOUTH

Rio Grande ●

HEAD
WINDS

URUGUAY

Buenos Aires ●

Montevideo ●

R. Plate

—40°
SOUTH

A R G E N T I N A

LEG 3 (part)

EYE OF DEPRESSION

CURRENT

ROARING

FOUR WEEKS OUT ○

FORTIES

—50°
SOUTH

FALKLAND
ISLANDS

CHILE

TIERRA DEL
FUEGO

Le Maire Strait

CAPE HORN *18th. JANUARY*

Diego Ramirez
Islands

70° WEST   60° WEST   50° WEST   40° WEST

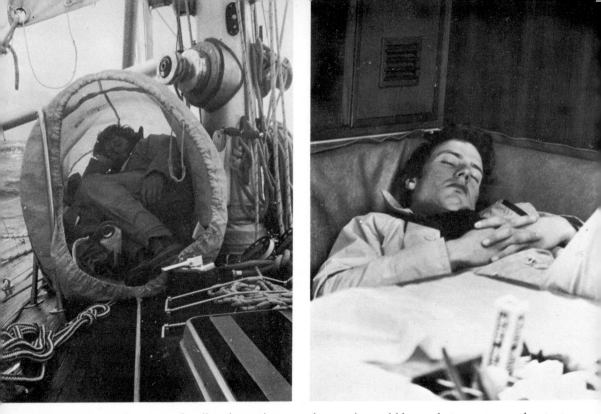

After eating, sleeping was the most popular pastime.

overhauling the engine to make sure it would be ready to start once the starter motor was repaired. Since the crew were tired much of the time anyway, these extra jobs would often exhaust them. Snoozing in the cockpit was a favourite way to make up sleep. As long as there was someone on the helm and someone keeping an eye on the sail trim, then the others were free to nod off. Sam was particularly fond of catnaps and often made a comfortable nest out of the empty sailbags we kept on the floor of the cockpit. Some of the others would stretch out on the seats, their hats over their noses and apparently dead to the world. After eating, sleeping was the most popular pastime on *ADC*.

North of the Falkland Islands the temperature rose rapidly and we were able to dispense with the thickest of our underwear. One day it was warm and sunny enough for us to open all the hatches and dry out some of our damp and clammy clothes. But the gentle weather was short-lived. We were still in the Forties and, although the South American continent sheltered us from the eternal, roaring westerlies, the weather was still vicious and unpredictable. It was normal for depressions to intensify over the continent and sweep down into the South Atlantic. Close to the coast the wind often came in violent squalls, known as Pamperros. We were well away from the coast and aiming to stay well off, so we should avoid these squalls. Our decision to stay off was governed by the winds we would meet north of the Forties. Here we expected headwinds, predominantly north-easterly. If we could make up to the east, we should gain the weather berth and avoid too much tacking.

Soon after leaving the Falklands behind, we were hit by a depression sweeping across from the west. Memories of the warm, gentle day we had just enjoyed were soon forgotten as we found ourselves plugging hard to windward. The wind eventually settled in the north – dead on the nose – and we made disappointing headway. the barometer plunged downward and the wind rose to forty knots, Force 8. The wind neither veered nor backed, but held constant, and we beat on for hour after hour, the boat wet, uncomfortable and steeply heeled. I got diarrhoea and some of the others got sick. It was reminiscent of our long South Atlantic trek five months before.

'Okay everyone,' said Fred. 'This is the good news. . . the wind's going to ease off and the sun's going to come out.'

Cheers and whistles.

'This is the bad news . . . it's not going to happen for another week.'

Boos and catcalls.

Fred was wrong. Not only did the wind ease that night but it completely dropped in the space of half an hour. The barometer still being low, it could only mean we were in the eye of a depression. For a long time nothing happened and, keen to make some headway, we put up a large genoa to catch the tiny whisper of wind that wafted from the west. Once the eye had passed over, I knew the wind would come up rapidly from the south or south-west – yet even I was unprepared for the suddenness of its arrival. One moment it was blowing three knots of wind – the next fifty. All hell broke loose. From sitting quietly in the cockpit or resting below, the crew scrambled for the halyard and the foredeck to hand the large genoa before it ripped and disappeared over the side. Next we handed the mainsail, a job that took five people several minutes as they struggled to tie the heavy sailcloth down to the boom. But we were too late for the mizzen. In all the furore we had not even eased the mizzen sheet and the poor, tired sail gave up the struggle – oversheeted and overstrained it split right across from luff to leech. When we had finished sorting out the other sails we lowered the mizzen and surveyed the damage – it would take a full day's work to repair, and even then the sail would be far from strong. Down went the mizzen for repair and up went a reefed main and boomed-out jib to send *ADC* scurrying along in the steady southerly, while we contemplated the suddenness of events. Beat smiled wrily and observed, 'I knew that rounding the Horn wouldn't be the end of the excitement but. . . this!' He rolled his eyes and shook his head.

For the next few days the wind gave us a hard time, veering and backing, falling away then blowing hard. Ahead, the leading boats had fallen into the light headwinds of the temperate latitudes north of the Forties. *GB II* reported thunderstorms and the extraordinary news that she had been almost crippled by lightning. They had been sailing along under a thundery cloud when they were blinded by a flash and two of them thrown across the deck. When they recovered they found that all their instruments were out of action, their wind speed and direction sensor at the top of the mast had melted into a lump of metal, and, worst of all, the boat had become highly magnetised, giving the compass wide and unknown deviations.

More serious news came on 27th January. *33 Export,* who was just behind us, reported that one of her crew had been flung across the cockpit and had broken his femur. When Nick heard this he was worried. He told us that it was not simply a matter of a broken bone – the man could die without proper treatment if fat released from the bone got into his lungs, or he had internal bleeding. It was important that he reached a hospital as soon as possible. *33 Export* were already aware of this, having spoken to a doctor on one of the French boats. Fortunately – or so we thought – we were able to make contact with Rio Yacht Club by radio relay, *33* to us, us to *GB II* and on to Rio. Some of the race organisers were there and promised to do what they could to get the injured man lifted off by a ship. Since *33* were also in contact with a vessel in the Eastern Atlantic who was trying to contact ships nearer the scene, we thought the man would soon be lifted off. Being relatively close to civilisation we all fell into the natural trap of believing that rescue would be a relatively simple and straightforward matter. However, this was far from the truth.

The next four days were a fiasco of confusion and misunderstanding. First, the race organisers told us that the Brazilian Navy were sending a vessel to pick up the injured man. The next day we were told that it would be a tug – but that it hadn't left yet. On the third day we were told that, actually, no tug was on its way, nor was there going to be one. *33 Export* was now heading for the nearest port, Rio Grande in south Brazil. *33*'s radio was weak so, to let everyone know her destination, we tried to call a shore station for them. No-one replied. We tried emergency calls to ships, but received no reply. Finally I contacted Portishead in England and asked them to relay the message to Race Control and also to the Brazilian Navy. When we made contact with Rio Yacht Club again, they told us all the shore stations were trying to alert ships plying up and down the coast. What no-one mentioned was that ships did not use the South American shore stations and would therefore be unaware of the emergency. The organisers told us that contact had been made with a Japanese ship but, since we never heard from her, we doubted this too. The South American coast was busy with shipping but we were unable to contact ships directly – the distress frequency, 2182 kilohertz, was drowned out by static. By the third day, *33 Export* were running out of pain-killing drugs and were very worried about the man's condition. There was very little we could do to help. *Japy-Hermès* was, however, on a course that would intercept *33*'s, and she had a doctor on board. Ironically, it was the doctor who had spent the first leg of the race on board *33 Export,* then switched to *Japy* in Cape Town. The two yachts met up and the doctor swam over to *33* with a bag of drugs held between his teeth. He found the sick man to be weak, distressed, and in bad pain, but no longer in danger of his life. When *33* finally arrived in Rio Grande and put their man ashore, the Brazilians did at last provide real help in the form of excellent medical facilities in the naval hospital.

It may be that the Brazilian Navy was unable to send out a ship due to lack of resources; if we had been told this, we would have understood. But it was a little difficult to cope with the South American habit of promising the earth in order to make everyone happy, while being unable to fulfil the promise. It must have been particularly hard on the sick man who daily expected to be relieved of the terrible pain, only to find he could expect several more days without pain killers.

With the drama over, we gave the radio a rest and concentrated on reaching Rio as quickly as possible. Entering the temperate latitudes of the Thirties, the

The first hint of warmth and John resumes his favourite state of dress.

weather changed dramatically. Almost daily the temperature rose, the wind became more variable and the air more humid. From the cold of only a week before we were suddenly hot and having to guard ourselves from the sun. From wearing face masks against the hail and freezing spray, we now wore them against the scorching sun. For me, the only tangible memory of the Southern Ocean was my dead fingertips, slowly coming back to life. Already the cold and the snow seemed a long way away.

The climatic change required some adjustment and we took salt tablets against dehydration and lethargy. However there was no possibility of becoming disinterested in the race – the competitive situation was a cliffhanger. It seemed that our strategy of trying to make up to windward was paying off. We had overtaken *Neptune*, caught *Disque d'Or* by several hours, and were well ahead of *Gauloises*. It was almost certain that we would improve our position to fifth.

The last few days were tense as we worried about falling into calm patches ahead. Our anxiety was not improved by *Tielsa* who played us a trick by

185

pretending to be behind us one day and ahead of us the next, so that we were immensely cheered one moment and very depressed the next. In Rio they apologised for such a rotten joke, but it cost them several rounds of drinks and a lot of friendly abuse.

With Rio only days away, there was the usual burst of preening, mirror-gazing and critical self-examination. After all, Rio was the most exotic of all the stops and didn't the most beautiful girls in the world adorn Copacabana Beach? Dreadful yellow T-shirts were removed, scruffy beards disappeared and hair was washed and combed. Robert, after much heart-searching, decided that there would be no rakish moustache this time, just a deep suntan. Since he, like the rest of us, was rather white, this would have to be developed in something of a hurry and for three days Robert fixed himself to the deck, as if with glue. John was also working hard on his all-over tan, wandering around in his favourite state of undress, frightening the sea life. Robin and Beat had a hasty shave and Jacques ran a comb through his hair, an event sufficiently rare that I noted it in my diary.

'Cor', laughed Bumble at the sight of so much order and cleanliness. 'Why don't you lot spruce up for me and Evey? What have these Brazilian birds got that we haven't, I'd like to know!'

'Glamour,' said Evey, 'and total ignorance of the nasty and unsavoury habits of this crew – that's what they've got!'

CHAPTER 11

No Carnival in Rio

We arrived in Rio in fifth place for the leg and, best of all, in fifth place for the race so far. It was satisfying to have gone from ninth to seventh and now to have a position that was extremely respectable – at least *we* were delighted with it and that was all that counted! *Gauloises* had won the leg on handicap, followed by *Flyer, Traité de Rome* and *Disque d'Or*. We had beaten *King's Legend, Neptune* and all the larger boats. Furthermore we had beaten *Sayula*'s Portsmouth to Rio time on the previous race by over three days.

The first thing that struck us about Rio was the heat. For the last mile to the finishing line we were almost becalmed and sat there cooking slowly in the setting sun. Bob Saunders had brought his BBC film crew out to greet us, a welcome sight. Later Bob told me he had been filming the carnival preparations on the other side of Rio when he suddenly had the feeling we were coming in. I thought he must have found out through the Rio Yacht Club, but it was pure intuition. I was only sad that my parents were not there as well. They had booked to fly out three days later, in confident expectation of being in good time to wave us in. But so fast was our time, we had beaten them to it.

Rio was as spectacular as all the photographs one had ever seen. Silhouetted by the bright orange sunset were the sharp, jagged peaks that surround the city. On one was the floodlit figure of Christ, and in the foreground the famous Sugarloaf. As we were towed into the harbour, the city itself unfolded before us like a glittering carpet. We heard the street noises and smelt the scent of exotic flowers. The yacht club itself was bright with lights, people and yachts. There is no feeling in the world like arriving in a strange port – a mixture of excitement, elation and relief. As we tied up between the other yachts the crews gave us a friendly yell and a wave, the organisers officially welcomed us, and we were free to go ashore.

We knew that the Brazilians were not great sailing enthusiasts and were not likely to show much interest in the race. We also knew that the Rio Yacht Club was primarily a social club for the very rich and that, despite its name, there would be little interest there either. The club had welcomed the previous race four years before but ever since the participants in another event, the Cape-to-Rio Race, had overstayed their welcome in a rather noisy and bad-mannered fashion, they were noticeably cool towards yachting events. This became clear when we were informed that we would not be allowed to eat in the restaurant or on the verandah, but only on the open terrace. Nevertheless, we enjoyed a superb meal that evening and collapsed into our bunks for a full night's sleep, happy and content. The sensible ones slept on deck, for the heat in the harbour was oppressive and humid.

The next day my usual round of jobs began. The first priority, as always, was money. Jacques and I hailed a taxi and, like innocents to the slaughter, stepped in unsuspecting. The driver was a cross between Fittipaldi and a kamikaze pilot and drove as if his life depended on it, which it did in a way. At one point he took to the pavement rather than give way to another car. Fortunately there were no pedestrians in the way. Jacques and I held on to each other, eyes agog and teeth bared in terror. The driver thought we were smiling with pleasure and took every whimper as a chuckle of delight. After smiling back he promptly accelerated. By the time we arrived at the bank we were like wet rags. It took an hour to draw the money, not bad going for Rio, then we were faced with the problem of getting it back to the club. Everyone had warned us about carrying money about in Rio so, assuming no-one would dare put their hand there, Jacques stuffed it down his underpants. We survived the return taxi ride with body, soul and money intact, and were luckier than the crew of *Traité de Rome* who, against all advice, sat on the beach with several thousand dollars in a bag, to find it stolen from under their noses. Once back at the club, our money was relatively safe because the club was heavily guarded by its own security force and no-one could enter without a pass.

The famous Rio Carnival was due to start a week after we arrived, so it was necessary to get things done in a hurry. Once the Carnival started everything would come to a complete halt – shops, offices and repair shops would close. First priority was to get the starter motor rewound. To begin with we could not believe our luck – not only did we find a Bosch agent but they said they could do the job in a few days. We did not appreciate that this was Rio and nothing could ever be as simple as that.

Next, we tried to arrange for the exhaust – which had leaked the water into the engine – to be repaired. Again, no problem! The naval shipyard would be delighted to do it and, what was more, they would lift *ADC* out of the water for a scrub. Thinking we had everything set up, Jacques and I started to look for somewhere to stay. Hotels were far too expensive at Carnival-time, but we managed to find a tiny apartment off the Copacabana (or the Choppabanana, as the boys called it).

After my parents arrived, we thought we would have time to relax and see some of the sights with them. Then difficulties started to appear. Every day we asked one of the Portuguese-speaking staff in the RNSA office to phone up the Bosch agent and ask how things were going with the starter motor. Every day there was great optimism. It would be ready tomorrow! After a week of tomorrows we began to be a little suspicious, but with the Carnival almost upon us there was nothing we could do. The exhaust repair was not proving so simple either. Suddenly there were 'difficulties' at the shipyard and concern about payment. Back and forth we rushed, trying to find out what was happening, but got nowhere. It was not until the RNSA representative, Admiral Steiner, had lunch with the head of the naval dockyard, a Brazilian admiral, that everything was ironed out admiral-to-admiral. Talk of money faded and everything was now possible again. Except lifting out, that is. It transpired that the dockyard possessed no slings to lift large boats. The skippers of yachts in desperate need of repairs, like *Disque d'Or,* eventually borrowed some and were lifted, but they hardly dared watch the operation for fear of the boat being dropped. We decided to leave the dockyard well alone. I thought I had been very clever to find another yard who would pull us out – until they quoted a price of £4,000.

All this dashing about in the stifling heat trying to cope with the Brazilian telephone system, as well as the language, left Jacques and me feeling completely drained. Carnival time should give us a rest. The rest of the crew had been working on the boat every day for a week in the burning heat and also took a few well-earned days off. Bumble went to Brasilia with Diana, the girl on *GB II,* and two of the boys from *Tielsa.* The others went shopping or walking along the Copacabana, girl-watching. 'It's no good getting friendly,' said Robert ruefully. 'Rio girls don't play with anyone less than millionaires.'

While it was so hot, leaping into the club's swimming pool was one of our favourite pastimes. But the club snubbed us once again by suddenly charging the boat crews an entry fee. This was too much, for no-one could afford a pound a time to jump in the pool. Not surprisingly there was a lot of bad feeling. It was one thing to be ignored and another to be made downright unwelcome!

My parents, Jacques and I obtained tickets for the Carnival on the principle that we would never have the chance to see such a spectacle again. It was an incredible sight as one samba school followed another down the long street, their costumes sparkling with dazzling colour. The parade went on all night but by three in the morning our stamina had faded and we slipped away to bed. Another night Jacques and I went to one of the famous Carnival balls but this we found very disappointing. Four thousand people were crammed into a shabby modern dance hall, jigging away to the rhythm but unable to move for the crush. It was far from the glamorous evening we had imagined.

The Carnival over and a week left to go before the restart, we tried to find out what was happening to our starter motor. Again we ran into communication difficulties but eventually discovered that the motor was in a workshop the other side of Rio and nowhere near the Bosch agent. With the help of an Anglo-Brazilian, we found the workshop and, after much bowing and smiling, established that 'it was highly likely' the motor would be ready soon. Our Anglo-Brazilian told us that 'highly likely' was strong language for Brazil and that we could expect our motor any day.

All the boats that had goods arriving from Europe by ship had encountered trouble in getting their stuff through the Brazilian Customs who did not recognise 'Goods in Transit' and wanted to charge duty on everything. Since we were waiting for all our food to arrive from England we became a little concerned. But BSR, who had arranged the shipping, came up trumps as usual by choosing an efficient shipping agent who had the crates through Customs and delivered to the quay in no time.

After a long wait, our exhaust pipe finally got repaired by the dockyard. And to our profound relief the starter motor was no longer going to be ready tomorrow, but today! Many people had told us that, in the end, everything gets done in Brazil – it just takes time. With the engine happily running, we could now sit back and appreciate the truth of this saying, but it had not made the previous two weeks any the less anxious.

Our last major task was to scrub the boat's bottom. Taking some tanks, masks and flippers, we motored *ADC* across the harbour to look for a quiet, unpolluted bay where we could dive over and scrub. *GB II* had recommended a certain bay and, thinking we'd found the one, we motored gently in. There were plenty of people on the beach but no other yachts in sight. It looked perfect. As we drifted in, anchor at the ready, a man in blue appeared among the sunbathers on the beach and started jumping up and down. He had a rifle in his hand. Suddenly we heard a crack and, looking up at a hill above, we saw several more men in blue, all with rifles aimed at us. One raised his rifle and carefully fired a shot in the air. It didn't take long for us to get the hint. Putting on full throttle, we turned and, trying not to be cowardly and duck, left with as much dignity as we could muster. The next bay looked better. No soldiers in sight and lots of bathers. Still no yachts though. Halfway in and Fred suddenly said, 'Look up there!' The next moment 'Crack!' The hillside was covered in unfriendly soldiers again.

'I have the feeling we're not too welcome around here,' Nick remarked. As we turned and fled, we felt somewhat shaken and it was only when we saw a bay full of boats that we dared enter it and drop an anchor.

Towards the end of our stay we managed to find time to visit the Sugarloaf and the figure of Christ. We also sneaked another couple of days at the nice soldierless bay where an immensely friendly yacht club hosted us royally.

The prizegiving for the third leg was held at the Rio Yacht Club and we wondered what kind of a party they would put on for us after their cool hospitality so far. Ironically, the party was at the swimming pool – but we were not asked to pay for this particular visit. The beginning of the evening was very pleasant – there were waiters with drinks, bits and pieces to eat, and a band who started to play samba music. The band was excellent and, to the boys' utter joy, four samba dancers suddenly leapt on to the floor and started to gyrate in the way that only the Brazilians can. These ladies were beautiful, dusky creatures, wearing skimpy silver costumes that made the boys' eyes boggle. In no time the evening had developed into a stupendous party. Everyone started to dance until the floor was a mass of leaping, shaking people having the time of their lives. The music was intoxicating, the atmosphere perfect, and everyone was in the mood to dance all night. In Brazil it is quite normal for people at swimming pool parties to end up in the swimming pool. The guests at the chic Hawaiian Ball, held at this same pool some weeks before, had all jumped in the water when they got too hot. We were now too hot, so we jumped in too. Soon everyone was going in the water between dances.

Then for no apparent reason all the lights went out, the samba dancers disappeared and the band started putting away their instruments. It was only ten o'clock. Of the many unnecessary measures that the yacht club had taken, trying to stop that party was the most foolish. Having behaved quietly throughout their stay in Rio, the crews were now enjoying the first opportunity to let themselves go, and they weren't about to stop. Although there was no music, everyone started dancing again. Those who had not been in the water were gently picked up and thrown in, among them my mother and by no less a person than Cornelius, the owner and skipper of *Flyer*. My mother, being an adventurous person, thought it was great fun.

Then the trouble started. A couple of screens around the pool were accidentally broken. Chair legs were pulled off to form drumsticks and a rhythm was beaten out on the chair seats to enable the dancing to continue unabated. Water was generally splashed around while the club security guards looked on helplessly, not knowing what to do. Some of them were thrown in, just so they could enter into the spirit of the party. The atmosphere was one of high spirits – very few of the crews were drunk and in time everyone would have gone back to their boats, tired but happy. But the next thing we heard was the shriek of sirens, and an army of men in uniform appeared wielding batons and looking very unfriendly. It was time to leave the party – these policemen meant business. After we left we heard that, although everyone was trying to leave the party quietly, tear gas and batons were used quite unnecessarily. The next day the restaurant manager, who had stopped the party and called the police, was fired by the club. But it was too late to save the evening. We would not be sorry to leave the Rio Yacht Club.

During the last few days we finished many small deck jobs and took the boat out several times to tune up the rigging. It was difficult to muster enough energy to carry out these tasks. Normally a person who never catches so much as a cold, I had the most appalling flu which knocked me sideways. I had fever, a temperature and then the worst head cold I have ever suffered, and all this in the oppressive, humid heat. Beat was laid low with fever, and stayed in his bunk for four days, sick and miserable. The others felt none too bright either, and we all looked forward to feeling a cool, fresh sea breeze on our skins again. Never had a restart been so appealing – never before had we so wanted to return to our small, wet world on *ADC*.

The route from Rio to Portsmouth was fairly straightforward. First we would meet predominantly easterly winds and have to stay close-hauled until we ran into the Doldrums. Once through – and if we didn't get through more quickly than the last time, we would probably give up there and then – we would meet the north-east trades and have another long windward passage to the Azores. Here a high-pressure area lay in wait for us. Like the South Atlantic High, this patch of variable winds was capable of travelling great distances or suddenly spreading across thousands of miles of ocean. However, the weather information in the North Atlantic was good, so we should be able to keep a better track of the high's antics. Once through, we should pick up westerlies and roar home . . . unless it blew from the east, as it often did in March. It was not impossible that we would meet headwinds the whole way to Portsmouth.

It had been suggested that the last leg would be boring after the excitement of the Southern Ocean, but as we set out for the start I think everyone was more excited than ever before. A dozen duels were going on within the race and we were as determined as ever to outwit our competitors. On this, our last

191

FACING PAGE
Above left: Bow
spray in the north-
east trades.

Above right: A long,
wet beat up to the
Azores.

Below: Pico in the
Azores, only a week
from home.

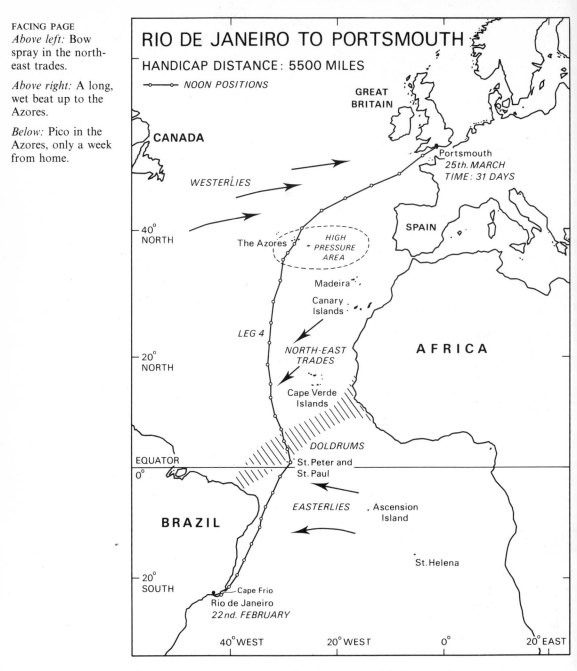

chance to compete against each other, we would all try to do better than ever
before.

For us there was little chance of improving our position in the race as a
whole. Indeed, it would be hard enough to hold off *Adventure* and *Gauloises*
who were breathing down our necks in the handicap table. Our ambition was
simple – to keep our fifth place overall and to try for a leg prize.

192

The wind around Rio was notorious for its absence and on the day of the start it lived up to its reputation, but there was a small sea breeze to take us out of the harbour and we had a splendid tacking match with the rest of the fleet to see who could be first to the harbour mouth. A last wave to my parents, another sneeze into my handkerchief, a final glance at Rio and we were away, happy to be at sea again.

The wind all but becalmed us a mile or so off the land and we settled down to a long drifting match. That night our secret weapon came into play. This was our floater – our gossamer-light spinnaker which could fill in almost no wind at all. When the wind shifted behind, up it went and off we shot – at all of two or three knots, enough to overtake *GB II*, catch *Flyer*, hold *Pen Duick* and generally do rather well. *Pen Duick* was still disqualified from the race, but had been invited to join the fleet all the same. We considered her to be a fully-fledged competitor.

By the next morning we were in line with *Flyer*, *Condor* and *Pen Duick* and feeling rather pleased with ourselves. *Disque d'Or* was well behind too. Yet again – it was getting monotonous – we had made an excellent start and shown that *ADC* had the speed. This time it would be wonderful, wonderful if we could go the right way for a change and keep our position.

We had some difficulty in identifying some of the yachts in sight because, search as we might, we could not find the binoculars anywhere. We looked high and low, in every locker and every corner, but no luck. They could have been stolen, but why not steal all the other valuables as well? It was a mystery.

It was soon clear that Bumble was not her usual bright self. She was quiet, pale and taking to her bunk at every opportunity. 'Think I'll just go downstairs and lie down,' she said. 'I'll be up to make lunch.' But she wasn't. Nick took her temperature, diagnosed a fever, and told her to stay in her bunk. Bumble crashed out and, apart from taking the odd drink of water, was not seen for two days. While Nick had the medicine chest open, I finally gave in and started a course of antibiotics for the very painful sinusitis I had developed. Others had headaches, sniffles and rashes. Never had we been such a rueful collection of aches and pains.

Clear of Cape Frio, tactics were vital. John suggested staying near the coast to keep out of the current, then sailing straight for the point where we wanted to enter the Doldrums – just east of St Peter and St Paul Islands – going for speed as before. Jacques, however, was keen to make up to the east, to windward, to get well into the trade winds and away from the coast and be sure of keeping a good, fresh breeze.

To begin with we stayed near the coast then, when the advantage of the current was lost, we gybed in a light southerly and headed out, well away from the land. It was a fine strategy which would have worked brilliantly, except that we had left the gybe a little too late and should have reached out to the east at an acute angle rather than the shallow slant we took. We were in good company. *Pen Duick* was in view behind us and *King's Legend* was to port, near the land.

For the next two days we held an excellent position towards the top of the fleet. The wind was fast coming round to the east and not allowing us to make

FACING PAGE
Tony tweaks the floater, to encourage it to fill.

the easting we would have liked, but at that time it did not worry us. Bumble emerged a little shaky from the fever, but feeling much better. It was not a very good awakening – she discovered that an entire sack of carrots was rotting, only four days after purchase. To save the last few, Bumble peeled, blanched and froze them. The next surprise came with the eggs, some of which were so bad that they stank through their shells. 'Never mind,' said Bumble, 'you're all too fat anyway!'

Sam was the next person to fall ill with fever. At first we thought it was a similar bug to the one from which Beat then Bumble had suffered and we put Sam to bed in the expectation of seeing him up and about in a couple of days.

The wind freed us again and we were able to make more easting. Things were looking up. Apart from Sam, we were all beginning to feel our old selves again. It was still hot and we were uncomfortable in anything more than sarongs, but the sea breeze was cool, the food good and the sailing exciting. John let slip there had been cockroaches on his *Tangaroa*. This met with loud gasps of amazement.

'John!' Nick cried. 'There *couldn't* be – not *cockroaches!* Well, well . . .' He shook his head.

'But they didn't stay long,' John added, laughing.

'We are still deeply shocked,' said Nick.

Eve burnt her hands on some rope and, not surprisingly, let go of the rope to nurse her sore palms. Nick, a smile at the corner of his mouth, said, 'Come on Evey, pick up that halyard!'

'Shurrup!' yelled Eve. 'You do it yourself or come and treat my hands!' Eve and Nick were off again – but as before they seemed to enjoy every moment of it.

Robert made tea for us one morning and we decided his standard had improved. Instead of British Rail Mark II, it was now British caff standard – still dark and turgid but with no oily deposits on the surface.

The Chat Hour conversations were particularly fascinating. *33 Export* were in their usual trouble. This time they had left all their pots, pans and cutlery on the quayside at Rio, hidden among the mass of junk they had offloaded in order to clean the boat. How they were managing to cook and eat we didn't dare ask. The skipper of *Gauloises,* Eric Loiseau (just call me 'Ze bird'), was giving me some educational French lessons. *'Le vent est vraiment merdique, n'est-ce pas?'* he said one day.

'Merdique?' I pondered. *'Ah oui! Ici, nous sommes décapités.'* I thought a literal translation of Jacques' favourite, 'We are beheaded', might fool him. It did, and he signed off to think about it.

The next day, our fourth day out, Sam was still flat out in his bunk, far from well. Nick had given him something to stop the sickness and dehydration, but without any lab facilities he could neither diagnose the virus nor treat it. As long as Sam could keep some liquid down he should be able to sweat his way through the fever. Nick suspected that Sam was suffering from a more virulent ailment than Beat and Bumble, and that it would take much longer to overcome.

As we pressed on north-eastward we daily expected to find the trade winds. On the fourth day the wind appeared to be settling in from just the right direction and we looked forward to a steady thrash up to the Doldrums, holding and consolidating our position behind the three maxi-raters, level with *King's Legend*, and ahead of *Flyer* and *Disque d'Or*.

On the fifth day we found and fell into our first hole. It was almost unbelievable but it was happening again – we were sailing into a Doldrums-type weather pattern. The sky was heavy with anvil-shaped clouds producing sudden squalls and large, windless patches. And we were still a week away from the Doldrums proper! It was a small consolation when we saw, a couple of miles to the west, a small, white triangle against the dark horizon. It could only be *King's Legend*. The next day our worst fears were confirmed. The other boats still had fresh easterly winds while we, under 100 miles to the west, had frustratingly slow conditions. Yet again we watched a promising position evaporating. By the third day it was flat calm and we were beyond caring.

Every morning the dark, sombre clouds would be sitting heavily in the sky, suspended and motionless. Every morning *King's Legend* would be there, shadowing us like a phantom, the two of us caught like flies in a web.

We had been foiled by the wind once again. There was a maxim to be learnt from this kind of long-distance ocean racing – it's *where* you are that counts! We were in a part of the ocean where the wind should have been blowing. But it wasn't and that was all there was to it. Best to keep cool and wait for a miracle.

After four days in his bunk, Sam finally emerged – pale, wobbly and very skinny. He had been slim beforehand but now poor Sam was hardly there at all. He was able to drink water without being sick and had even sniffed at some broth. When he asked what sails we were going to blow out to celebrate his recovery, we knew he would be all right. Nick confessed that he had been rather worried about Sam's condition and had taken a look at the chart to see the distance to the nearest port.

Just a few hours later, when we picked up a small following breeze, we blew out the light spinnaker. Or to be more accurate the tapes broke again, just as they had done on that first night in the Channel. Being a sensible fellow, Sam took one look at the mounds of nylon in the saloon, said 'There, I knew you lot would have it in for me,' and retired to his bunk. Evey settled down to do the repair and, so there would be no recurrence of the tear, stitched on a complete new tape around the sail. It was cheering to see *King's Legend* tear their spinnaker too. It was not that we wished them ill, we just liked to share our problems!

The breeze heralded the return of the wind and our speed slowly went up from three to five then nine knots. It was marvellous to be moving again! In the evening we heard that many of the other boats had also run into light winds so, despite everything, we still had a chance to make up lost ground. *Flyer* and *Disque d'Or* had slipped past, which was a disappointment, but there was still a long way to go. We had kept an edge on *Adventure* and *Gauloises,* the two boats we had to beat to maintain our position.

We raced for the Equator, aiming to pass just to the east of the islands of St

Peter and St Paul. Then? Then it would be the Doldrums again, not our favourite place. We would tackle them with determination – and of course hope. As we approached the latitude where the sun would pass directly overhead the heat became intense and, with all the hatches closed against the spray, it became stuffy down below. 'God, it's nasty in here!' declared Bumble. 'How about compulsory bath time?' We chucked buckets of water over ourselves throughout the day and wandered about in sarongs, trying to cool down. At the same time we couldn't stay in the sun for too long for fear of burning.

With the sun overhead the fixing of our position became a question of taking two sights either side of noon. The sun was overhead for such a brief moment that it was not possible to take the usual meridian passage, or noon sight. John frequently took morning and evening star sights as well, so that our position was fixed twice or three times a day, a great luxury after the difficulties of navigating in the cloudy Southern Ocean.

Making radio contact with England was getting marginally easier too. I could now get through to Portishead every day, as long as I chose off-peak times. I spoke to my parents and Jacques to his. Now that we were nearing home, all we wanted to hear was news. The BBC World Service was coming through loud and clear on the radio and we listened to it at least once a day. The extraordinary thing was that nothing seemed to have changed. Somehow you expect the world to have made great strides over a six-month period – but the news was remarkable only for its similarity to all that had happened before.

When the engine stopped for no reason one day, we were not surprised. After all, this would not be the first time it had given trouble. However, this time it was not actually the fault of the engine. Being low on fuel and heeled hard over, the pipe was sucking air from the tank. The problem could be remedied quickly enough when we came upright and could redistribute the fuel between the eight tanks. In the meantime we economised on power. We had done it so often now that the procedure was automatic.

At the Equator we opened a bottle of champagne kindly donated by *33 Export* in thanks for relaying their radio messages off Brazil, and a day later we passed the St Peter and St Paul rocks, sighting them off to port. Any moment we would hit the Doldrums. The wind was already falling away and the heat was intense. We had caught the boats ahead but, as before, this meant nothing. The important thing was who escaped from the calms first. When a familiar black cloud loomed up on the horizon and the wind started to behave strangely, we knew the signs and settled down to battle our way through the frustrations of calms, small gusts and ever-changing wind direction.

Oddly enough, we enjoyed our two and a half days in the Doldrums, mainly because there was enough wind to give us something to work on. Our daily mileage dropped from 190 to about 100, still good progress. Never did we have to endure a flat calm for very long and at no time did we feel that blank, blind despair of the first leg. The Doldrums still managed to play a trick on us, though. Having gone through them once and found the trade winds, the weather forecast predicted they were about to move north. And indeed they did, so we had to sail through them a second time! This allowed *Disque d'Or* to escape once again but she was the only one, so it was no disaster.

In contrast to the first leg, we enjoyed the long windward slog through the trades to the Azores. Although it was wet and humid and the boat was heeled hard over, the race was so exciting that every day was a cliff-hanger. On the first leg we had felt the despair of a hopeless situation; now we were duelling with *King's Legend* and *Tielsa* while trying to cover *Adventure* and *Gauloises*. Ahead, *Flyer* was having trouble in keeping up with *Disque d'Or* and we could only hold up our hats to our old adversary, who was holding *Flyer* for mile after mile, and had a good chance of winning a prize for the leg.

During the long haul to the Azores there were several days without a single sail change. Sam complained about his last two standbys – on the first he had actually had to get up during the night to switch off the fan above his bunk and on the second he'd had to get up to go to the loo. This, he said, just would not do!

The major events during those windward days were domestic. The aft loo outlet got blocked and, being unable to free it, Jacques and Robert rigged up another outlet pipe. There was only one problem – the pipe was transparent and ran inside the loo compartment. This gave a whole new meaning to voyeurism. The point where the pipe left the pump was labelled, inevitably, Crapham Junction, and a notice appeared above the pump handle, PLEASE DO NOT LEAVE TRAINS STANDING IN THE STATION.

One day I was at the wheel and heard a fantastic roar come up from the cabin. Loud booing and catcalls followed. It transpired that the binoculars had been on board all the time, lost in the dark, deep locker behind the chart table which was known as Tanner's Hell-Hole. John was not allowed to forget that one easily.

Bumble also surprised us all. She suddenly decided to learn how to take a sun sight, work it out and plot it. And not only did she learn in no time at all, but she became very proficient at the art.

For nine days we were hard on the wind. The sparkling sun and flying spray of the trades burnt our already suntanned faces until they were red and sore. Spotty botty was widespread and our bedding was damp as dribbles of water seeped down bulkheads. Yet the trades were so beautiful, the sea such a deep, sparkling blue, the sky so clear that we enjoyed each and every day. We raced past turtles as they paddled slowly along. We were overtaken by dolphins swimming and leaping effortlessly beside the boat. We watched hundreds of flying fish scattering over the waves in panic-stricken flight from the cutting bows. At night phosphorescence lit our wake and the sky was dark velvet pinpricked with a multitude of stars. It was magically beautiful and made even more intoxicating by the nearness of home, now less than 2,000 miles away.

'Might as well toss a coin,' said Tony, 'but I'd go for the gamble every time.'
   'Me too,' said Beat.
   'I'm all for it,' added John.
   The matter was settled. We would try to get through the Azores high by

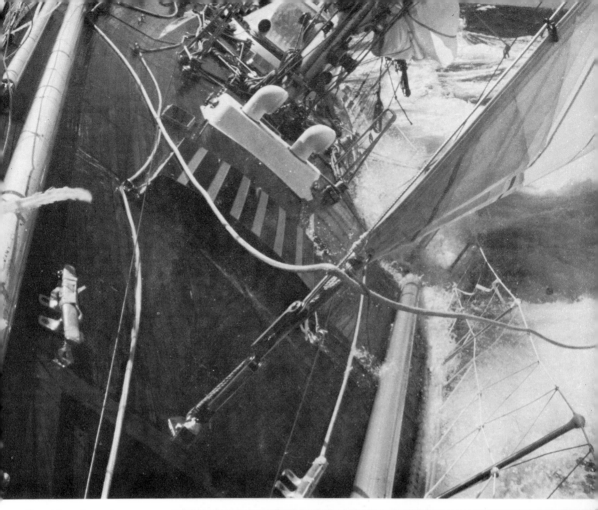

Spanking through
the north-east trades,
with companion
(*photo* [right]: Nick
Milligan).

skirting round its western edge. As usual, the weather forecast did not give us much information on the extent of the high, but there was reason to believe we might do better by going the long way round. It would be a gamble – but what had we got to lose? The sheets were freed and *ADC* accelerated on her new heading.

Two days later we were becalmed – but only for eighteen hours, a much shorter time than many of the other boats. As it turned out, we would have done better to free off even earlier and take a longer detour. Nevertheless we emerged from the Azores in a strong position to keep our fifth place and possibly to beat *King's Legend* and *Flyer* on the leg. A westerly wind sprang up as Pico and several of the other beautiful Azorean islands came into sight. We altered course for the English Channel. If the westerlies held, we could be in Portsmouth in six days.

The grey, windswept North Atlantic reminded us of the Southern Ocean, so hard did it blow and so large did the seas become. For me it evoked other vivid memories. Twice I had crossed the North Atlantic in this kind of weather – gale- to storm-force winds and seas as large or larger than anything we had seen in the Southern Ocean. However, the circumstances had been somewhat different – I had gone from east to west, against the wind, and singlehanded. Here on this big, well-tried boat running fast downwind, with my large family aboard, it was another kind of sailing.

The last few days were fast and furious. *ADC* flew along with a bone in her teeth, the foam and spray white around her bow. The waves made steering difficult. There was a large sea – perhaps thirty feet high with twelve seconds between crests – and a vicious cross sea which twisted the stern and corkscrewed the boat. Nevertheless we were making 230–250 miles a day, fast enough to get us to Portsmouth some time between the afternoon of Saturday, 25th March, and the Sunday morning. Bets were taken as to the precise hour of arrival, something we had done on all four legs. It was not a lucrative proposition for the winner, however, since we always forgot to pay our debts.

With our arrival only days away we suddenly realised that the long race was nearly over. 'Only three more days of cooking, Bumble!'

'Oh,' murmured Bumble, rather quiet, 'I don't know whether I'm glad or not. I've got so used to you and your appetites . . . and who am I going to shout at when the washing-up's not done?'

Sam, spurred on by the proximity of land, was inspired to greater heights of prose. Always exchanging remarks with John, he eyed him and announced, 'Here we have Spanner, wearing the latest Paris outfit in beige with white accoutrements highlighted by a double-handed winch handle embedded in his skull and a jockey pole wrapped delicately around his neck.' By Sam's standards, this was an expression of great endearment.

All kinds of plots were hatched. John was famous for spending as little time as possible on deck, so Sam and some of the others secretly attached a line to him at the chart table and, without warning, winched him up on deck. Robert suffered the same fate at the change of watch. Late as usual, he suddenly found himself disappearing up the companion-way.

Jacques had his last mutter about the mad British and their strange habits –

OPPOSITE

Roaring along in westerlies again.

200

cricket, warm beer and eating jelly with meat – while Sam complained about there being something wrong with the radio (it was tuned to a French station). Robin and Jacques had long and heated discussions about politics – a subject we had managed to avoid for most of the 27,000 miles – and decided to disagree, which met with loud cheers.

After so long, it was strange to imagine a so-called normal life again. Although we had often longed to return to dry land, now it was almost upon us we began to appreciate what we would be missing when our close-knit, interdependent community broke up.

The wind held all the way to the Channel and, despite a considerable amount of frisky spinnaker work, we managed to sail 1,000 miles without breaking a sail. We spoilt this record on the Friday when we blew the starcut for the very last time. Three days from home, we nearly ran into an enormous telegraph pole which was lying straight across our path and, just before we crossed the continental shelf into calmer waters, a large sea swept Robin and me off our feet where we were working in the scuppers.

In the Channel approaches the sea moderated considerably, but the wind did not. A Force 10 was forecast although it blew no more than 9. Like several of the other yachts we fell into the trap of putting up a lot of sail because the seas were making it so much easier to steer. As a result, our last day was memorable and a little more exciting than we intended.

First to go was the Number Three genoa. We poled it out before noticing that one of the hanks had made a small tear in the top of the sail. Before we could lower it, the rip extended straight across the sail. We fought it down, but in the strong wind it flipped out over the pulpit and into the sea. The next moment it was under the boat. I asked Bumble to let one sheet go, so we could drag the sail up on the port side, but on the bow Fred took matters into his own hands and cut away the other sheet. Result – we lost half the sail down the Channel. Perhaps it had gone to join the spinnaker we had left there seven months before? 'Just look at the cool and collected way we blundered our way through that one,' remarked Nick.

Next the mainsail went at a seam which had been worn away by chafe. Down it came and through the centre hatch it went to where Eve waited with the sewing machine. 'Could it be the last time I repair a sail?'

'No,' said Sam, 'give 'em time and they'll bust the rest.'

The next casualty was me. During a squall we tried to lower the mizzen staysail and, like a beginner, I stood behind the sail as it started to come down. Suddenly it twisted, collapsed and refilled, slamming me to the deck. My head hit the teak with a loud clunk and beautiful stars appeared before my eyes while a loud whistle filled my ears.

'Darling, will you please *not* do that!' said Jacques in some agitation, picking me up and sitting me down in a less dangerous place.

'I'm fine,' I said, adding 'Let's get some more sail up' to prove it. Fortunately I was not badly concussed, but I must have been the only person that night who saw two sets of lights on all the buoys and lighthouses, and two complete finishing lines.

As a final fling we tore the storm spinnaker. We hoisted it in a powerful

An Easter egg for an Easter finish (*Photo: The Observer*).

wind, got it set and drawing when the guy, a large heavy rope, broke. As the spinnaker flew out to leeward, it cut itself on a piece of wire.

We finally managed to put up some sails which stayed in one piece and were then free to concentrate on the navigation. It was a little embarrassing – although not surprising – to find we were lost. There had been no sun for several days, and to my chagrin my old enemy the radio direction finder was being even more unco-operative than usual. It whined and shrieked but produced no null at all. Even when we strongly suspected we might be a few miles off Start Point, the gadget refused to acknowledge the fact. The only indication as to our position came from the direction and size of the ships we saw coming out of the misty distance, and the VHF radio operator, who told us we must be somewhere near Start Point because of the strength of our transmission. This information was better than nothing, but still not enough to ensure we would find the Needles Channel into the West Solent. We'd be travelling at fifteen knots over the bottom, allowing for a strong tide, so there would be no room for mistakes in the thick mist.

But we were lucky. In the afternoon, a weak sun peeped through the thick cloud and, although John's first hasty sight put us several miles inland, the second looked more or less right. In the early evening the cloud lifted away and allowed the sun to light up the scene. The sea was a startling bright, translucent green capped with angry white crests, while away to port land appeared through the mist, dark and never more beautiful. Portland, St Alban's Head, Anvil Point, murky shapes, then clearer in the sharp light of a perfect sunset.

Voices on the radio from patient, anxious families waiting on boats, conversations with Race Control and with the other yachts ... excitement, anticipation, and yet everything unreal.

A final dash under spinnaker up the Solent in the light of a moon, going so fast we hardly had time to pick out the buoys before they had flown past. A glance at the lights of Lymington and a thought for our house, empty so long, then Portsmouth just ahead. A last-minute panic as we search for the buoy which marks the end of the line ... no-one can tell me whether we're rounding the right one ... then a struggle to lower the spinnaker before we run up the beach.

We finished at 10.58 pm, local time, to hold our fifth place overall. *Flyer* had won the Whitbread Trophy, but we had the satisfaction of beating her on this, the last leg.

As we motored into Portsmouth Harbour, I felt everything from relief to happiness, to sadness and anticlimax. It was a moment of tremendous adjustment. But then ... here was the *Golly* motoring alongside ... and a motor boat filled to overflowing with Francises, Bonhams and Ogilvy-Wedderburns. People in the waterfront pubs cheered ... and the quayside was lined with waiting figures. We laughed and cried. It was good to be home.

EPILOGUE

We had finished the race and we had finished it in one piece – and that was the major part of the battle won. Furthermore, fifth place out of fifteen was not a position we were unhappy with, considering our disastrous performance on the first leg. We might have done better if we had chosen our routes more carefully and had a bit more luck – but I don't believe we could ever have done better than fourth. The first three boats were either lighter, faster, and built to attract the best possible handicaps (*Flyer* and *Traité de Rome*), or sailed so hard that the crew must have had nerves of steel (*King's Legend*). With *Disque d'Or* it was different, however, Having usually managed to beat her when racing side by side, we felt certain we would have taken fourth place from her . . . if only . . . !

Ocean racing is always full of 'if onlys'. If only we had been racing under the same conditions, if only we had met the same winds . . . . But of course the essence of the Whitbread Race was to find the most favourable conditions and stay in them. A deep study of the wind and weather patterns and a wise choice of route were vital, and we certainly fell down on this during the Southern Ocean legs. But the first leg was different. Here our choice of route was good, but we ran out of luck. And luck was undoubtedly the other essential ingredient for success.

Of course, we were not the only ones with a hard luck story to tell. Nearly every boat had fallen into a windless hole at some point or another and the amount of time each boat lost in this way probably cancelled out over 27,000 miles.

Once sailing in the most favourable part of the ocean, it was boat speed that counted. On the two Southern Ocean legs it had been very hard to find the right balance between good seamanship (that is, staying in one piece and not breaking vital gear and equipment) and competitiveness. The dividing line between safety and foolhardiness was very thin; sometimes we had erred on the side of safety, losing time to the other boats, and on other occasions we had pushed too hard and broken gear unnecessarily.

Certainly there was no room for holding back – the second Whitbread Race was hard fought and hard won. To stay ahead it was necessary to push hard and sail right up to the limit of that thin dividing line. A comparison of the second race with the first revealed a major improvement in elapsed times. Although the first race had stopped in Sydney rather than Auckland, the total distance was about the same. Yet we had beaten the time of *Sayula II,* a sister ship and winner of the previous race, by nearly seven days. Undoubtedly the next race in 1981–82 will be even faster.

As we sped up the Channel at the end of the race, we all decided that, as far as the sailing went, we were just about ready to *start* the race. It takes so long to get to know a big boat really well and to become familiar with her habits in large seas that 27,000 miles was about the right distance for proving trials prior to a major race! We had learnt many things which would have been impossible to discover off the coast of England, or even crossing the Atlantic. In this respect I was left with an itch to do the race again. With all our accumulated knowledge, it seemed a pity not to put it to good use on the next Whitbread . . . assuming, of course, that one had a boat specially built for the event – ultra-light, very strong, and a real downwind flyer. But then I was always dreaming about what I could have done with such-and-such a boat in this or that event (a lighter, stiffer boat in the Transatlantic and another two days off my time?). It did not mean I wanted to do the race again! Indeed, when the subject of doing the Whitbread again came up among the crew, the answer was a unanimous no.

The race had been an unforgettable experience with outstanding highlights: the passage round the Horn, the wild rides down the Southern Ocean waves, the occasional excitement of being ahead – but there had been many other moments which passed slowly: times of boredom, discomfort and longing for home. Seven months was a long time to be away and, when the going had been repetitive and undemanding, I think many of the crew wondered why they had agreed to come in the first place.

It is difficult to compare the Whitbread Race with long-distance singlehanded passages, because its nature is so very different. To sail an ocean singlehanded you need stubborn willpower and determination. Unless you are racing and want to do well, you don't even need much skill, just a basic knowledge of seamanship. The essence of the Whitbread was sailing hard up to the limit of safety, a different idea altogether and one which demanded skill and experience.

Sailing with a large crew had involved special difficulties. A group of twelve individuals cannot live in a confined space without making tremendous adjustments – or trying to, at least. On *ADC* we were lucky – on a personal level we all got on famously. Everyone possessed a well-developed sense of humour and a desire to make the venture a success. This atmosphere succeeded in reducing most problems to insignificance.

Nonetheless I occasionally found leadership to involve very difficult problems. In many ways the boat ran herself – most of the crew were people who took on responsibility gladly and fulfilled their obligations without prompting. However, there were moments when hard decisions had to be taken. If it was a question of looking at the facts and drawing conclusions, then the matter was reasonably straightforward. But when personalities and egos intruded it became very much more complicated and conflicts arose – on the one hand I was anxious to maintain harmony in the family by smoothing over the differences that cropped up over sailing techniques, tactics and so on, but on the other I was aware of a need to establish the best and safest way of doing things, based on our joint experience and judgment. In the end, we still differed in our approach to spinnaker-handling and several other matters, but short of running the boat like Captain Bligh I don't think it was possible to iron these problems out, considering the personalities involved.

Without Jacques I would have found the job as skipper very much harder. For the most part we worked as a team, discussing problems and decisions together. In this way I was able to share the burden of responsibility and to benefit from the advice of someone who could see problems from the overall standpoint.

And yes . . . being a woman *did* make the job more difficult! Not much, because I had tremendous support from my crew . . . but just a little. When I couldn't lift the spinnaker pole and had to ask one of the boys for help, I felt guilty. Here I was asking people to do things that I couldn't do myself!

After a few celebratory days in Portsmouth, we sailed *ADC* back to Lymington. The realisation that the long voyage was over finally soaked in. The crew had kindly promised to stay on in Lymington for two weeks to help put the boat back in good order but not surprisingly their thoughts were already on the summer ahead.

'Well, I think I'll retire now and become rich,' said Sam. 'Just lend me a stocking and a cosh and I'll saunter up to the Post Office with intent . . . .'

Sam went to work in a local boatyard as a general fitter and dogsbody. After a few weeks he had enough money to put his motorbike back on the road and take some of the local belles to a disco or two. We all noticed that, despite his earlier ideas, Sam showed little enthusiasm for sailmaking.

Eve positively blossomed on dry land. She scooped up the remains of her small business and started to rebuild it, working long and hard hours. As if this wasn't enough, she started another business and was last seen rushing around the country selling sweaters bearing embroidered sailing burgees.

After a short holiday Robin returned to his job as a chartered accountant, while Robert quickly made the rounds of Henley, Lords and Epsom before taking a job selling skateboards. Rumour has it that this didn't prevent him from making a quick visit to Ascot with a tall blonde on his arm.

John returned to Italy to take up his old job as skipper of *Tangaroa* and, after a long, warm summer, faces a tough winter in the sunny West Indies. As a job, it has its compensations!

Tony is looking after a brand-new, hot One Ton racing machine, quite a bit smaller than *ADC*, but involving just as much work – so Tony tells us as he speeds past our door on his way to the sailmaker, the rigger or the boatbuilder. We ask if the boat is likely to do well. Tony, his eyes sparkling, thinks yes, although he doesn't fancy heavy weather because the mast's a bit thin, and there's only a centreplate, no keel . . . . He thinks it'll be fun.

Beat, too, will be racing all summer. On returning from Switzerland after doing his two weeks' national service, he'll be taking part in the two-handed Round Britain Race with his old crew Albert, sailing in the second *Petit Suisse*.

And Beat is not the only one doing the Round Britain. Fred has been loaned a long, slim 6-metre and, despite lack of sponsorship, is entering the 2,000 mile event. With both Fred and Beat in the race Jacques, Eve and I will be going down to Plymouth to wave them off, bringing back memories of the last Round Britain four years ago when the three of us also took part.

Nick has a temporary job at a Birmingham hospital while he looks for a permanent post nearer the sea – it's not that he's so desperate to go sailing again, but he does enjoy chasing those elusive fish.

Somewhere in Scotland, Bumble is cooking for people, or on a dig, or rebuilding crofts for the National Trust – we're never quite sure with Bumble. However, we do know she and Eve are going to the Hebridean isle of Barra to welcome Fred and Beat at the second stopover on the Round Britain Race.

Here in Lymington, Jacques and I have been busy settling back into our house which is just as lovely as we remembered it. Our only problem is in the garden. Working from the top of the small garden down, Jacques has been madly planting vegetables, while I have been almost as busy planting flowers in the opposite direction. Where the radishes met the wallflowers we compromised – Jacques pulled up some paving stones to plant more lettuces while I was allowed to create another flower bed around Jacques' tomatoes.

The ground floor of the house is almost decorated now, and we have high hopes of doing the guest room in a few months' time, after our holiday. We're going for a small cruise to Brittany, just for a complete break.

Lymington
June, 1978

APPENDICES

Clare Francis

Spinnakers and Broaching

The spinnaker has long been considered unseamanlike and unnecessary by those who like to sail in a dignified and sensible manner. However, for those who race it is an essential sail to carry, providing very significant increases in speed when sailing downwind. Not only can hull speed be reached in a moderate breeze but as the breeze stiffens the boat will quickly exceed her hull speed and surf. Under plain sail (jib, main and mizzen) surfing can only be attained in a large sea and a very strong wind.

HANDLING
The spinnaker is not an easy sail to handle. First, a lot of work is required to put it up. The spinnaker has to be prepared, usually by running it through a bottomless bucket covered with elastic bands. As the sail is pulled through the bucket, the bands are slipped off onto the sail until it is trussed up into a long sausage. In this way it can be raised and the guy, sheet and pole set up before the sail opens and starts causing trouble.

Second, the spinnaker is controlled by a large number of lines and pieces of equipment (guy, sheet, pole, foreguy, topping lift, etc) and all these have to be set up, then trimmed . . . and retrimmed, and retrimmed. Setting a spinnaker is a time-consuming business.

The diagram opposite shows how we set our spinnaker on *ADC*. We always rigged a lazy guy and sheet in case we should want to gybe. Apart from the gybe around Bembridge Ledge Buoy at the start of the race, we never did a dip-pole gybe as it was usually far too dangerous to leave the spinnaker without a pole even for a moment. Rather, we stuck to twin-pole gybes, setting up the lazy guy through the second pole – and hopefully keeping the whole operation beautifully under control.

On the second leg, when we had only one good pole for most of the time, we took the spinnaker down, repacked it and rehoisted it on the other side rather than risk the chaos of trying a dip-pole.

When the wind got up we would flatten the spinnaker by lowering the pole at both the mast and outboard ends, and feeding the sheet through a snatch block placed further forward on the toerail. In this way the sail was pulled downwards at both corners, making it flop around less, catch less wind and generally become more controllable. In calm waters and a gentle breeze we found it was possible to trim the pole aft so that the spinnaker was carried well to the windward side of the boat, was not masked by the mainsail, and was therefore at its most efficient. But in a fresh wind or any kind of sea at all we

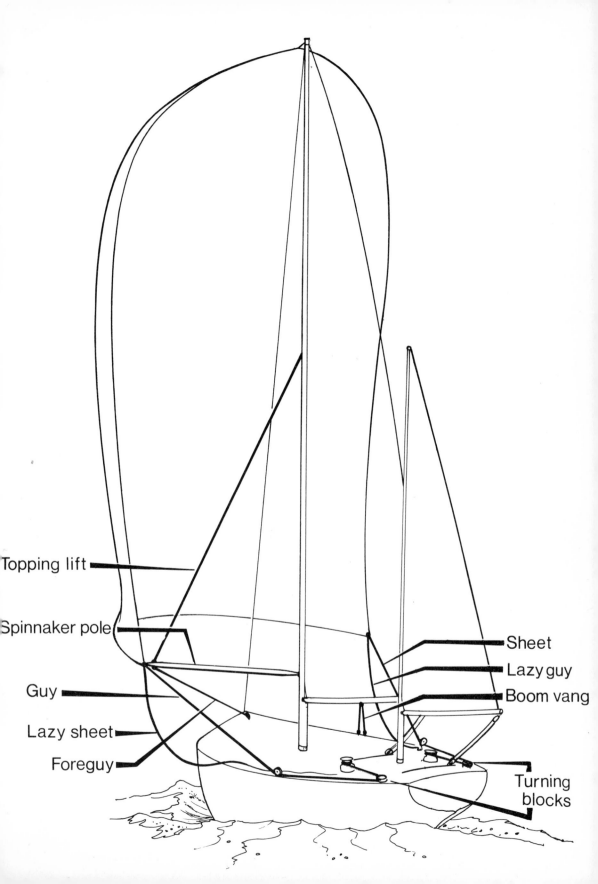

Topping lift

Spinnaker pole

Guy

Lazy sheet

Foreguy

Sheet

Lazy guy

Boom vang

Turning
blocks

found that *ADC* started to behave very badly unless the pole was eased forward. Most of the time we carried the pole at about 45° to the centre line of the boat, so that the spinnaker's centre was straight in front of the bow. Trimmed in this way, the spinnaker did not pull too much to one side or the other.

If, after flattening and carefully trimming a spinnaker, it was still uncontrollable we would take the sail down and put up a smaller one.

BROACHING

There are several reasons for broaching, but the three most common are bad spinnaker trim, sailing dead downwind, and wave motion. All these cause the boat to roll and, depending on the wind strength and sea state, to go out of control and broach. To this should be added another cause – the carrying of too large a spinnaker for a given wind strength, although you could put this under the heading of bad trim.

Taking bad trim first, a spinnaker which sags out to windward or leeward and is not properly flattened down will pull the boat over to one side or the other, setting up a violent rolling motion which will end in a broach – unless something is done about it. A spinnaker which is allowed to pivot freely around the mast head will respond to the slightest roll by swinging round and accentuating the movement by a considerable factor.

Even if a spinnaker is properly trimmed and is not allowed to throw the boat around, violent rolling can still start up if the boat is allowed to sail dead downwind. Without the steadying effect of the wind on one quarter or the other, the boat becomes extremely unstable, rolls and goes out of control.

However, the major cause of broaching in ocean sailing is a big sea. Assuming you are sailing happily along with a well-trimmed spinnaker and the wind safely on the quarter, you will still have a hard job controlling the boat if a large wave twists the stern round. As the quarter lifts to a wave, the boat tilts over to one side and tries to turn. The helmsman corrects the turning movement but in so doing can cause the boat to roll over the other way. The spinnaker, even when well-trimmed, will inevitably accentuate this movement. It is then that the vicious circle of roll and counter-roll can start up.

A cool, calm and alert helmsman (and one rarely feels all three simultaneously) will counteract a turning movement so well – that is, not too violently but just enough to be effective – that he or she will stop the boat turning, yet prevent a roll. But in a sudden squall or just too much wind it is often impossible to bring the boat safely out of a twist on every single occasion. Sometimes three or four nasty, twisting waves will come at the boat in quick succession, and catch out even the most alert helmsman.

The drawing opposite shows a yacht rolling over to leeward (A), which causes her to turn to windward and broach (B). The spinnaker has pulled the boat right over on her side and, if the boat tries to come upright, the head of the spinnaker fills with wind and pushes the boat sideways and over again. Only by easing the spinnaker sheet and forcing the spinnaker to spill wind will the crew usually be able to make the boat right herself.

During a windward broach the main boom is dragged along in the water,

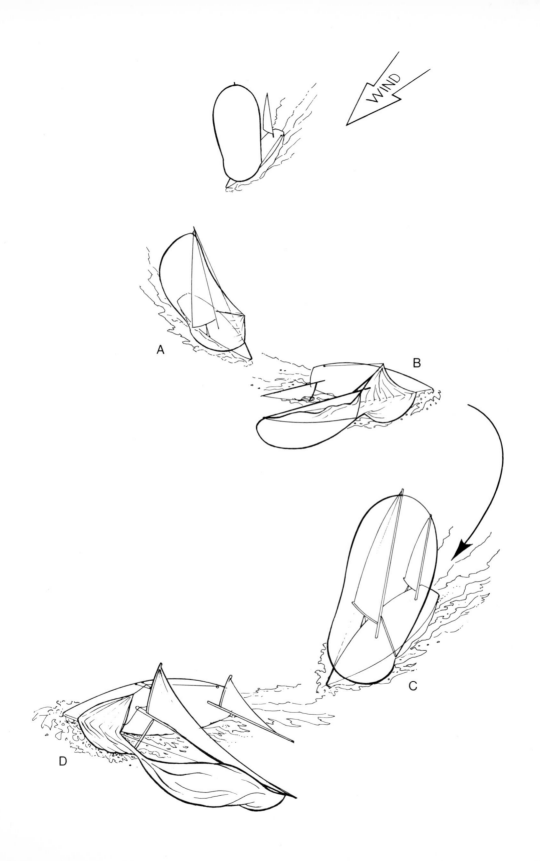

and it is essential that the vangs holding the boom down to the toerail break, otherwise a weak main boom would bend or fracture and the mainsail would be torn. In fact, rather than break expensive vangs every time, we used short strops between the vang and the toerail which were designed to break before anything else.

A windward broach is not usually dangerous because the mast is not at risk. Everything shakes and shudders and it seems everything must inevitably break, but in fact it rarely does.

Far more dangerous is the leeward broach. Here the boat rolls to windward (C) and turns to leeward (D). This time the spinnaker pole is in the water but, unless the foreguy breaks, it will stay there and, since a big boat will still be doing a good five knots sideways, crabwise or forwards when broached, the pole will normally bend, break or tear away from its mountings.

Even if the pole stays in one piece, the major worry comes from the main boom. This time you want the vangs to *hold,* despite the tremendous pressure on them from the wind blowing into the *back* of the mainsail. If they do not hold, the main boom will come crashing across and probably take the backstays with it. Without backstays, the mast will usually fall down.

Thus it is far better to broach to windward and, by careful trimming, it is possible to give the boat a small bias in that direction so that she is more likely to broach the right way should she go out of control.

Therefore the worst thing a helmsman can do is fail to notice the spinnaker is badly trimmed, then let a wave turn the boat dead downwind, make no effort to bring her out of a roll and finally to let her broach the wrong way. Still, we all do it. . . but hopefully never more than once.

Spinnakers are great fun once you develop nerves of steel and forget all the risks. When not racing, Jacques and I like to do some quiet cruising on *Gulliver G.* . . she's got two spinnakers, but one never goes up and the other blows out in Force 2. We always manage to have a beautifully relaxed time.

Tony Bertram

General Breakages and Gear Failure

When planning to enter a yacht in a long offshore race it is essential to study the deck gear, masts, spars, and running rigging in some depth. The Whitbread Race, however, poses extra problems due to the length of each leg and also the fact that fifty per cent of sailing time is spent in the Southern Ocean, where average wind strengths can be expected to be higher and conditions generally harder on the yacht.

In *ADC Accutrac*'s case we were lucky both to have a well-tried production yacht and to be sailing in *Sayula II*'s wake. Many of the modifications we made were learnt from her experiences. However we soon found problems of our own.

On starting from Portsmouth probably the first thing you discover is that a heavily laden yacht needs more power to pull it through the water and adds to the strains the boat would normally have to take. It soon became apparent that our worst enemy would be chafe. A rope led against what looked like a smooth surface, stanchion base of toerails shackle would be cut through and rendered useless after a night's sailing – and a sheet once chafed in the centre is of very little use.

The standing rigging on *ADC* was completely checked and much of it renewed before the start, all the Norseman terminals being replaced by swaged ends. The rigging gave no trouble in the early stages of the race. The cordage and deck blocks were also new. Our biggest trouble on the first leg was the failure of one of the backstay hydraulics. The backstay was split twenty feet above deck and came down to a Kruger hydraulic pump either side of the bridge deck. All we could do was to take up the bottlescrews above either ram and use the remaining pump. The result was a somewhat slacker forestay than would have been desired but we had to put up with it for the remaining 3,000 miles to Cape Town.

Before leaving England we decided to have Sparcraft snapshackles and Barient bear claw spinnaker pole ends sent to Cape Town. This decision proved to be justified. Although our standard piston-type spinnaker pole ends lasted to Cape Town, other yachts in the race did report breakages with theirs after only ten to twelve days' use. The chromed bronze Lewmar snapshackles (now manufactured in stainless steel) proved unusable, however. After twenty-four hours hard running the knuckle burred over sufficiently to prevent it opening, even with the piston pulled out. We also decided to do away with the snapshackles on the pole lift, foreguy and spinnaker halyards and attached them by using bowlines which proved entirely satisfactory.

The only other damage on Leg One was caused by one of the mainsail tack reefing hooks which worked its way forward out of alignment. When we gybed in a light breeze and heavy swell, it went hard against the mast and severely strained the mast track by exerting leverage.

In Cape Town a general inspection of the masts and rigging revealed some wear on the spinnaker crane U-bolts, so these were removed and built up with weld so that the bottom of the U became oversized and could stand being worn away without lessening the actual diameter of the bolt. This proved successful and no further attention was necessary. While in Cape Town our new spinnaker fittings arrived and these were fitted. The Barient pole ends, while being an extremely robust stainless steel claw, have a weaker aluminium casting to take them on to the spinnaker pole tube. We remarked on this at the time. However these fittings have an extremely good reputation and so at this stage we did no more. The Sparcraft snapshackles also arrived and after some deliberation we decided to try wire guys with rope tails. This, we found out later, was a mistake.

On Leg Two after four days we picked up the westerlies and began what was going to be a nearly all downwind leg. The first major breakage came shortly after, with our first bad broach. *ADC* rolled so heavily to windward that the spinnaker pole end dipped into the water. The resulting force pulled the foreguy attachment out of the deck, and we then had to use the alloy toerail to secure the foreguy. After this we always had a back-up block and strop to prevent further incidents when it blew hard. We also had rope strops on all the blocks in the event of a break. This incident also shook the outer pole end fitting loose and although we tried locking the machine screws first with Locktite and later resin it was only finally solved when we glassed around the entire fitting.

Another problem was that, since the cordage had been stepped up in size to provide greater safety, it was not always possible to get the required number of turns on the spinnaker halyard winch barrels. So, for the rest of Leg Two we had the spinnaker halyard led back to one of the four Lewmar 65 cockpit winches, and the foreguy to the other.

During such a long race it is obviously necessary to keep a constant check on all the deck gear, so it was quite alarming to find that the turning blocks (used for both the headsails and spinnaker guys) were lifting from the deck. The only thing we could do at sea was to put three extra bolts through the toerail. This proved sufficient and we had no further trouble with them.

In Auckland, with half the voyage over, we had a fairly comprehensive idea of what was needed in the way of further modifications and we decided to renew the spinnaker halyards with a slightly smaller-diameter New Zealand braid to enable us to go back to the deck-mounted winches. The spinnaker guys we modified again, and had a small stainless steel ring welded to the cage which was attached to the Sparcraft shackle allowing us to pass the guy inside and make an overhand knot. This allowed the pole end to come against the cage and the guy itself was only exposed to chafe for the three or four inches of guy preceding the snapshackle. This section we kept bound with tape.

On Boxing Day we left New Zealand and came face to face with a new

216

problem. Coming from Cape Town the voyage had been almost entirely off the wind and the main mast had always seemed to stand quite well, so that all that had been done to the rigging was generally taking out the stretch which you get on such long spans of wire. On heeling, however, the main mast was dropping off above the intermediate shrouds rather alarmingly. A fault with the rigging was that both the intermediate shrouds which ran from the first spreader to the inboard end of the top spreader, and the cap shroud which ran over the second spreader (and shared the same lower span of wire), were of the same diameter. The caps being three times longer than the intermediates, they stretched more, and to compensate we had to slacken off the intermediates until the leeward wire flayed around rather alarmingly. I think on a race of this nature it is probably desirable to have a rig where both shrouds lead down to the deck and facilitate easy adjustment.

The fourth and last leg brought no new problems, mostly because the gear was well tried by this time. I have mentioned the major problems but to list all the many small ones would be impossible, and you can be sure that on the next race a great deal more will come to light.

Eve Bonham and Sam Badrick

Sail Repairs

Eve: When Clare asked me to join *ADC Accutrac* it was as a normal crew member, participating in watches, taking my turn at the helm and doing general deck work along with the rest of the crew. However, I was aware that there would be times when I might not be strong enough for the deck work, so I decided to learn how to mend sails and improve my usefulness aboard. I spent a few days with a Lymington sailmaker, and was taught the essentials. We were kindly loaned a Sailmaker sewing machine by Reads, and used it an immense amount. Sam was also going to mend sails and having two of us turned out to be very useful.

Sam: In my job of sail repairer I was able to draw on my experience gained aboard *British Soldier* in the first Whitbread Race, and also on the experiences of sailmakers aboard the other yachts (advice was free and available, so I took it).

Eve: We had twenty-seven sails on the boat (a list of which is given below), many of them new. During the race we ripped nearly every one and many of them were mended more than once – the starcut spinnaker we repaired seven times!

Sam: Not to mention the old Number Three genoa, which we repaired ten times!

Eve: We took with us a lot of sailmaking equipment and a large quantity of sailcloth of different weights. We used miles of thread and broke numerous needles. The first leg was my apprenticeship. It took some time getting used to handling a huge spinnaker with 3,000 square feet of cloth in the confined space of the saloon, with the boat pounding through rock-hard waves, or heeling over. Fred had made a metal frame which screwed into the saloon table and kept the machine from sliding off the table.

Sam: Yeah, but there was nothing to stop *us* sliding around! Sail repairs were not easy when you had to keep thousands of square feet of sail under control. You needed about three pair of hands to push the sail through the machine, to turn the handle and to hold yourself down – all at the same time.

Eve: The first really major repair was on the working spinnaker, on the first leg. We blew it out completely when the wind suddenly strengthened and the weight of cloth was too light – it ripped to let the wind blow through it. We cut out and sewed on some sixty or seventy patches, and it took forty-eight hours of continuous work. Every patch was cut with a hot knife to prevent fraying and every seam was sewn twice. We made a beautiful job of it and this may account for the fact that no further repairs were needed on it, until the last leg. Or perhaps we were more careful.

Sam: We didn't have to mend the first sail we blew out though! The old heavy spinnaker went on the first night of the race and most of it went back up the Channel. The rest of the sail was put to good use in Cape Town when we made it into a banner with WATCH THIS SPACE written across it. It was also used as a sun awning to keep the boat cool in the scorching heat of Rio.

Eve: As the race progressed we learnt quicker and more efficient methods of making repairs. On average we used to rip a sail every two to three days and often we had two hanging dripping in the saloon, waiting to dry out before work started on them. Meals became rather chaotic at these times, and I remember one day, when the boat gave a nasty lurch, I and my lunch were thrown across the saloon. The spinnaker waiting to be mended was deluged with macaroni cheese and salad. When we put it up later pieces of soggy macaroni and lettuce fell on top of us.

Some of the repairs had to be done by hand, which was quite difficult in the Southern Ocean when it was necessary to do repairs on deck and our hands were very cold. We used leather palms to push needles through and it often helped to have another person on the other side of the sail to return the needle.

Sam: We used our old mainsail on the two downwind legs because we didn't want to chafe and wear out our new one. The old sail was a bit stretched and worn, but it had a deep third reef and was ideal for bombing downwind. Only trouble was, it was horrible to repair. The material was very thick and rigid and generally difficult. It ended its working life left on the quay at Rio, with all the valuable slides removed.

Eve: It was on the last leg that Sam and I began to feel victimised by circumstances. We always seemed to rip a sail on our twenty-four hour standby and spent the entire time sail-mending. In fact every fifth day (when our standby came around again) was known as 'sail-breaking day'.

I think we did more damage to sails on the last morning of the race than on any other previous single occasion. We blew the starcut for the last time. . . .

Sam: And didn't have to repair it, thank goodness!

Eve: . . . we tore another sail, a seam in the main parted. . . .

Sam: . . . and the Number Three genoa was finally put to rest when half of it was lost over the side. . . .

Eve: . . . all in the English Channel! We repaired the main and wept crocodile tears over the genoa (which had caused us a certain amount of heartache).

Sam: But really, the sails stood up well to the bashing we gave them over 27,000 miles of very hard use.

Eve: Yes, it sounds as though we spent all our time turning the sewing machine handle or pinning patches. Luckily this was not true but I won't be upset if I don't have to mend any more sails for a while. I certainly won't miss being confronted, at three in the morning when cold and tired, by another wet and shattered sail! It was all good experience, I suppose.

Sam: Yeah, wouldn't have missed it for the world. But if there's ever a next time, the sails will have to be cast-iron and never let out of their bags.

SAILS CARRIED ON ADC ACCUTRAC

Headsails

Drifter	2.2 oz	Mizzen	7.0 oz
No. 1 genoa	6.0 oz	Light mizzen staysail	3.5 oz
No. 1 genoa	6.5 oz	Heavy mizzen staysail	6.0 oz
No. 2 genoa	7.0 oz	Trisail	12.0 oz
No. 3 genoa	8.2 oz		
No. 1 jib topsail	6.0 oz	*Spinnakers*	
No. 2 jib topsail	8.2 oz	Floater	0.5 oz
No. 3 jib topsail	10.0 oz	Light radial head	0.75 oz
(storm jib)		Light triradial	0.75 oz
Working fore staysail	8.0 oz	Medium triradial	1.5 oz
Storm staysail	10,0 oz	Heavy radial head	2.2 oz
Genoa staysail	7.0 oz	Heavy triradial	2.2 oz
		Starcut	2.2 oz
Main and Mizzen Sails		Storm	2.2 oz
Mainsail – new	10.5 oz	Mizzen spinnaker	0.75 oz
old	10.0 oz	Big boy shooter	1.5 oz

APPENDIX D

Bumble Ogilvy-Wedderburn

Food and Feeding

It was only after I'd accepted Clare's amazing offer of a job to cook in the Round the World Race that I realised what I'd let myself in for. I had no idea of the hours I was to spend writing lists and calculating how much food twelve people would eat in eight months. I tried various ways of working it out but they weren't all successful. I even went to a Captain in the Army Catering Corps, who said, 'Easy – we work out that each man has ¼oz butter, ¼oz jam, one slice bread, one rasher of bacon etc. a day.' I knew from the start their method wouldn't work, as I could quite happily eat 4oz of butter at breakfast, and Beat could eat half a pot of jam or honey at a sitting! How I eventually worked it out I still don't know, except that I had lots of help from Clare, who would take one look at the list and write back, 'FAR TOO MUCH!' She was right, and I think I probably cut it down by half.

We were very lucky to be provided with most of the dried and tinned food for the whole race. I supplemented the processed food with lots of fresh meat, fish, vegetables, and fruit. We had a small deep freeze which would hold 120 lb of frozen meat or fish off the bone, and I had storage space for lots of fresh vegetables and fruit. Eventually I was also to have a whole bunk as storage space for boxes of fruit and more delicate vegetables. The yacht looked like a cross between a grocer's shop and an extremely cramped bed-sit, with sacks of potatoes nestling up to Evey's feet when she was in her bunk, and string bags of cabbages, carrots and onions hanging over the saloon table, swinging with the motion of the boat.

I had to go through all the vegetables once a week, turning and ejecting any bad or rotting fruit, an extremely irritating job, as the yacht would usually be well heeled over. I'd have to wedge myself in a corner and try to catch the apples and oranges as they rolled around. During their clean-up the standby watch would often find the odd orange, dirty fork or tube of mustard lurking under the saloon seat.

The standby also had the job of washing -up. Usually I did the saucepans, because there wasn't the space in the galley for a mass of plates, cutlery, mugs and pans, and since I'd made them dirty, I'd clean them myself – then there would be no complaint from me about dirty pans when I next came to cook. But in my own sadistic way, if the standby watch had really irritated me or if I thought they had been particularly lazy, I'd leave them the pots and pans after all! This didn't always work because, in return, they'd feel cheesed off and wouldn't wash them properly!

The galley was fairly large compared to some yachts, and it included a small

221

deep freeze, a slightly larger fridge, twin sinks with fresh hot and cold water (practically never used) and one salt water pump, and a cooker on gimbals (which was the bane of my life). It was a fairly dry galley with few leaks or damp lockers, but I did have trouble with liquids when they spilt on the working surfaces – they would immediately seep down through the insulated lids of the deep freeze and fridge. Every now and then the smell in the fridge would become too much and I'd have to clean it out. This meant standing on my head in the fridge with a bowl of seawater and bicarbonate of soda, sloshing water around in the hope that it would remove the smell.

Another job I really hated was 'shopping'. Once a week – and I had to choose my time carefully – I would remove all the very warm, smelly bedding and mattresses from the two forward bunks (hoping that the owners weren't about to leap into bed), unscrew the bunkboards and grab roughly what I thought we'd eat during the following week. All the tins had previously been marked and the labels removed, to ensure that there was no chaos caused by soggy paper labels clogging the bilge pumps and hundreds of bare unmarked tins. I had a horror of opening cans of fruit salad only to find that they contained tomatoes and sauerkraut. After I'd been through the lockers and removed all the tins, rice, macaroni etc which I wanted, I'd have the job of putting back all the nausea which seems to collect in bunks – magazines, books, paper hankies, cameras, all sorts of stiff clothing, diaries and pens. Then I would organise an unwilling chain of hands to pass the tins and packets into the galley. I always prayed that there wouldn't be a sail change or a tack in the middle of this operation because everyone would willingly drop what they were doing and thunder backwards and forwards, squashing the macaroni into pasta crumbs and bursting bags of rice with their big smelly feet.

I worked out that we would always have a cooked breakfast, porridge or cereal, some sort of bacon, eggs, or sausages and bread. (Not toast as the cooker had a hopeless grill – either the bread was so close that it touched the flames, or it was so far away it never toasted.) I got extremely baity at breakfast, especially when they all went on diets and wanted something different.

Lunch, depending on the weather and what I had left in the veg. line, was either cold meat and salad and tinned or fresh fruit, or risotto and cheese, or soup and fried 'sarnies' (sandwiches). We had two sittings for each meal, first one watch, then the other half an hour later. Supper was always a hot meal, the meat or fish taken from the deep freeze, then a hot pudding with custard or cream. I would really have to use my imagination to make meals different and often, in despair, I'd ask the boys what they'd like for the next meal, hoping for some new ideas. 'Spaghetti,' they'd say! I think I could have given them spaghetti three times a week and they would never have noticed.

I had to plan my meals, since I only had three burners on the cooker and, because of the size of some of the saucepans, I knew some wouldn't fit on with others. Also I had to be careful to distribute the weight evenly because of the stove being gimballed. Most of the cooking was done in seawater, or seawater diluted with fresh. We had a fairly limited supply of drinking water, five gallons a day for twelve. The only seawater pump was in the galley and sometimes I'd find I was scraping carrots while Fred and Tony were trying to clean their teeth at the same time in the same sink!

Cooking in a heavy sea didn't upset me much – I think I enjoyed the challenge. The only mishap I had was when I forgot to wedge a saucepan and a second later I'd hear it whizz across the working surface and tip over when it reached its destination. Shouts of rage and abuse would follow!

The only real disaster we had was when the generator broke down and the deep freeze had to be turned off. For three days we'd eat like pigs before all the meat and fish went off, then we'd resort to soya bean meat texture, which, when flavoured, wasn't too bad. We had fresh vegetables practically all the time. Cabbages, beetroot, onions, potatoes etc would easily last the whole leg, and if the lettuces were kept cool they would last three weeks. The tomatoes lasted most of the time – I bought them in three stages of ripeness. There was plenty of fresh fruit which was eaten at any time of the day or night.

Most of my cooking was done in pressure cookers, an essential piece of equipment in any yacht. All the tin openers, sieves, cheese graters, roasting tins and any other non-stainless steel equipment went rusty. It was essential never to lend any kitchen knives to the crew (even for a moment); either they never got returned or they came back with a serrated edge, a broken point or covered with fast-hardening fibreglass!!

If asked whether I'd ever do it again, the answer would be 'Well. . . I'll have to think about it!'

FOOD FOR 12 PEOPLE FOR WHOLE RACE

Tea bags	64 packets of 100	Dried peas	16 lb
Instant coffee	24 catering tins	Dried beans	16 lb
Ground coffee	40 lb	Dried lentils	12 lb
Cocoa	32 × 1lb tins	Dried carrots	12 lb
Ovaltine	64 × 1lb tins	Dried onions	12 lb
Orange squash	12 gallons	Dried mixed vegetables	20 lb
Powdered orange with added vitamins	28 packets	Dried sultanas	64 lb
		Dried raisins	64 lb
Powdered grapefruit with added vitamins	28 packets	Dried currants	64 lb
		Dried apricots	40 lb
Powdered lemon with added vitamins	28 packets	Dried prunes	56 lb
		Dried apple (flakes)	20 lb
Dried milk	288 gallons (made-up)	Dried mixed fruit (ie pears, apples, prunes etc)	40 lb
Packet soup	240 large packets	Custard powder	32 × 11 oz tins
Cornflakes	128 large packets	Self-raising flour	128 lb
Oatmeal	12 lb	Plain flour	128 lb
Porridge oats	168 lb	Brown flour	200 lb
Alpen	64 catering packs	Cream of tartar	½ lb
All-Bran	16 large packets	Pastry mix	40 lb
Long-grain rice	192 lb	Baking powder	4 lb
Round rice	24 lb	Sugar	384 lb
Spaghetti	64 lb	Salt	40 lb
Noodles	120 lb	Pepper	2 lb
Instant potatoes	32 Maggi catering tins	Curry powder	4 lb
		Bicarbonate of soda	½ lb

Mustard	48 × 2 oz tubes
Stock cubes (chicken)	192 cubes
Stock cubes (beef)	192 cubes
Mixed herbs	2 oz
Dried parsley	2 oz
Dried thyme	2 oz
Mixed spices	100 g
Cinnamon	100 g
Bay leaves	4 oz
Ryvita	128 packets
High-baked water biscuits	100 packets
Digestive biscuits	100 × 1 lb packets
Penguins	1,000 biscuits
Clubs	1,000 biscuits
Jaffa cakes	128 packets
Shortbread	80 × 1 lb packets
Ritz crackers	32 boxes
Tuc	60 × pack of two
Oatcakes	40 × ½ lb packets
Assorted sweet biscuits	16 large tins
Hellman's mayonnaise	32 pints
Worcester sauce	4 × 5 oz bottles
Tomato ketchup	16 bottles
Vinegar	8 pints
Olive oil	40 pints
Corn oil	32 pints
Blackcurrant jam	32 lb
Marmalade	48 lb
Strawberry jam	32 lb
Raspberry jam	32 lb
Apricot jam	32 lb
Black cherry jam	32 lb
Mint jelly	4 lb
Honey	32 lb
Syrup	40 lb
Marmite	4 jars
Semolina	24 lb
Butter	240 lb
Cheddar cheese	80 lb
Philadelphia cheese	20 lb
Gruyère cheese	80 lb
Emmenthal cheese	80 lb
Peanuts	200 lb
Sardines	160 × 5 oz tins
Pilchards	80 × 1 lb tins
Kippers	160 tins
Shrimps	128 × 6½ oz tins
Prawns	128 × 6½ oz tins

Tuna	128 × 1 lb tins
Ravioli	80 × 1½ lb tins
Bacon	120 × 1 lb tins
Sausages	120 × 1 lb tins
Baked beans	120 × 1 lb tins
Tomatoes, large	48 × 1½–2 lb tins
Tomatoes, medium	100 × 1 lb tins
Tomato purée	32 × 5 oz tins
Creamed sweetcorn	128 tins
Carrots	80 × 1¾ lb tins
Mushrooms	64 × 1¾ lb tins
Spinach	80 × 1¾ lb tins
Ham	40 × 2 lb tins
Rhubarb	80 × 2 lb tins
Plums	80 × 2 lb tins
Peaches	80 × 2 lb tins
Mixed fruit	80 × 2 lb tins
Pears	80 × 2 lb tins
Pineapple	80 × 2 lb tins
Gooseberries	80 × 2 lb tins
Apricots	80 × 2 lb tins
Blackcurrants	80 × 2 lb tins
Washing-up liquid	15 bottles
Soap powder	6 packets
Matches	20 large boxes
Vim	16 × 1 lb 2 oz drums
Jeyes' fluid	4 gallons
Bleach	8 litres
Toilet paper	70 rolls
J cloths	24 packs of 12
Brillo pads	8 packs of 10
Kitchen paper	96 packs of 2
Large sponge cloths	12
Scotch-Brite	12 packs of 2
Mars bars	800
Chocolate (milk, plain, fruit and nut)	160 lb
Boiled sweets	32 lb
Fox's Glacier mints	32 lb
Toffees	32 lb

Fresh fruit – apples, oranges, grapefruit, bananas, lemons.

Fresh vegetables – cabbage, beetroot, potatoes, onions, cucumbers.

In fridge – tomatoes and lettuce.

Plus other fruit and vegetables in season at various ports of call.

Frozen meat and fish – 120 lb per leg.